# Avoiding the
# OS Phase®...

Second Edition

**Robert Baim**

*Avoiding the OS Phase®...*
© 2010

Robert Baim

ISBN: 978-0-9845166-1-2

Second Edition

First Edition published in 2006
ISBN 0-978369-7-X

No portion of this book
may be reproduced in any form
without the written permission
of the author.

Warwick House Publishing
720 Court Street
Lynchburg, VA 24504

This book is dedicated to
my mother and father
who supported my education, career and family
and always encouraged independent
and creative thinking.
Frank Baim (1909 – 1994)
Lucy Baim (1912 – 2004)

# Contents

Acknowledgments ................................................................................. vii
Foreword ................................................................................................ ix

### Defining the OS Phase
Chapter 1    Airplanes and Project Management ................................. 2
Chapter 2    Experiencing the OS Phase — Not a Resume Builder ..... 8
Chapter 3    Cleaning Up After the OS Phase Strikes ........................ 11

### Understanding the OS Phase
Chapter 4    That's Not the Problem…This is the Problem! .............. 24
Chapter 5    Managing the Stuff ......................................................... 28
Chapter 6    Changing Current Wisdom ............................................. 39
Chapter 7    Capturing the Right Stuff ................................................ 45
Chapter 8    The Objective to Understand Objectives ....................... 51
Chapter 9    Objectives Burnout ......................................................... 57
Chapter 10  Finding the Magic Pill ..................................................... 66
Chapter 11  It's Customary to Say Everything is Fine! ..................... 78

### Avoiding the OS Phase®
Chapter 12  The Relentless Pursuit of Scope ................................... 96
Chapter 13  Defining Roles and Responsibilities ............................ 114
Chapter 14  Who Do I Really Work For? .......................................... 127
Chapter 15  Risk…The 4-Letter Word That Scares
                the Bajeepers Out of Executive Management ............. 142
Chapter 16  Exactly How Do You Plan to Execute the Project? ....... 153
Chapter 17  You Want It Done…When? The Lighter Side of
                Managing a Critical Path Schedule .............................. 167
Chapter 18  What Story Does Your Schedule Tell? ......................... 179
Chapter 19  An Estimate is Just an Estimate .................................. 190

| Chapter 20 | Managing Behavior — Someone Has to Do It! | 203 |
| Chapter 21 | In Search of the Perfect Project Manager | 214 |

**A World Without the OS Phase**

| Chapter 22 | Understanding the Processes of Project Management | 226 |
| Chapter 23 | Welcome to the P.O.T.P. Convention | 234 |
| Chapter 24 | It's All About Data! Pass It On! | 239 |
| Chapter 25 | The Attributes of a Great Project Management Organization | 245 |
| Chapter 26 | Tracked, Discussed, But Never Managed… the Real Life Cycle of Risk Management | 259 |
| Chapter 27 | Avoidance Metrics | 267 |
| Chapter 28 | Understanding Earned Value Management | 280 |
| Chapter 29 | Avoiding That Déjà vu Feeling | 297 |
| Chapter 30 | Managing Vendors | 309 |
| Chapter 31 | Strategic Chief Projects Officer | 319 |
| Chapter 32 | Multiple Projects | 325 |
| Chapter 33 | Rewriting History— the Unpleasant Saga of Rebaselining | 337 |
| Chapter 34 | Are You Doing What You Said? | 344 |

**The Organization in Crisis — The OS Phase Expanded**

| Chapter 35 | Organization-Wide Implications | 350 |
| Chapter 36 | Reaching Maturity in Project Management | 353 |
| Epilogue | | 359 |
| Glossary | | 361 |
| Index | | 373 |

# Acknowledgments

Family might be the secret ingredient for avoiding the **OS Phase** in our personal lives. A heartfelt thank you is given to all members of my immediate and extended family for their support and encouragement.

I especially wish to thank my wife Kathy for her constant support and the confidence she gave me to keep persevering with the writing of this book. Her insight was profound and resulted in countless improvements. Her willingness to provide candid comments demonstrated an important **OS Phase** avoidance strategy.

A special thank you to my children who helped me translate my passion and convictions for project management into written words…

Eric, who took time away from his MBA studies to provide so many challenging and constructive comments (I think he enjoyed critiquing his dad's work).

Stacia, who provided excellent formatting and content suggestions while busy completing her medical residency.

Jim, my son-in-law, who used his experiences with electrical engineering technology projects to question as well as to validate this book's recommended strategies.

It is also important to acknowledge everyone and every company that has hit the **OS Phase** and as a result provided many of the examples used throughout this story.

And finally, to Joyce Maddox, who spent countless hours editing each draft and making each so much more readable, I am very grateful.

www.avoidingtheosphase.com

# Foreword

My son, Eric, sent me an e-mail after I asked him for any comments or suggestions for a second printing of *Avoiding the OS Phase*®. As part of his response, Eric wrote a foreword-type note. Although it's unusual to include a son's comments as a foreword to a book, Eric's words were so profound and spoken from the heart that I had to choose his comments.

For those of you that offered to write the foreword, I thank you. Please forgive me for not choosing yours. I hope you will understand. Our children represent the next generation and it is important that we ask them for advice, as well as hear their concerns and expectations. The following is taken from Eric's response to me and his note will serve as the foreword to the second edition printing.

...

Dad,

I was just playing around with some thoughts or comments for a second edition and I came up with this. Let me know what you think, or if you would ever be willing to include something like this in a future edition of your book. I could shorten it, lengthen it, or I could tone it down. I shouldn't have to wait to write an introduction to one of your books till it's being published post mortem; that's just depressing, and too many sons do it. Let me know what you think...

Since the first edition of *Avoiding the OS Phase*® was printed, the world has hit its own version of the OS Phase. Basic processes and underlying financial systems systematically failed in a way the world has never seen.

For those of you who are unfamiliar with the OS Phase, you are not alone. This is not a term you learned in business school. It was initially used to define a project that had flown past its deadline or outspent its budget. Essentially, the OS Phase begins when a project has hit the hypothetical "wall" and the only thing left for managers to do is hope to maintain their current job or look for a new one. After studying hundreds of companies and more projects than most could imagine, it was all too clear for my dad, Bob, that the OS Phase was very common. Depending on a variety of factors, this phase may be a bump in the road or a show stopper. Bankruptcy is the ultimate corporate or personal OS Phase, and is usually the result of multiple underlying problems, often in the operational processes. The current worldwide economic situation is the result of fundamental process problems. The problems have centered on people trusting those whom they shouldn't have, and no one wanting to take accountability. Instead of taking accountability, they have ignored the warning signs, ignored the risks, and ignored the approaching cliff. Even the US Government cannot be held without blame. Since the turn of the US housing market in 1995, to the oil spill in the Gulf of Mexico, there have been no governmental actions, only reactions. This sort of reactive management will always be one step behind the curve, and will never see the OS Phase in time. Economists still argue over how fast the economy will recover, with optimists feeling we are on the verge of an upswing. The sad reality is that the economy is fragile and there still are not processes in place to prevent another OS Phase.

We must learn not only how to survive the OS Phase, but hopefully how to avoid it.

I was sitting in an airport years ago when my dad whispered something to me. I thought he was just being weird, or maybe a little paranoid, but he swore me to secrecy. He's usually an animated person, but at this particular moment, he was oddly reserved. As he whispered to me what was to become a profound basis for his first book and a rather radical paradigm change, I was spellbound. He was presenting a new look at predictive project management. The basis for the book was consistent with his personality and his approach to managing people, processes, and projects. They were simple, they were credible and they were predictive. These attributes were perfect for avoiding what he had referred to for years as the OS Phase.

Years later, when he asked me to read the preliminary draft for his book, *Avoiding the OS Phase*®, I realized that not only were the concepts and strategies in the book more comprehensive than several of my new MBA classes combined, they were incredibly easy to understand and to apply as well.

In order to validate my feelings, I quietly bounced several of the strategies from the book off of other MBA students and professors and was quite pleased with their responses. All agreed that the OS Phase Avoidance Strategies, as well as the lessons contained in the chapters, could change the way projects are managed for the better. Sadly, the term OS Phase is not something we learned in business school, but it should have been, and hopefully it will be in the future.

Bob's simple strategies for predictive project management begin with education about the OS Phase. Learning to avoid the OS Phase involves taking a new look at project and institutional processes. Starting with the relentless pursuit of scope, Avoiding the OS Phase® is a step-by-step plan to define and guide roles and responsibilities, project execution and risks, scheduling and estimating, as well as the overall management for any project.

The OS Phase Avoidance Strategies, as well as the lessons contained in each of the chapters, make this book a must have for any project manager, and as useful reference for anyone from a student to a seasoned professional.

Eric J. Baim, May 2010

# Defining the OS Phase

# CHAPTER 1
# Airplanes and Project Management

The *OS Phase* can occur in any aspect of our lives.

The *OS Phase* on a project is when you admit that you've overrun the authorized budget limit or zoomed past the target end date without warning anyone ahead of time.

The *OS Phase* is when a perfect plan stops coming together.

The *OS Phase* is synonymous with the experience companies encounter just before they file for bankruptcy protection.

The *OS Phase* is when chaos reaches its peak and careers begin to change.

The *OS Phase* has always been troubling us, but it's much more evident today because of the speed and pace with which we execute projects and other operational activities.

Most professionals experience the *OS Phase* at some time in their career.

Many professionals are actually in the *OS Phase* now!

There are many names and clichés that we use instead of the term *OS Phase*.

*...the project hit the wall...everything hit the fan*

*...the project is in the ditch...our project is hosed*

No matter what you call it, the *OS Phase* is real. It happens and, when it does, it is an unpleasant experience.

The origin of the name *OS Phase* was purely by accident. Despite the absurdity of the name, the designation seems to have stuck. Maybe the ridiculous nature of the name itself is the staying power.

The *OS Phase* represents a light-hearted depiction of the time period on projects that many of us have experienced and don't ever want to visit again.

> As with any abbreviation, the letters **OS** could have many different meanings. During a project management international satellite broadcast in 1999 that reached South America, the translator, uncomfortable with the American version of the name **OS**, coined the **OS Phase** the "Oh Senor" Phase. As far as I know, this is the only time someone has formally attached a precise meaning for the name. Regardless, though, of its precise meaning, the only good part of the **OS Phase** is when it happens to someone else!
>
> If you've ever hit the **OS Phase**…then maybe…just maybe …you're ready for some suggestions to avoid ever having that experience again!

It was just another hectic day at O'Hare Airport in Chicago. The weather outside was wonderful but the atmosphere inside the airport wasn't so calm. Loudspeakers were busy blaring details of departing and arriving flights.

Today, though, I was feeling great, despite the unsettling chaos. My flight to Dallas was on schedule; there was a plane at the gate, and the pilots just headed down the ramp to start their preflight check. These are positive signs to a seasoned traveler. It was indeed a great day!

Even with such good fortune, it was obvious that other travelers were having difficulties. Constant announcements over the intercom seemed to get louder and more annoying as each moment passed. I couldn't help but notice two travelers sitting adjacent to me who were very upset about something.

My curiosity grew, and with good reason. As a frequent traveler, you learn to stay in tune with changing conditions and potential flight interruptions. I was concerned that something was wrong with our flight to Dallas and maybe they knew something I didn't. If a traveler doesn't act quickly on an unexpected change or delay, they might find themselves in for a long night.

With little hesitation I blurted out to the fellow travelers, "If you don't mind me asking, is there a problem with our flight to Dallas?"

The question seemed to annoy both strangers as my abruptness caused an interruption to their serious discussion. Even with their obvious frustration, they were still polite enough to answer the question.

The man, a well-dressed professional in his late thirties, provided a simple but direct response. "No, we didn't mean for you to get alarmed, we were just stewing over the earlier flight to Dallas that we missed."

Relieved, I acknowledged their comment and continued with my novel.

Although I made every attempt to block out their continuing discussion, the loud conversation was difficult to ignore. Curiosity again took over my thoughts and reading the novel became trivial. If I didn't join in on their discussion, curiosity would consume me.

My family usually tells me to relax and leave others alone, but they were not with me today and I decided to be just a little extroverted!

"What kind of problem did you have with the earlier flight?" I questioned.

Both seemed taken aback by my bluntness but responded that they had expected the earlier flight to Dallas to leave on schedule, but instead the flight had left over forty-five minutes late. This meant they could have taken that flight since there were plenty of seats available and they hadn't checked any baggage.

In a way, this was a strange complaint. We know that the passengers scheduled on that flight weren't happy that it was late, but sometimes one's misfortune is another's gain. If this couple had gotten on the delayed flight, they would be on their way to Dallas sooner.

Since the earlier scheduled flight is often late due to the increased traffic at the end of the day, they called the airline to check on its status. Unfortunately, the automated message announced that the flight was leaving on schedule and would not be late today. Based on this information from the airline, they decided to stop for a bite to eat, only to go to the gate and discover that the flight was late and had just left.

After listening to an all too familiar story, I exclaimed, "Yes, it's a shame. All we want is for people to do what they say they are going to do! It is just as frustrating when someone that should know better brags that everything is on schedule, and then at the last minute, always a most inopportune time, the same person turns around and announces a major delay.

"I've often wondered how long they knew about the delay before they told us the news, recognizing that the bad news in itself isn't the worst part. If the news arrives too late, we've possibly lost other options to consider alternative flights."

Both of the strangers laughed, and one of them responded to my comment, "You're right, all we want people to do is what they say they will do...simple concept, but hard to achieve."

As these new travel companions and I continued to complain about the hassles of flying, the man, who I later learned was Troy, commented, "I guess the airline is no different from the project manager who told us today that the project we need to have completed this month is actually three to five months behind schedule. Alice and I traveled to Chicago to discuss the project's closure and to review the planned turnover steps, only to find out that the project was in the ditch, a very big ditch!"

With only gentle nudging necessary, Alice, an executive in both appearance and demeanor, began to describe the project. A little over a year ago, their newly formed company, appropriately named Mountain Adventures, had embarked on a concept to market and sell complete backpacking trips, using a web site on the internet. It seemed simple enough, but yet innovative. They would sell guided backpacking trips that would include all travel arrangements to the trip's origin. Adventurers would meet their guide at the appropriate location and pick up the necessary pre-ordered equipment. It was a one-stop shopping proposition. The customer would find their internet site, learn about their offering, and then schedule a trip to any number of locations in the country.

The web site would guide them through the process of obtaining airline tickets, hotels, and rental cars to get to the base camp. After arrival, they would receive all of the equipment, such as backpacks, tents, and food, as ordered through the web site.

The concept was a great idea, but the complexity quickly became apparent. The project entailed real time coordination with airlines, hotels, and rental car agencies. A supply distribution system would be required to get the camping equipment delivered to the right location for the right customer at the right time. If they requested a guide, that person would meet them there. There was no room for mistakes.

"Sounds like a pretty interesting venture," I responded. "What is the problem with meeting the project's schedule for starting to provide the mountain adventures?"

Troy hesitated only a second, "A lot of items never considered previously seem to have surfaced this week. The project manager apparently agreed at the beginning of the project to attempt an unrealistic schedule. The sad part is that this is quite common on projects, but no one considered it a significant concern on this particular project.

Everyone was so excited with the idea that few thought seriously about the reality of meeting the commitments."

Alice joined in with the depressing news. "Now some large loan payments are due and we are still spending money, not making any!"

Smiling, I said, "Sounds like you hit the OS Phase on your project."

Puzzled looks, turning quickly to scowls, appeared on both of their faces, so I began to clarify my comment.

It was good to see their looks of frustration turn to slight grins as I explained the new phase of the project they had experienced. "The OS Phase represents a time period occurring when a project, which seems to be on track, hits a brick wall.

"On most projects, we define the elements of the project in terms of phases. We have the conceptual or requirements phase, the design phase, the building or construction phase, the testing phase, and then the final turnover and systems integration phase. These phases represent a time sequencing of project activities. The OS Phase, however, can emerge at any time, although it happens most often towards the end of the project, always at the worst possible time. Ironically, sooner would be better, but often it's very late, too late!"

As further explanation I said, "The actual timing of the OS Phase varies from project to project, but it most often occurs past the originally scheduled midpoint of the project and usually appears without warning. At least we want to believe there was no warning. It's always so amazing to see everyone's surprised reaction when they reach the OS Phase. The sad part is that it's preventable. It doesn't have to happen!"

"What you experienced today was probably avoidable, but that's not what is on your mind now and the last thing you need is for me to 'Monday morning quarterback' your problem."

Troy grinned, "When you think about it, I bet no one wants to admit they saw this thing you call the OS Phase coming on the horizon. It would be career limiting to say they knew it would happen and then did nothing to prevent the disaster."

I smiled while acknowledging Troy's comment. It appeared that he and Alice understood this new name for their recent experience. It was clear, though, that they couldn't joke about it —yet!

---

*OS Phase* **Avoidance**
**STRATEGY 1**

*If your project is in trouble, chances are that you've hit the OS Phase.*

*The sooner you understand and appreciate the reality of the OS Phase the sooner you will be able to start the recovery process.*

# CHAPTER 2
# Experiencing the OS Phase— Not a Resume Builder

Reference to the *OS Phase* puts a smile on faces…most of the time! During seminars and training sessions, I ask participants to indicate by a show of hands those who have visited the *OS Phase* at some time in their career. After a few in the group bravely raise their hands, it seems to encourage others not to be ashamed of admitting the truth. In a few moments time, it is common to have everyone in the assembly holding their hands up high.

It is not a badge of honor; neither is it something to be ashamed of in front of others. The mere fact that so many hands are waving in the air is an inspiration for anyone of us to seek out a cure for the ills that often beseech our projects.

After first learning of the *OS Phase* concept and realizing that there is actually a name for that time on a project, most people are eager to describe their actual experience. Those that laugh and smile probably have distant positive memories, because that's what we usually remember, the positive stuff. When someone glares after hearing the phase mentioned it could be an indicator that not only did that individual hit the *OS Phase*, but they're still there!

The cliché, *you'll laugh about this tomorrow*, probably originated after someone hit the *OS Phase*.

**W**ow! Imagine the frustration felt by Troy and Alice after traveling all the way from Dallas, only to find out that the project they came to wrap up was in fact far from complete. The sad reality is how this same scenario plays itself out with projects in countries around the globe every day!

Using care not to frustrate them anymore than they already were, I spoke in an upbeat and encouraging tone. "Troy and Alice, your problem is not unique. The current situation with your project is a common example of the OS Phase. Unwarranted optimism by your project manager and an eagerness by you and other senior management to overlook the real project status created an environment that was far from reality.

"The fact that the project's problems were disguised for so long should in itself be troubling," I said carefully, not wanting to scold them for their previous misguided reviews of the project. "When the OS Phase starts to approach, the project manager has the choice to respond in different ways. The most damaging reaction is denial and cover-up. Denial may not be intentionally deceitful at the time, but the results will be the same, maybe worse."

Adding more details to the discussion of the downside effects of the OS Phase, I went on to explain, "If a deliberate cover-up or diversionary tactic is attempted, most chances for project success will be lost. The corresponding activities will do nothing to support the project and will ultimately consume so much of the project manager's time they won't have a chance to resolve the real problems with the project itself."

Alice broke her silence and spoke forcibly about how she was starting to feel. "Time spent hiding or managing the news is wasted, absolutely and categorically wasted! It turns out that we have all wasted a lot of time on this project and it's hard to put into words how frustrated I am now. In fact, the more I think about it, it's a good thing Bruce, the project manager, is not sitting with us at the airport."

Responding to her comments, I tried to calm Alice's current anger and frustration. "Alice, how you're feeling now is normal. You are frustrated at being misled, and now your mind is in a fog trying to figure out how you and your associates are going to survive all of the expected criticism."

I explained again to both of them that the OS Phase represents the moment in a project's existence when you realize that the project is not really in good shape after all. At this moment, the project is in serious trouble and no simple solutions will materialize anytime soon. Resumes often come to mind when entering this OS Phase of a project.

Troy quickly saw the correlation of the OS Phase to their project. After reflecting he said, "Even though I'm thinking about this OS Phase thing for the first time, it seems that I've observed it a hundred times in my career.

"Remembering what I've seen in the past, I think when symptoms of the OS Phase start to surface, the project manager and others lose focus and begin spending most of their time dealing with damage control and ignoring the actual project."

Continuing, Troy became more dramatic, "At this moment, no one is looking at our project as a whole. The project is spiraling out of control. The ultimate magnitude of what you call the OS Phase is increasing. Life is not good. It's resume time!"

Alice smiled for the first time. "Now that you've motivated me, Troy, I think I'll catch a plane to the North Pole instead of Dallas."

"And miss out on all the fun getting the project back on track?" I interjected, while watching both Troy and Alice's interest in turning the corner on the project's problems. "The resumes might come in handy later on, but today you need to get motivated to get your project finished."

---

**OS Phase Avoidance
STRATEGY 2**

*The cover-up must never begin. If it has started, it must stop! Time spent on spin control is wasted.*

## CHAPTER 3
# Cleaning Up After the OS Phase Strikes

You might not completely understand all of the **OS Phase** concepts yet, but given some time, it's easy to realize the importance of avoiding it. The tendency is to feel that your projects are unique and special and that your problems are unique and special. I'm reluctant to admit it, but you might be right. Your project may be special, but by the time the last shoe drops, the solutions will inevitably be very similar.

When considering projects in the workplace, it's amazing that most project personnel ignore the **OS Phase** or the **OS Phase** concepts in general as a potential occurrence. "We're special; it won't happen to our project." If you've ever thought that, even for a minute, consider the analogy of a medical doctor's warning to us or any one of our loved ones. *The earlier you catch the problem, the better chance we have to obtain treatment that will work. Wait too long and we hit a very sad, personal* **OS Phase**.

A participant in a seminar asked, "What should you do or what should you say to executive management when your project hits the wall?"

My response was simple. "Go into their office and tell them the project hit the wall."

This blunt response will usually get everyone on the edge of their seats and create a lot of conversation because of the culture not to just drop things on our supervisors or managers. The cliché, *don't bring me a problem if you don't have a solution*, creates an environment hindered by the unpleasant ultimatum.

To the extent that we shouldn't wear out our welcome by having a revolving door of problems, it is still imperative that we let management know as soon as humanly possible when we have a project that is getting into serious trouble.

> We can only hope that the shock value of the term ***OS Phase*** brings enough attention to the problem and wakes up executive management to the consequences of ignoring it before countless future projects fail.

Maybe it wasn't resume time yet for Alice and Troy, but future activities on their project were going to be uncomfortable. It was time now to start getting both of them focused on their next step.

Turning to Troy, I asked, "Troy, what would you have said if the project manager reported a month ago that the project was in trouble and wouldn't meet the deadline? How would you have reacted?"

With no verbal response yet from Troy, I continued the questioning. "Would you have done anything? Would you have tried to motivate the project manager to work harder and get everything back on track? Would you have acknowledged an occurrence like the OS Phase or would you have employed the management skills of motivation to try, and I emphasize the word try, to make the problem go away? Think about it!"

At this point, their silence was normal. Both of their minds were traveling in circles thinking of all the scenarios, many of which were only occurring today due to their recent introduction to the OS Phase concept.

Interrupting the silence, I added, "Tell me today that you would have done something proactive last month. Think about it and make sure you are comfortable with how you feel. And don't worry; it's okay to second-guess how you would have reacted."

Reluctant at first, Alice joined the discussion. "This conversation is wearing me out. I'm personally upset at what we learned today, but the more I think about your questions, I'm not sure that I wouldn't have glossed over bad news last month. I'm not sure that much of anything would be any different than it is today. That's sad when you think about it!"

The serious look on Troy's face indicated that he was listening to Alice's every word and agreeing with what she was saying. "When you work on projects, you get used to hearing things that are upsetting.

The challenge, I guess, is to understand when the problem is really a problem and not just someone whining. Regardless of how either one of us would have interpreted the project manager's announcement, I'm sure we would have used the standard motivational buzz words to try and get him to step up and meet the challenge. We would have raised the bar!"

Alice admitted that her reaction would also be just as shallow. "Now that I think about it, I'm embarrassed to admit that I would have done something as ineffective as the pep rally chant you're joking about. What a waste of time when you actually think about it from the perspective of what we've talked about today.

"Now that we've hit the OS Phase, it is imperative to get the problem on the table to the rest of the company," Alice continued, while trying to remain composed. "If we don't act immediately, we will compound the situation by wasting more time trying to cover up or mask the problem. In fact, I'm not sure we have anymore time to delay. We're up against the proverbial wall and have run out of time for any excuses. I'm so frustrated; it's difficult for me to even discuss the problem anymore."

Listening with obvious interest to Alice's comment, Troy joined in with his personal thoughts. "Alice is right; we are against the wall and have no choice but to let the executive committee know what happened. It would seem like a perfect time to figure out how the politicians develop strategies for *spin control*. I've heard the cliché spin control used many times recently to put that positive spin on a bad situation, but I've never thought about the process itself."

Troy's comments actually brought a smile to Alice's face. "I'm not sure we could spin this problem with any positive slant. It has already spun out of control. We need to figure out instead a good way to *manage the news*."

Alice's use of another worn out cliché lightened the mood a little. Summing up their thoughts, I added, "As many times as we hear both of these clichés, they are quite pathetic. Whatever happened to the concept of stepping up and admitting responsibility and getting the pain over with before it gets worse? Nothing other than a lot of wasted time ever derived from spin control."

After the discussion of managing the news dissipated, Troy and Alice had to get back to the current situation. The new reality faced by both of them was a little unsettling. Even with their high level of frustration, it was important to keep addressing their key concerns.

Continuing with another question, I asked, "Troy, Alice, do you have any idea when the project started to get in trouble?"

After a couple of moments of thought, Alice answered the question. "It's funny that you asked that question because we never even considered failure. That wasn't an option. We're all smart enough to know that our creditors wouldn't accept any sort of delay. Whenever anything started to look like we were slipping, I think we unconsciously ignored the warning. Bruce, our project manager, is so competent we never gave up the faith."

Joining in, Troy added, "It's as if we were wearing blinders and never wanted to see anything bad. Again, as Alice said, failure was not an option. We all focused on always looking at the project from the *glass is half-full* perspective. Until today, everything was always positive and upbeat. We've completed many small projects leading up to this point. I don't think any of these projects had any type of problem."

"That's right. We might have just become complacent," Alice added. "We all wanted to live in a happy world. Our personal lives and other concerns at work might be wearing on us each day, so a little positive performance on the project was refreshing."

With both Alice and Troy still shaking their heads in a somewhat disgusted motion, I thought it appropriate to change the focus of the discussion just a little. I started by asking another direct question. "How would either of you have reacted if the project manager reported at your status meeting that the project would finish precisely on schedule and precisely on budget and would complete all of the features and functionality as was originally proposed?"

With a slightly puzzled look, but without any hesitation, Troy responded, "I'm not sure where you're going with that question, but if I'd heard that kind of news I would think it was the best news we'd ever heard. It would be very exciting and we would thank the project manager and then pass on the news to the big brass."

Turning to Alice, I asked her if she agreed with Troy.

"Absolutely," she responded. "But you're being cruel with that hypothetical question. We never had a chance to hear that kind of performance report."

Trying to keep the mood light, I looked at both of them and said, "Let's stop and think about this whole process for a few minutes. Please let me play with your mind a little. What do you think the odds are that any project manager could bring a complex project similar to this one in on budget and on schedule and within the defined parameters?"

"Anything is possible, I guess," Troy answered quickly, but without the assurance in his voice that he had earlier. "That kind of performance is what we were looking for from the team, but after today it seems a little far-fetched."

Looking at Alice, I waited for her answer.

"Actually, I've never thought about this before and I'm not real sure where you're going with this scenario. I think any manager would be pleased with that type of performance. As Troy said, that's what we expected."

"That's the problem. Your expectations set the wrong tone and create a culture of compliance that might not be realistic," I responded with a firm tone. "I know the scenario I presented might seem odd. I did it to challenge your traditional thinking of what we have grown to expect from our project managers. I defined a status that's actually quite difficult to reach. When you understand the sheer volume of activities going on at any point in a project, it is illogical to think even for a minute that anyone could be tracking so successfully."

"Are you saying that project management and perfection are often not synonymous?" Alice questioned.

"You're quick," I responded. "When a project manager announces perfect performance, it is more likely that they are telling us what we want to hear or are telling us something they themselves hope is true. No one wants to hear bad news. Actually, though, an alarm should ring in our heads anytime we see a project projected to be perfect."

Troy did not see any levity in the conversation and asked bluntly, "What difference does it make? The project is in trouble and we need to figure out a plan to get it back on track, not worry about something that never happened on the project."

"It's hard to argue with your reasoning, Troy," I said, while trying to get his interest back into the conversation. "The significance of these comments is to show that we really have a great misconception when it comes down to what we want from a performance reporting perspective. If we hear good news, life is good. If the project manager confesses to having problems and the project has already hit the OS Phase, then life is bad. In your world there appears to be no in-between. That's where the problem lies. We have to have an in-between status. We need information that predicts we might be getting into trouble and is conclusive in its accuracy."

"Troy, I would like to change your mind about your previous comment," Alice said with a renewed energy level in her voice. "On Monday, less than three days from now, we are going to have to explain how this delay could have happened. I would feel a little more comfortable having some sense of where we are, how we got here, and how we're going to avoid the same problems again. Up until now, we've been spoon-fed what I now realize was unrealistic perfect progress. Unless a meteor dropped on the project this week when we weren't looking, it's going to be difficult explaining what happened. Just as we are in shock today, the executive committee will feel the same way when we drop the news on them."

With even more energy in her voice, Alice went on to say, "The concept of perfect status should have been a clue and it wasn't."

Turning and pointing to Troy, she continued with even more intensity, "I feel that we must take the blame, but the more I think about this perfect reporting scenario, the more I feel the executive committee was just as duped as we were. If we can deal with this fact without rubbing their noses in it, we might be able to soften the blow on Monday."

It was encouraging to see Alice's reaction to the performance reporting concern. This deficiency alone might be the biggest clue that a project is in trouble, and ironically, it's a clue that we most often miss because we're hearing the words we want to hear. What makes matters worse is that a project manager who is describing perfect performance is actually using the laziest approach. They're not working very hard to deceive us. A person doesn't have to be very creative when just repeating the approved project baseline values.

Troy now began to change his viewpoint somewhat as he was relating the discussion to the project. Summarizing what he heard, he said, "I guess the problem is that it's easy to exaggerate progress and hide the real performance of any project. When progress is exaggerated, we can expect the exaggeration to be close to the targeted baseline values."

"That's right," I responded, and then moved the conversation to a little different twist by asking another pointed, but relevant, question. "Did either of you see anything from your recent meeting that was indicative of a meteor falling out of the sky? If the previous reports were good news, what aspect of them changed today? Where were they wrong?"

Alice smiled and commented, "I'm just as curious as you are, but I have the advantage. All of the previous performance reports are here on my laptop. I saw where the conversation was going so I retrieved the most recent electronic files for the project's performance reports. After a quick glance, I'm embarrassed to share them with you."

"What's wrong?" I asked. "Were the previous performance reports a little too positive?"

Alice shook her head in agreement and then related her findings. "It's absolutely amazing. Up until last week, every aspect of the project was right on track. Like you said, on budget and ready to deliver the complete package in two months as scheduled. We had a fantastic project."

With a great deal of reflection bouncing around in her head, Alice said, "It became so chaotic today with the shock of the news that I for one didn't even think about the previous reports. The more I think about what happened, the more troubling it becomes. Troy and I became so fixated on how we were going to present the news when we got back to Dallas we actually lost sight of the project itself."

I tried to convince them that their reaction was normal considering the situation. The project manager is in a corner and hopes to catch everyone off guard by using a shock factor. The inevitable is now here and the result will not be pretty.

Troy was beginning to get either very nervous or very anxious. His pacing back and forth was obviously beginning to annoy some of the travelers closest to us. Abruptly, he stopped in mid-stride and, with almost a tearful exclamation, spoke quietly to both of us, "You have to understand that the roll-out of this project is the heart and soul of our company! Failure is not an option! We have already said that we have investors ready to start seeing some payback. Instead, we might even be hitting them up for more cash. This is devastating! This may even be career limiting for both of us. Yes, Alice, you and I might be facing dismissal when the investors hear the news."

Troy continued with even more veracity, "Whether you call what happened to the project hitting the OS Phase or just plain hitting the wall, we have failed and that is all anyone will see. We are going to look like fools when we meet with everyone on Monday."

The scene with Troy's emotional realization was classic, considering what had happened. I couldn't help but remember, from seminars I've taught, the description of the Seven Phases of a Project.

...*Wild Enthusiasm*
...*Disillusionment*
...*Chaos*
...*Search for the Guilty*
...*Punishment of the Innocent*
...*Promotion of the Non-participants*
...*Definition of the Requirements*

Months ago, Troy and Alice were definitely in the *Wild Enthusiasm Phase*, only to switch abruptly to the *Disillusionment Phase* after this afternoon's meeting and now Troy is feeling the effects of certain *Chaos* emerging in his life. With his latest comment about Monday, certainly the idea of blame and finger pointing were on the horizon.

I had to convince them to concentrate on the project and not on spin control. It's not always apparent, but the worst part of spinning bad news is the time we waste doing it.

It turned out that letting Troy vent his frustration was helping. He needed to get his feelings out in the open and now that he felt better, it was time to get them focused on Monday.

Careful not to exploit Troy's current mood, I asked about the next step. "You both mentioned a meeting on Monday. I realize that today is Friday and you probably don't want to make a call now, but don't you think that a little heads-up to the executive committee is appropriate before Monday?"

"Yes, we need to pass on some information," Troy agreed, "but I'm not sure what to tell them. We were blind-sided today and we still don't have all of the facts. I'm not sure we will have anymore explanations by Monday either."

Alice took Troy's lead and began to call the members of the executive committee today and ask for their support Monday morning in looking at strategies to improve an unexpected delay in the adventures project.

Her avoidance of details in the phone conversations was appropriate. Despite any attempt to get more information from her, Alice had to stay firm and hold everyone off until Monday.

As she finished her last call, we were getting close to boarding our plane to Dallas. I thought it might be appropriate to bring Troy and Alice back to where they needed to be to get ready for the next step. With care not to add fuel to the fire, I summarized the situation as I saw it. "Please consider what you're doing. You have a complex project, with urgent completion needed so some hungry investors can be satisfied. You discovered at the last minute that some major project problems exist. You're getting ready to fly back to Dallas for a meeting on Monday to tell senior management something. Realistically, you won't have more information Monday than you have today."

Alice was now feeling the pressure. "What do you think we should do instead?"

The response was easy. "We met forty-five minutes ago, you're in trouble; this is what's happening. What you do next is up to you, but you might want to call your travel agent and delay your flight to Dallas until Sunday night. Then you need to get on your mobile phone and call the project manager that you so kindly let off the hook when you left today and you should get his butt back into the office tonight. You need to meet with Bruce and begin to lay out a plan of action that has some level of credibility when the three of you present it to the executives on Monday in Dallas. Better yet, you might even want to set up a video telecom on Monday so that you will appear to be dealing with the problems directly."

Continuing, I added, "The biggest problem is that you have to make a decision in the next couple of minutes and you better make sure Bruce isn't leaving town and is accessible this weekend."

Troy and Alice agreed and were able to line him up for two hours this evening and then for the rest of the weekend. Troy thought it best to return Sunday with the project manager as they could negotiate the compromise much better in person than over a video. Considering the possible reactions on Monday, he made a strong point about the advantage of being physically present at the meeting.

With the recovery plan now in motion, Alice seemed relieved. She smiled for the first time and looked directly at me. She then began, "Well, Troy and I are perfect strangers to you. We've spent the last forty-five minutes pouring our souls out to you and you've certainly helped us get focused. Is there even a slight chance that you could spend some time this weekend explaining the OS Phase to us?"

Also smiling, Troy added, "Actually I was hoping you could tell us how to get out of the OS Phase before Monday. I think we both know what the OS Phase is; now we need to know what on earth we should do to save the project."

At this point, it was difficult to resist. My wife will say I should have just minded my own business and kept reading my novel, but whenever a project is in trouble, it's not easy to turn away from it, so I agreed. "If you believe I can help, I will meet with you Saturday. Tonight you need to get with Bruce and do everything possible to squeeze out the details behind what happened today. My only limitation is that I have to leave for Dallas Saturday evening. My next engagement isn't until Wednesday, but my wife is flying in from Virginia to meet me late Saturday evening. It is important that I'm there in time to take her out for a late dinner."

"Or you might hit the OS Phase in your marriage?" Alice added with a smile, as everyone acknowledged how the OS Phase links to our personal lives as well.

"Absolutely," I responded without hesitation. "I've spent thirty-two years avoiding that OS Phase, and when I look back at it, it was a lot easier to avoid it than experience it.

"If I am able to change my flight and meet in the morning, it is imperative that we have a productive session. To accomplish that goal, I must stipulate that you two and Bruce spend the first four hours in the morning working with me on process related problems. You have to agree that you will not talk about project specifics. If we get wrapped up in the project itself, we will never get out of town on time."

Alice and Troy took a step back, but didn't challenge me before I finished my comments. "Your project is not in trouble because it's a bad idea or it is impossible to actually do. Your project is in trouble because you have routine process issues. The solution will probably not be difficult, but you must be ready to introduce the process issues and not drag the discussion down into a ditch by getting into the gory details of the project."

The response was simultaneous, "Okay, that's a deal. We'll look at those gory details you've referred to tonight and start off with an open mind in the morning."

They were both intrigued with the discussion of the OS Phase.

I think they would have rather heard about it, though, and not actually experienced it!

Taking Troy's business card with the address of the office, I headed back to see if I could extend my hotel stay for another evening. The earlier discussion energized Troy and Alice for the moment, but I suspected that they would get a little down in the dumps after I met with them again in the morning. At this point, ignorance is bliss!

Alice waved and said, "Get plenty of rest. We plan on working hard tomorrow morning."

---

### *OS Phase* Avoidance
### STRATEGY 3

*Beware of the perfect status report. If a report seems overly optimistic then there's a possibility that the team is embellishing the performance to date and ignoring the future.*

*If in fact all of your projects are as perfect as their status reports indicate, pass this book on to a more deserving associate before reading any more pages and enjoy life; you've earned it!*

I hope they will get rest too, because they are the ones that have to deal with a complete reversal of the way they do business. On the other hand, I will be doing something I love to do!

# Understanding
the OS Phase

## CHAPTER 4
# That's Not the Problem …
# *This* is the Problem!

Entrance into the **OS Phase** is not a good experience. The first reaction is most often denial. When reality finally sets in, either our mind goes too fast out of control and we grasp at any task that will make us feel like we're doing something, or we sit in a daze. Either way, nothing productive is accomplished.

Criticism by others often accompanies project failure. For the project manager or team, it is only natural to become defensive. Many clichés come to mind.

*"Try walking in my shoes, even for one day, and then you would understand!"*

Ironically, the worst part of being defensive is when someone says, "don't be defensive." Courses in anger management come to mind at this point. Behavioral issues explode, self-esteem is low, concern for future employment is high and unwanted help is out of the question.

We believe our problem is the biggest in the world. Charles Schultz created a cartoon years ago that I've carried with me since the first time I read it in the newspaper comics….

Remember, we all have problems. The difference is how we choose to deal with them.

Everyone arrived Saturday promptly at 8 o'clock in the morning at the moderately appointed offices of the project team in Chicago. The meeting room was a typical conference room, with a boardroom-style table in the middle, surrounded by whiteboards and flip charts. There were a couple of project schedules hanging randomly on the wall. Decorations were scarce.

Meeting Bruce, the on-site project manager, for the first time was a little awkward. Apparently Troy and Alice confronted him last evening about the problems and briefed him about my planned participation during the Saturday events. After a few short pleasantries, and with a fresh pot of coffee brewing in the adjacent break room, we sat down in the sterile but comfortable conference room.

"How did everything work out last evening?" I asked, breaking the uneasy silence.

"We developed a lengthy list of problems and worked on some strategies for presenting them to management on Monday," Alice commented, while moving to the whiteboard to show how the list was organized.

She explained that they sorted the list of issues by category and identified the group on the team responsible for resolution. The list was extensive.

As I began my discussion, I could see Bruce getting tense. It was clear he was uncomfortable with my presence. Keeping him on task was going to be a challenge. Defensiveness is a common trait of a project manager after they hit the OS Phase. The fact that a consultant was here to help compounded everything!

*Welcome to my world!*

Turning to Bruce, I asked, "Last evening, did Alice and Troy discuss my stipulation for our session this morning?"

Given the opportunity to share his opinion, Bruce didn't waste a single moment, as he blurted out, "As a matter of fact they did talk to me about the stipulation, and that leads me to ask why we're wasting time at this point in the project looking at basic processes. An even bigger question is 'who are you?' It seems like they picked up a stray dog at the airport, someone they didn't know before yesterday and now you're here asking questions that are none of your business."

Continuing, after catching his breath, Bruce went on to complain, "As far as any of us know, you might even be a competitor. I'm supposed to listen to someone I don't know about processes that aren't important because we hit what you refer to as the OS Phase? I dare anyone to look at what we're doing this morning and then criticize me for my actions."

Bruce wasn't bashful with his comments and overall concern about the meeting. Although it wasn't necessarily up to me to explain my presence, I thought it might be best at this point because Troy and Alice might be developing the same apprehensions in their own minds now that Bruce brought the subject up.

Calmly facing the frustrated project manager, I started responding to the concerns on the table. "Bruce, your comments were expected. In fact, had you not questioned the process, it would have seemed odd. Nevertheless, I would like you to think about what I have to say regarding the current situation. You have nothing to lose by listening for a couple of hours this morning. Your project is in trouble and it's natural to feel uncomfortable talking with a stranger about it. That's why we're talking about process first and not the project. I don't have time to understand the details of your project. That is your responsibility. We will not divulge any big, dark secrets. What I can help with is how you manage the effort from this point forward and work with you on how to present some recommendations to senior management on Monday."

"But we don't have time to get you up to speed with the details of our project," Bruce said in a whining voice. "No offense to you, but we need to get going with our ideas for Monday and not spend valuable time talking with you about processes and details of a project that you just heard about yesterday."

After letting his comment drift off without impact, I waited for what seemed like an eternity to respond in a calm but professional voice. "Troy and Alice have a realistic concern about what might happen on Monday. It is conceivable that all three of you will be unemployed by Monday evening. Casting blame on anyone but yourselves and reeling off a lengthy list of excuses now will not prevent that from happening."

Now, with Bruce's full attention, I continued, "The most important thing you must do on Monday is admit that you all messed up and messed up really bad! Then to survive, you'd better give everyone the confidence that you have a clue about what you have to do and how you intend to manage the team from this point forward."

"You're right about what might happen," Bruce interrupted, "but we need to get going right now with solving the issues listed on the board, and sitting here with you is only frustrating me more. We need to capture these items in the project schedule and start assigning dates for resolution to each one of them. I'm not sure what you are going to add, but I just described the proper way to manage a project. We can't just sit around and talk about it forever."

Bruce was obviously getting anxious and, as a result, losing his cool. It was important for me to keep calm but unrelenting in the need for the process reviews. I continued without staring him down, "If I had any reason to believe the list on the board to be complete, I would support your comment. But, realistically, the list is probably deficient and anything that you learn from your work on those items will not help you solve any of the items that might be missing. When you find the additional items next week or even the next, you will, in effect, hit the OS Phase again.

"Even if by some slim chance you survive on Monday, you won't last past the next crisis," I continued. "Let's make sure you get the list right this time and then management will feel comfortable that they have the proper team to bring the project home. On Monday, you won't be selling your knowledge of the performance of the project, but, instead you will be selling your strategy for getting the project completed. Now let's get started."

> **OS Phase Avoidance**
> **STRATEGY 4**
>
> *If other team members aren't familiar with the concept of the OS Phase, then take the time to bring them up to speed.*
> *It's time to get everyone focused on fixing the process problems, not covering them up!*

# CHAPTER 5
# Managing the Stuff

Fascination with predictive project management, and the *OS Phase* in particular, stemmed from seeing several catastrophic project failures and my curiosity at how these projects had gotten to the point of complete collapse before anyone even noticed. The more I thought about the failures and the possible causes, the more perplexing it became. Certainly, someone had to know that something was wrong.

It was reasonable to expect that the team could hide problems from the sponsor or client, but what about those people directly related to the project on a day-to-day basis? They wouldn't be able to ignore what was going on with the project.

How was denial possible? Why weren't the problems obvious to everyone? These questions kept surfacing on every troubled project I reviewed. It was clear that the predictive tools were not working well. None of the project management *processes* worked properly.

Upon further review, it was clear that the peril these projects faced wasn't totally a secret. However, those closest to the projects discounted the severity of the problem and, in many instances, no one felt it necessary to stop the project or alert senior management about any impending doom. After all, the team could fix the problem. Management challenged the team to make it happen, and now the team needed to make some corrections but without any meddling or micromanagement from senior management. Unfortunately, this mixture of optimism and pride resulted in many members on the teams overlooking the *process* problems until it was too late.

As it turns out, many of these failed projects did have a common problem...a glaring deficiency! These projects lacked a comprehensive *process* for managing the actual work items comprising the project itself, something often called *scope*.

This is where I had to make sure I was looking at the cause and not the effect.

When projects miss their scheduled completion dates and the team overruns the cost targets, everyone links the failure to an execution issue, not a *scope* management problem. Actually, it was much easier to blame the entire list of project problems on management's unrealistic target date, resource deficiencies, priority changes, or just lack of management support in general. After all, these excuses were out of the direct control of the project manager.

Even with a project manager's admission to a total lack of a *process* to manage the work of the project, any serious discussion criticizing *scope* management *processes* draws empty stares or sarcastic comments from the project manager, team members, and even senior management. It might be the simplistic nature of *scope*, but most project managers think they have a complete grasp of the *scope* management process.

Bottom line, *scope* is routine and is nothing special, or is it?

Based on my unplanned involvement with their project I needed to understand what processes the team had in place before getting too far ahead and trying to fix the project itself. It was important to make sure everyone understood that projects don't fail…processes do!

Although I doubted that Alice, Troy, and Bruce needed any basic instruction in project management, it was, nevertheless, still important to make sure we were all on the same page as far as project management processes were concerned.

Stopping and reviewing project management processes at this stage of a project is challenging because of the emotional explosion that accompanies hitting the OS Phase. It's not surprising that most team members are chomping at the bit to fix things, hopefully before too many people find out!

A technique that I use when beginning project management training classes, seminars, or consultancy sessions is to ask the participants as a group to describe key areas where a project manager must focus attention each day. In most cases, the groups will hit several areas, e.g. scope, time, cost, communication, quality, or risk but will forget others.

The Project Management Institute (PMI), a fast growing international professional society of project managers, describes nine Knowledge Areas in their Guide to the Project Management Body of Knowledge (PMBOK®Guide). These Knowledge Areas represent what they feel are important for the successful implementation of a project management program.

In order to engage any group into the discovery process, I draw a circle on a board or flip chart (Chart 5 – 1), place the symbol **PM** in the middle to represent the project manager and then draw several arrows pointing inward. I then ask everyone to suggest areas that require a project manager's focus each day. I title the flip chart *Project Management Focus Areas*.

One at a time, I then capture the suggested areas and add them to the chart. Without being specific or giving anything away to the group, what I'm actually looking for are the PMI Knowledge Areas. Quite often it's necessary to make subtle suggestions in order to capture the complete list.

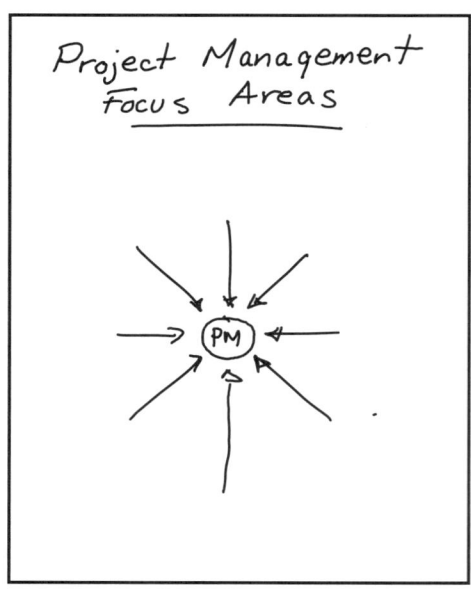

**Chart 5 - 1**

For emphasis, I purposely save Integration for last. Drawing a circle encompassing the other eight areas is a powerful visual of the role of the project manager to integrate all facets of the project (Chart 5 – 2).

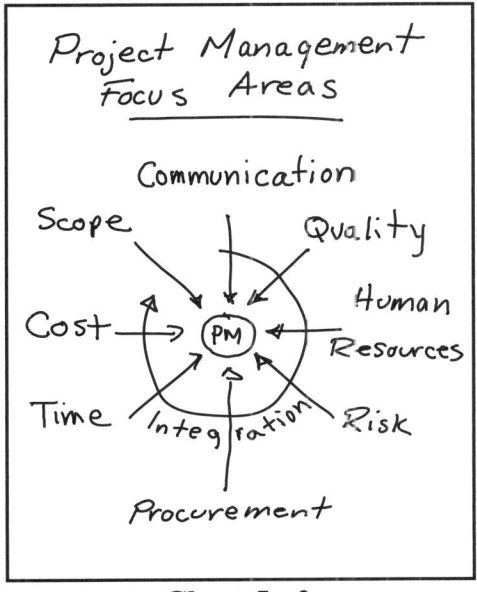

**Chart 5 - 2**

Not sure where I was heading with the discussion, Bruce reluctantly contributed some of the items on the chart. Even with his participation, he was less than impressed with the process.

Bruce's impatience surfaced again as he addressed Troy and Alice, purposely leaving me out of his sight path. "He's right. In a perfect world, a project manager has time to sit and contemplate for a few minutes everyday as to what is important. The problem is that our project is far from the perfect world and there's hardly time to stop and do what's on the daily agenda, let alone ponder the mysteries of project management. We all have heard of the Project Management Institute and at one time or another we have referenced their guide, but, again, this was not a perfect project and standard processes and solutions wouldn't work. This project is special and we all knew that it was special when we started it eight months ago!"

Bruce's blunt comments were starting to concern Alice and Troy. It's not that they were saying anything to Bruce specifically, but their non-verbal cues were quite telling. Before either one of them said anything, I reminded Bruce about his promise to be patient. His concern for the future of the project was important, but he needed to listen and turn his attention onto process issues rather than specific project issues.

Bruce's passion for his project was a good thing. We just needed to get him to concentrate on the right areas. Getting him to calm down, however, was going to be a challenge, one hopefully worth the effort.

After a short break to grab breakfast snacks and drinks, I decided that we had better get Bruce engaged quickly because his promise of patience might not last much longer.

Addressing Bruce, I stood again, moved towards the whiteboard, and said, "Bruce, we will all agree that this project is special, but at the moment I want to bring us back toward the processes of project management on the flip chart and not dwell on specific aspects of the project."

Acknowledging Bruce's somewhat reluctant agreement, I turned to all three and started the next discussion. "When we embark on any project, it's a classic behavioral tendency to make the management processes more complicated than necessary, especially if it is thought to be a special project. The irony is that the resultant effect of imposing complicated or unnecessary processes might end up being the first step towards failure and ultimately the OS Phase. In order to avoid anything like that for the balance of the project, the suggested approach I will take in the next half hour will be simple, very simple!"

Making sure that Bruce understood the concept surrounding the OS Phase, I began by asking the group a rather straightforward question. "What do we mean when we refer to something as a project?"

Not surprisingly, the simplicity of the question set Bruce off again. In a rude outburst, with his attention directed my way, he spoke in a sarcastic tone, "Whoa! This is too basic. We have a million dollar project that's hit the wall, and you're asking us the definition of a project. We need to move a little faster. I think we all know what makes a project!"

Replying in a directed tone, I continued with another question. "We know that a project manager has to manage the project management focus areas we drew on the flip chart a few minutes ago. Now getting to Bruce's question, what is it that the project manager is actually managing?

"Stuff!" Bruce shouted. "Stuff is what we're managing. All kinds of complicated stuff that in our case is way behind schedule and is going to get us all fired if we don't get it done!"

"Great answer," I said excitedly. "I'm pleased that we're on the same page. From a purely simple perspective, all we do as project managers is work on stuff. Every project is made up of stuff and everyone is going to have to help get the stuff completed."

"I was only kidding when I used the word stuff," Bruce shouted in a joking but sarcastic tone. "You can't be serious if you think that projects are made up of stuff."

Alice smiled and turned to Bruce, "You're the one that mentioned the word. Let's use your term and move on. We have a lot to do today, and arguing isn't helping."

Leveraging off Alice's comment, I again took charge of the conversation. "Okay, let's focus on a concept about stuff. Every project consists of something that needs completion by a certain date and usually with a limit of money or just plain physical effort. Calling that something *stuff* is just a way to depersonalize it. That's an important step. The stuff could be a rocket fired towards Mars or it could be a file of computer code to perform some type of business transaction. No matter what it is, it's still just stuff."

"Wow, I'm not sure I agree, but I'm still listening," Troy said while shaking his head.

"Great!" I continued. "Now that we've agreed on the stuff, let's give it a more proper name. In the formal project management world, it's common to refer to the stuff as scope, the same scope we referred to on the other diagram as a Knowledge Area."

"Great, scope's a term I've heard before," Troy exclaimed, "although we actually use a different term on the project. We use the word 'requirements.' The project requirements are the stuff we're doing. Each of the requirements is put into action and included in the project schedule for tracking purposes."

Bruce was becoming agitated again, and commented, "If you use the term scope, why in the world did you beat around the bush playing games with the word *stuff*? We would have understood scope and would have understood sooner."

It was apparent that Bruce was going to argue about everything. It would be easy to strike back at him by saying that if he really did understand scope then the project wouldn't be in trouble. Instead, I realized that I had to keep Bruce focused, without being too critical of anything he had done up to now.

Bruce's impatience is a common personality flaw in project managers bred to feel that they must do something at all times or they are wasting time. Listening skills are hard to teach to project managers, especially when time is limited. More times than necessary, I had to bring Bruce back to his commitment to sit and listen patiently for a couple more hours.

Responding to Bruce's comment, I said, "Most of the time I do use the word scope, but in today's project management world it has so many meanings that the resultant confusion causes many to misunderstand what is meant. I like to use words that get attention. If we can't get everyone's attention, it's difficult to get everyone to understand and to change."

For the first time I received a positive nod from Bruce, so I continued. "Now that we've beat the word stuff around so much, I don't think there will be any confusion as we move forward. But maybe, Bruce, you can use the word scope when you report to executive management on Monday."

"Instead of the term scope, is it acceptable to refer to it as requirements when we meet on Monday?" Alice asked.

"To answer that question accurately, let's look at the supporting process first and then decide on what we'll call the term for scope on this project." I continued, "You were correct when you used the term requirements, because it is common for many project managers and customers to refer to scope as requirements. After all, requirements represent what has to be completed."

"Then why don't we use the term requirements on all projects?" Troy asked.

"When you sit down and assess requirements you realize they are only part of the scope on your project," I responded.

"What do you mean, part of the scope?" Bruce asked.

Thinking aloud, I responded to Bruce's question. "Requirements represent an item that must be delivered or they represent a condition that has to be met. Often they don't include the work you have to do to get a sub-tier supplier's contract in place. They don't include the work you have to do to attend performance meetings and prepare performance reports. Requirements might only include what we refer to as product scope, that is, scope related to the product or the result of the project itself.

"In fact, a very common way to describe scope is to show its relationship with time and cost," I said, while drawing a big triangle on the flip chart (Chart 5 - 3). "If you write scope, time, and cost on each side of the triangle you can see an important relationship. This triangle will become one of the most relevant project management tools we will discuss today. Sometimes it is referred to as the triple constraints."

Smiling, Alice said, "I've heard a phrase used to describe the triangle. You can have any two out of three…good, fast, or cheap. That kind of means the same thing, doesn't it?"

Acknowledging her comment with a grin, I responded with an agreeing tone, "Absolutely! Now isn't it a real shame that we never pay attention to a cliché that's been around for decades. Why do we continue to attempt to do the impossible?"

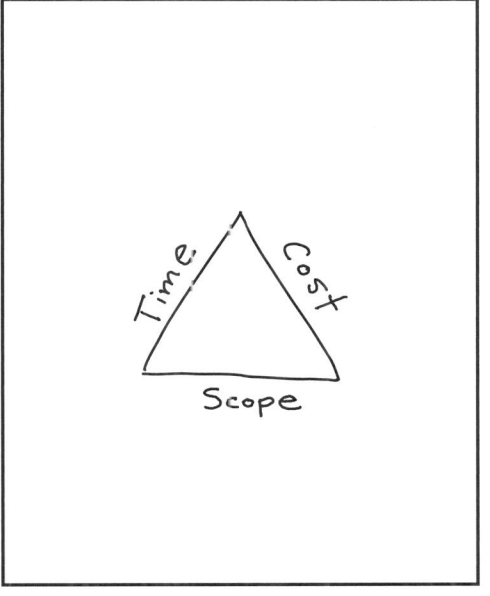

**Chart 5 - 3**

After answering the obviously rhetorical question, I continued by describing the triple constraints in a way that tied directly to the project. It was important to get the idea of the relationship between the attributes of these three components fixed firmly in each of their minds.

I spent additional time reviewing the relationship of scope, time, and cost, and then validated the relationships by providing several pertinent examples of how this simplistic tool becomes such an important concept in the realm of project management. All three now understood the need to have a "balanced triangle." If any of the three elements of the triangle is out of kilter with the other two, then that imbalance needs addressing immediately.

Given the fact that their project hit the OS Phase, they could complete what's left to do on the project fast and cheap, but the quality would be poor and the sales of adventures would plummet. If they decided to complete it fast and good, it might not even be possible, but if it were, it would be very expensive and might make it impossible to break even on the costs in enough time to keep the company solvent. The other choice, to do the balance of the project good and cheap, would take a lot of time. It is more than likely that it wouldn't even be possible to consider that option at this point.

The reality of the triangle does not vanish with wishful thinking or motivational pep talks. For the first time this morning, Bruce was attentive and even appeared interested. I wanted to get him engaged in the discussion on scope so I made sure to address him personally during the discussion. "Bruce, do you have any suggestions as to what scope is made up of on your project, or any project for that matter?"

Before he could answer, I wrote the Requirements in parenthesis below the scope label (Chart 5 – 4) and then turned back to Bruce for any other elements that we should capture. As so often happens, Bruce had never considered the details of what is included in scope.

He thought for a minute, then added Quality and Performance.

After that change in the makeup of scope, everyone started to understand the actual significance of scope. It included many project parameters that were obvious and probably many parameters that were not so obvious.

In a change of roles, Troy was showing signs of uneasiness with the discussion, so I

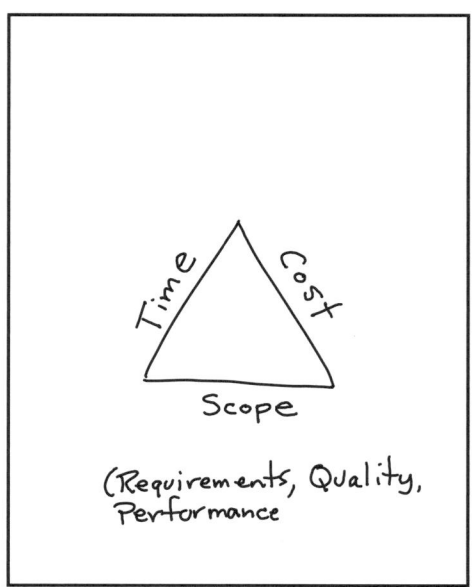

**Chart 5 - 4**

challenged him personally to make sure he had a good grasp on what scope was before we went any further with the discussion. I joked that I was a scope-aholic and hoped that he would become one as well.

It was important for Troy and everyone else to recognize that scope was possibly the most important element of any project.

Even though Bruce understood the purpose of requirements, performance, and quality, he joined with Troy in questioning the definition of scope. He went further than Troy and asked for a formal definition of scope.

It was obvious that he wanted to understand why scope was so important and he wasn't going to accept just any answer. Eyeing a project management text sitting on a shelf in the corner of the conference room, I asked Troy to grab it and see if there was a definition for the term scope either in the text or in the glossary.

Troy was able to find the word in the glossary and read it aloud. "Scope represents the sum of all project elements. It represents the product of the project."

Listening intently to the definition, Alice joined in with a milder paraphrasing of the book's definition. "Scope is what we're doing on the project. It is the stuff!"

Everyone laughed at Alice's use of the term stuff. Although an unconventional word for what we call scope, the term stuff does get you to thinking a little about words and their starchy definitions.

Even with the current levity in the room, none of these definitions struck a chord with Bruce. Like a broken record, he kept up his persistence, "Be specific!" He said, "What is scope in the project context? How can I be sure I'm managing all of the scope if you can't get me to understand what it is or what it's made up of?"

Bruce was very challenging, but his persistence turned out to be a blessing in disguise. Even though I was getting frustrated at his stubbornness, it was vital that he understand the meaning of scope. I could see Alice and Troy's mind also working feverishly. My brain was considering many different options for presenting a better definition, but nothing different popped into my mind.

I understood what scope was, but how could I share that vision with Bruce?

Everyone in the group now focused on me, waiting for a response.

Continuing the discussion, while walking and pointing towards the triangle drawn on the flip chart, I said, "My best definition of scope is not the one in the project management textbooks. Scope is *anything that takes time or costs money*."

Alice appeared to like the definition. She turned to Bruce and asked, "How's that for simple, Bruce?"

After Bruce smiled and acknowledged the simplicity of the definition, Alice said, "Based on this definition, it turns out then that scope is more than just requirements or specifications. Scope is more than just the product, it is much more than just technology, and it is more than services provided. Scope is everything a project manager must do to satisfy expectations of all of those associated with a project, and in our world, those people would be what we refer to as the stakeholders on our project."

It was clear that everyone was satisfied with the new definition, so it was important to validate that point. I moved back to the flip chart and said in a firm voice, "We need to move on with our discussion this morning and as far as this scope thing is concerned, scope is something that we won't know for sure what it will include on any project until we relentlessly seek it out!" Then beating my hand again on the flip chart where the triangle was drawn, I repeated what I said earlier, but this time with more oomph. "Forget all of the fancy definitions, just remember that scope is anything that takes time or requires some type of effort!"

"It's the stuff!" Alice shouted.

"It's what we have to do to complete the project," Troy added.

"It's the most important feature of any project," Bruce said with a new air of confidence.

> *OS Phase* **Avoidance**
> **STRATEGY 5**
>
> *You can spend a lot of time doing project work, but until you find all of the stuff, you will only be spinning your wheels. You must seek out all the scope in a relentless manner.*

# CHAPTER 6
# Changing Current Wisdom

Being able to convince professionals that a failure to manage *scope* could result in complete project failure is difficult. Everyone recognizes the importance of managing *scope*, but very few, and I say it again, very few professionals draw the correlation between the lack of *scope* management and hitting the **OS Phase**. When this misconception changes, significant improvements in project management will be possible, but until then, the **OS Phase** will remain a common phase on most projects.

There are many clichés describing the phenomenon associated with managing the *scope*, but the bottom line is this: if you don't have a proven *process* for managing the elements of the project, what we've referred to as *scope* or *stuff*, success is not in the cards. In most cases, only sheer luck could guide these project teams to successful conclusions.

A vital step is the recognition that *scope* is more than something you document in a set of specifications or requirements documents. Instead, it is an organized grouping of little triangles, each with *scope*, time and cost encompassing every element of work performed on the project.

It is so important to understand that you can't manage a project until you "have" a project. The "have" is the *scope* or *stuff*. You must get your arms around the *stuff* before you can ever successfully move forward.

Alice was leaning back in her chair visualizing the significance of our conversation. She then spoke, presenting a summary of her thoughts. "When we fail to consider everything we do on a project as part of the stuff, we will end up with costs that are greater than expected. The concept of scope or stuff linking so directly to time and cost or effort is fantastic. If we do things right, we shouldn't have problems at all."

"Just think how easy it will be to find the stuff. All we have to do is perform a simple test. If it takes any amount of time or relates to time in any way, or takes any type of effort or cost, it is stuff. Even a milestone, a point in time marker, is stuff, because it has a time component related to it. Remember, anything that takes time or has a cost is stuff," Troy said, with everyone else nodding in agreement.

As it so often turns out, the word scope, or stuff as we call it, has many definitions, but what we're looking at there is the work related to the project. After our earlier effort to seek out the textbook meaning of scope, Troy found the definition in a dictionary located in the conference room. He read the definition aloud. "Scope is the extent of a situation, activity, or subject."

After we digested the words and thought about that definition for a few minutes, we all agreed that the definition was consistent with what we might have expected. The key word in the definition is the word *extent*. We want to define every element of the work to every *extent* or boundary that has to be completed, not just the requirements, not just the physical portion of the work, but every element to the fullest *extent* of the work.

After Alice bounced the definition around in her mind a few minutes, she shared her thoughts with the rest of us. "The use of the word *extent* is indeed powerful. It directs us to capture and manage all work associated with the project, not just certain portions, but all of it!"

"That's right," I responded, while agreeing with her comment and making sure that Bruce was listening to the discussion. "Just the fact that we are arguing about the definition of scope demonstrates one of the basic concerns with project management. Project management processes have become so complex that we have actually moved away from handling the most basic elements of the project, like scope. We talk about it a lot, but we do very little with it."

"I agree," Troy interjected. "It's easy to sit here and say that we need to find the full extent of the scope, but to actually find it is another story entirely. There are many times that we start projects without even a semblance of the scope we will eventually end up with at the completion of the project."

"I agree with Troy," Bruce added with his impatient voice again surfacing. "Dealing with scope in the beginning of the project is difficult. It makes more sense to start working on what we know about and leave the rest of the scope to the point in time when we figure out what it is all about."

In order to avoid future confusion, I took the time to explain the terms a bit more. When we say, "Takes time or costs money," we have to remember that some projects track hours and not money. It would be easier to say "takes time or effort," but that might get confused with some "time versus effort" discussion we are going to have later on in the day.

"Do you have a name for the triangle, other than just triangle?" Troy asked.

"As a matter of fact, I refer to it formally as the Avoidance Triangle," I answered as I added those words to the flip chart (Chart 6 – 1). "If we pay attention to the triangle's relationships between scope, time, and cost, we will be taking our first step towards avoiding the OS Phase. Unfortunately, so few professionals take it seriously that I've nicknamed it the Stupid Triangle, not because it's stupid, but because any time we ignore the relationship between scope, time, and cost, we're stupid."

Bruce loved the introduction of the Avoidance Triangle, but, not surprisingly, he preferred the nickname to the formal name. Now he had a new word to add to his project management vocabulary. Let's see, first we had stuff and now Stupid Triangle. It must feel like he's having a dream, or maybe a nightmare!

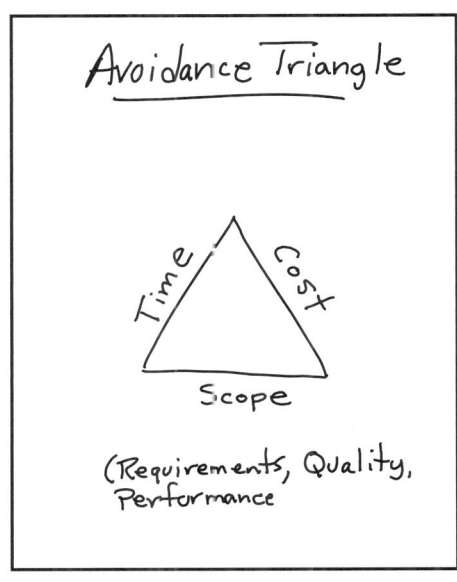

**Chart 6 - 1**

Alice got my attention and commented, "Hey, the Stupid Triangle is great. If I understand it correctly, any requirement associated with the project should either take some amount of time or take some type of effort or both. Is that correct?" she asked.

"Yes, Alice, you win the prize," I responded. "Here, let me give you a couple of examples of requirements."

Everyone was listening while I presented some examples. "A requirement could be that the new web site be available 24 hours a day / 7 days a week / 365 days a year. That condition will require the design and integration of certain web hosting equipment and it will drive how the system design is completed. It will consist of many activities that will take time and cost money to develop and test. Another requirement could be that we provide adventures at locations in Jackson Hole, Sun Valley, Vail, and the Grand Canyon. This requirement clearly requires logistical support to be available at those locations. Again, time and money will get involved. These examples are why we call requirements…requirements."

At this point, I used the broken record technique relating to the limitations of just using a requirements document. "It might sound redundant to mention again, but we must always remember that our projects are much bigger than just the items included in the requirements or specifications document."

Troy added a supporting comment. "In fact, with many smaller projects, there might not even be a requirements or specifications document at all. If the details related to smaller scale projects are presented informally, we still have to evaluate what we're given and make sure we supplement it with the necessary information. Until we do that, the scope will be incomplete and our ability to understand the expected cost and schedule will be lessened."

"Perfect," I responded. "I hope everyone followed Troy's thought process."

At this point Bruce made a profound comment. "What I'm taking from all of this discussion is that anything we failed to identify for the project will ultimately take time and money. Just the fact that they weren't included doesn't mean that they won't happen. We actually hit the OS Phase when we realize we don't have the time or money to cover the scope and to complete the project."

"Yes, Bruce," Troy added, "Time and money that we don't have because we never said we needed it in the beginning of the project, which meant we didn't include the time or cost resources up front to accomplish it. Sometimes we call that scope creep because it usually sneaks onto the project in little bits and pieces. It creeps slowly, but without the proper attention it grows to uncomfortable levels."

For the first time, all three team members seemed to be thinking seriously about the discussions and soaking in the conversation. In order to be certain that they totally understood how we had come so far, I continued to take it slow for a little while longer. "What we want to do is describe what work needs to be completed to deliver the web site and supporting locations and then estimate the time and cost of the work items required to finish."

"This is now sounding a lot more like project management," Troy added.

"That's right," I responded and then asked, "is the concept of the OS Phase getting clearer in your minds?"

"Yes, the OS Phase is when we discover that we didn't manage the Stupid Triangle."

Smiling I added, "If we would only take the time to thoroughly capture the scope on every project and capture it in the beginning, the need for project management consultants, like myself, would be reduced significantly or even eliminated."

"Are you worried about being unemployed?" Alice questioned with her own devilish smile.

"Not any time soon," I said. "But eventually the need to hire someone and pay them large fees to direct you towards processes that you already knew existed will decrease."

"Maybe you want to keep it complicated for job security!" Troy added.

"Simple is better," I responded without any hesitation.

Bruce's mood was getting a little better and he said, "The idea of managing scope and the importance of recognizing its significance in a successful project is making sense. Now that we understand the scope management process, can we move on to dealing with the specific project issues that we wrote on the board last night?"

"I don't recall anyone ever mentioning any type of scope management process," I responded, aware of Bruce's anxiousness to skip the good stuff. "We have a lot of steps to take before we are even close to having a scope management process in place. You see, Bruce, when you develop the balance of the scope for the project, I predict that you will have only one shot at it. If you miss something this time, any level of forgiveness might disappear. Let's stick with looking at the processes themselves for a while longer and not the small details."

Bruce's eagerness is quite common among project managers. This is such a difficult time for any project manager, even the best of the best. We want to see someone that is eager to get started, but we need to make sure they're starting on the right things.

I convinced everybody to take a stretch break and then we would return to start detailing scope management processes that we needed to put in place.

> *OS Phase* **Avoidance STRATEGY 6**
>
> ***Don't let anyone ever convince you that the lack of a scope management process is okay. Projects depend on numerous internal support processes. The scope management process is, without question, the most important.***

## CHAPTER 7
## Capturing the Right Stuff

A key focus of project management encompasses the *processes* necessary to evaluate those items that contribute to the complete *scope* of the project throughout the project's life cycle. We reviewed the relevance of requirements and concluded that they provide a lot of the "what." The effort of gathering requirements is a critical part of the *scope* management process.

In fact, when looking at requirements, another scope feature called project *deliverables* emerges.

In the simplest of definitions, a *deliverable* is something that the project will have to "deliver." It is an element of *scope* because it takes time and money to complete. The Project Management Institute's PMBOK®Guide states that completion of "all" *deliverables* signifies completion of the "project" itself.

In other words, the project isn't complete until all *deliverables* are completed—not the majority of the *deliverables*—but all of them. This is an important point because in order for the project to be completed we must make absolute certain that all *deliverables* are identified.

Failure to identify a *deliverable* up front would mean that we have missed some of the *scope*, which in turns means we have omitted some time and cost considerations.

Failure to identify all *deliverables* is in itself catastrophic!

Even though everyone was starting to see where we were going in the discussion, pre-meeting panic continued to bounce in and out of everyone's mind, and again it was about to glare its ugly head!

Alice was the first to express her concern with the morning's events. "Monday is getting closer every minute. I'm beginning to see

Bruce's point. If we don't start dealing with some of the details, we aren't going to be ready for any type of executive briefing."

"Your concern is normal," I responded. "Since we haven't actually discussed the scope of the Monday meeting, the three of you are starting to get a little anxious. Let's look at the upcoming meeting as a mini-project and make sure we consider the details before we go too much further."

Bruce smiled as he said, "Well, everyone, I guess the first step is to figure out what kind of stuff we're going to be doing on Monday. As I'm thinking about it, we probably should determine what we want to walk out with at the end of the meeting. Are there any specific deliverables?"

Troy was listening intently to Bruce but nevertheless added a little of his dry humor to the discussion. "I'm not sure about the rest of you, but the biggest deliverable for me is to walk out of the meeting keeping my job!"

Alice laughed and seconded Troy's comment by saying, "I know that Troy was joking around, but I would like to take his comment as a serious target. In fact, from my perspective, keeping our jobs is an important deliverable from the meeting for all of us."

Troy's candidness had indeed lightened the mood a little, but it also brought a focus to the serious nature of the meeting itself. In fact, his comments were very timely, because they would help to get everyone interested in the concept of deliverables.

Bruce seemed to be thinking about something and before anyone could ask, he shared his thoughts. "Based on what we're saying, I agree that we should be looking at the Monday meeting preparation as a project. We definitely have an end date to consider and the cost side of the Stupid Triangle will be the hours or effort it will take to get ready and then conduct the meeting. It's clear that the time or end date is fixed, so before we can understand the extent of our effort and even validate that the date is possible, we need to understand the scope of the meeting. We need to know what stuff we have to do in the short amount of time we have left."

Alice was pleased to see Bruce's new enthusiasm and followed up his comment with the suggestion that we take the time to understand the significance of deliverables related to the meeting. "We haven't discussed the details around the Monday session, but the more I think about it, the more I think we should stay away from any comments or formal recommendations. We won't have the facts we need by Monday and I'm realizing the importance of not presenting an arbitrary end date for the project until we've really assessed what stuff has to be completed."

Bruce agreed with Alice's comments and added, "The best we will have in place Monday are processes necessary to manage from this point forward. I'm going to try my best to be satisfied with that, but you know how impatient I am!"

Bruce's comment brought everybody back to reality. I kept the discussion moving and commented, "It was important to set realistic expectations for Monday. The Stupid Triangle's allocation on the time side of the triangle makes it important to understand what stuff the team can accomplish in the next forty-eight hours."

With everyone focused once again, I put myself in the character of a member of the executive committee. Taking a spot at the front of the conference room, I turned and addressed all three managers. "If you have any chance of finishing this project successfully, you need to get to the root cause of the process issues that contributed to hitting the OS Phase and then you need to fix it. Everybody at the Monday meeting will need to be convinced of how—not what or when—the project will be completed."

Continuing, I said, "Don't get me wrong, the executive committee will want the project completed tomorrow for the original budget. They will demand that you meet both of these targets—period!

"Their strategy will be to keep pressure on the team. You have to respect their passions and understand where they might be coming from.

"It is difficult to be certain of the reactions on Monday without ever meeting those that will be sitting at the meeting. I could only speculate, which in itself is a concern, but at this time, there are only limited options."

I started with what would be a lengthy discussion of deliverables related to their project and provided a couple of relevant examples. In order for all three to grasp the terminology and to be able to continue after I left, I thought it was important to get everyone on the same page with project management terminology. "Deliverables are things that we have to deliver and will on many occasions result in payment or reimbursement. This differs from a requirement in that a requirement can represent a condition or a thing; deliverables represent only things."

"This is just great," Bruce said, laughing. "First we defined stuff, then the Stupid Triangle, and now we're looking at things. I'm not sure, but I'd be willing to bet that these words aren't in any official project management text!"

Responding quickly, before letting his levity dissipate, I said, "There you go, Bruce, saying things you know I'll agree with. It's great to see that you're starting to understand these new terms. Now you know my strategy. If we used official terminology you might get bored and might even forget our discussion today."

It was clear that Bruce was still not sure where we were going with the discussion, but he was a little more relaxed than earlier in the morning. He even demonstrated a little humor as we discussed project deliverables. We limited our brainstorming for deliverables to twenty minutes. It turns out that many of the items were near completion, but it was also becoming apparent that there were bits and pieces of each deliverable that were still outstanding. It was interesting to add new items to the project that were in fact required but undocumented.

Glancing for a moment at the list of project problems put on the whiteboard last night, and comparing those items to the list of deliverables, there were several references to User Acceptance Testing (UAT) on the problems listed, but no reference to UAT on the list of deliverables.

User Acceptance Testing occurs near the end of the project and is an important final step in the development of any software or web-based system. It was easy to see an obvious discrepancy, because there wasn't a deliverable on the brainstorming list that made any mention of the UAT. On Bruce's project schedule, hanging on the front wall of the conference room, UAT appeared as an activity with a two-week duration, but that was the only reference to this testing effort.

Since UAT was a great item for illustrating the importance of understanding deliverables, I focused the group on how we can use that project feature as an example. I began by directing a question to Bruce. "When you considered UAT on your project, what type of detail did you put in your schedule?"

I moved to the flip chart to take notes.

Bruce answered, "User Acceptance Testing is a test, or maybe I should say, a group of small tests, and we allocated two weeks. I've never directed an acceptance test myself, but the software developers assured me that the test was routine and was only necessary to prove that the web site could be accessed easily by any potential customer."

Alice followed up with a pertinent question. "How did you choose two weeks for the duration? And I know you said that you're not real familiar with the test itself, but what types of things do we have to do to complete the test?"

Bruce wasn't prepared to provide a lot of details, but he very willingly summarized what he knew about the activity.

After he finished I asked a question that usually makes a person reach for the answer. "Is the deliverable the test itself? Or is there something else we should be considering?"

"Actually, I guess we want the test results, not the test," Bruce said confidently.

Taking this comment as a way to drive the deliverable discussion to a good closing point, I wrote a few items on the flip chart (Chart 7 - 1).

"Wow!" Alice exclaimed, while Bruce just stared with a depressed look on his face. "That's much more detail than we were tracking in the schedule, I can tell you that for sure. In fact, some of the problems

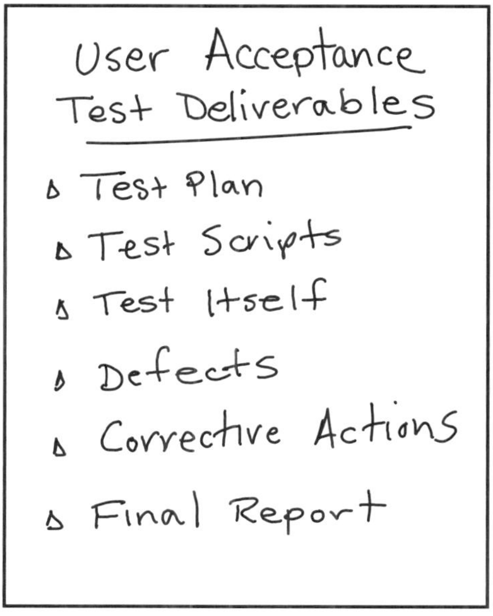

> User Acceptance
> Test Deliverables
> ⋄ Test Plan
> ⋄ Test Scripts
> ⋄ Test Itself
> ⋄ Defects
> ⋄ Corrective Actions
> ⋄ Final Report

**Chart 7 - 1**

we have listed on the back wall are related to the 'Corrective Actions' reference."

"This is unbelievable," Troy added. "We've only spent a few minutes looking at the project, only really discussing processes, and already we have found important items that were forgotten. I wonder how many we will find when we really start to drill down?"

"It may scare you if you sat down and drilled down each area of the schedule," I said, while pointing to the Stupid Triangle. "Now you're starting to understand why you just can't leap into a project without understanding what it's all about. It's all about the Stupid Triangle. We have to relentlessly pursue anything that will take time and cost money on the project. What we're going to find is that in order to find the whole scope we are going to have to approach it from several different angles or processes."

"I give up," Bruce said with a smile. "You've converted me to the Stupid Triangle and the value of looking for deliverables. What's next?"

"We're going to look at what will make the project successful," I said with renewed confidence.

"We're ready; let's do it!" said Alice.

---

*OS Phase* **Avoidance**
**STRATEGY 7**

*Early definition of project deliverables is the first step in understanding the real size and shape of the project itself. The Avoidance Triangle provides the visual reminder of the importance of finding everything that takes time or costs money.*

## CHAPTER 8
# The Objective to Understand Objectives

Management has always shown a fascination for the term *objective*. Since popularized by Peter Drucker in the fifties, we've studied *MBO—Management by Objectives*. During the eighties we began to evolve into a broad-reaching quality revolution that's still present today. It was common for the popular quality gurus to rely on specific and measurable *objectives* to validate the success of the various quality improvement initiatives.

It's impossible to travel in any type of management circle without encountering the term *objective*. Many personnel organizations identify performance *objectives* for each employee. A popular business journal selected at random used the word *objective* 167 times in 83 pages. This gives a perspective of how closely *objectives* tie to financial evaluations and considerations.

Despite their importance from business and quality perspectives, the use of *objectives* in project management is often soft and unfocused. After the start of a project, traditional time and cost *objectives* provide a source for measuring variances, but beyond those, there is little discussion.

The fanfare at the beginning of the project when original project *objectives* are set in place is met later with denials and finger pointing when it's realized that these original project *objectives* were not possible after all. Not surprisingly, once the project hits the *OS Phase*, new *objectives* are created, again with great fanfare, but with little validation or confirmation.

Here we go again!

The only thing worse than experiencing the *OS Phase* on a project is experiencing the *OS Phase* twice on the same project!

It's difficult to describe in words, but whenever you meet with a project team to discuss objectives, everyone contributes, everyone supports the process; the objectives are captured, and then everyone moves on to work on "real" project actions.

It is common for project team members to "tolerate" the objective setting process, but few stand up and applaud the effort as one of the most important steps on the project. In fact, when introducing the objective setting processes in classes or seminars, it is common to see the rolling of eyes and other expressions of boredom or that "can we do something a little more important" look on their faces.

I expected the same reactions from this trio and wasn't disappointed! The energy created by getting everyone to focus on deliverables quickly vanished. Considering the degree of reversal in enthusiasm, it makes one wonder if we shouldn't derive another name for objectives so we could disguise its introduction.

If given enough time, maybe Bruce will come up with a new term!

Being careful to prevent everyone's regression back to the panic mode, I introduced some important, but brief, elements of the objectives setting strategies. "Before we can proceed with finding and validating details of the project, we need to first review the purpose and appropriateness of objectives on the project."

Trying not to be negative, Bruce smiled and responded, "Hopefully this discussion will be brief. We've all dealt with the objectives on this project before. I think we're ready to move on to the important processes."

Knowing that Bruce's comments were all too common, I nodded my head in a positive way and then went on to explain how many project managers define the term objective. Paraphrasing their definitions off the top of my head, I said, "Objectives are measurable criteria that must be met if the project is to be considered successful."

This definition seems simple enough, but is easy to ignore when more pressing project problems surface. Bruce smiled at the definition and then said, "That's a great definition. I support the concept entirely."

Continuing, he spoke his true opinion of objectives. "We should take from the definition that our most important objective on our project is to get our butts in gear so we can finish up with this project management process review and get our scope identified and ready for Monday!"

Everyone laughed at Bruce's comments. Interestingly enough, he was right in his suggestion. It is important to get through processes quickly and not bog down with unnecessary steps. To most, the objectives setting process is just that…unnecessary.

"That's right," Troy commented. "We're all taught about their importance, but, when it comes down to taking the time to discuss objectives, interest usually drops like a rock falling off a cliff. On this project, we met the minimum requirements for setting objectives. We documented several objectives for the important schedule and budget parameters. Additional objectives focused on quality and safety targets, but the quality items didn't get much attention."

Bruce was listening to Troy's comments, but then he added the typical "nail in the coffin" relationship to objectives. "Every project has to have objectives. On our project we had objectives, but in all honesty, those objectives had no effect on the project whatsoever. They were something we did, we missed them, and now we need to move on and fix the real problems. When you look at causes and effects of the OS Phase, objectives are effects…nothing more."

It was hard to argue with Bruce, because that was his perception about objectives, and perception is most often reality in a person's mind.

Troy, who listened to the bantering back and forth about objectives, presented a level-headed comment relative to objectives. "Everyone blows off objectives, but they are important to me. Maybe no one else paid attention to them, but I did. I just didn't realize their impact, but I do now!"

Leveraging off Troy's surprise comments, I presented some important considerations for managing objectives. "Two problems surface with development of project objectives. First, most objectives are not comprehensive enough to work. This means that even when the team meets the objectives, there still might be some dissatisfaction with the project. The objectives really weren't as comprehensive as they were touted to be. Secondly, we don't track objectives adequately during the course of the project. This often is one of the major factors leading to the OS Phase, when it becomes too late to implement corrective actions."

Alice was listening to the discussion, but she wasn't on board yet. After letting everyone finish their thoughts, she asked, "Aren't objectives identified at the beginning of the project to support the original budget or contract and not at the end of a long duration project, like we've experienced on the project? I just didn't see the point of setting objectives when we're almost finished with the project."

It was clear that everyone was anxious to hear my response to this question. I took the time then to explain that one benefit of objectives is that they are best identified at the beginning of the project, but they don't have to be. It is acceptable to add new objectives if the need arises. In fact, for projects with a very long duration, objectives may only be fully identified six months to a year prior to the completion date of the project, well after the project is initiated."

Alice jumped back with a good comment. "I thought you had to make sure that each objective supported the project baseline. If that's true, then how can we possibly set objectives until we determine a new completion date for the project?"

"Great point, Alice," I responded. "Objectives are often limited to the high level parameters of the project. Most projects have an objective tied to the baseline budget and schedule values. We can still add objectives without knowing the details of the new baseline. In fact, if we do it properly, the new work we do is necessary to guide us through some very important points of the project.

"Objectives might be included with the original project initiating documents or surface as you proceed. Without question, key stakeholders need to review the objectives. The listing of objectives should include representatives from the key project management focus areas (Time, Cost, etc.). The relationship of objectives to the OS Phase is profound.

"The OS Phase is when we realize that we won't meet our key project objectives. As with deliverables, if we don't have all of the project's objectives identified and identified early, the ability to please everyone is lost. Moreover, the project itself is out of control."

# THE OBJECTIVE TO UNDERSTAND OBJECTIVES 55

Turning to Bruce, I asked, "What were the key objectives on this project?"

Responding, Bruce went to the flip chart and wrote a couple of bullets (Chart 8 - 1) representing some very generic objectives.

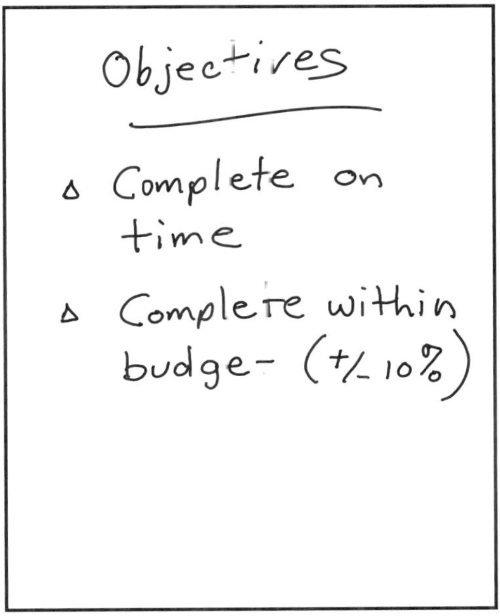

With frustration in his voice, Bruce continued by saying, "Sitting here and looking at objectives that we're obviously going to miss is not helping."

Bruce's frustrations are quite common after someone hits the OS Phase. Project managers are encouraged to "make it happen." Reviewing objectives just doesn't fit into anyone's definition of making it happen.

Speaking to all three in the room and not focusing on Bruce, I responded, "Your frustration is warranted!

> Objectives
> 
> ▵ Complete on time
> 
> ▵ Complete within budget (+/- 10%)

**Chart 8 - 1**

Absolutely! Your reaction is expected and quite common. What project manager worth their salt doesn't want to get going? The problem is that we are back to where we were with deliverables earlier. If we don't know what all the deliverables are, then we can't possibly know if we are really finished. The same holds true with objectives. How can a project be considered successful if we don't know all of the objectives?"

This time Troy spoke up and defended Bruce by saying, "Bruce is right. We set the objectives at the beginning of the project for the schedule and budget, and at that point Bruce was given the charge to meet those targets. We had our very own Stupid Triangle. Unfortunately, it wasn't balanced between the three sides and now we've missed them. Someone on the executive committee will ask us on Monday about the new targets, or as you call them, objectives, and I thought we had decided not to commit until we had more information. I'm beginning to feel like a yo-yo…"

Alice jumped into the argument, also criticizing the objective setting process. "When I worked on my Master's degree, we looked at the importance of objectives, but that was at the business level. Bruce is dealing with day-to-day problems and doesn't manage with objectives per se. He always reported to the executive committee the project's performance towards achieving the objectives, but that is the extent of his responsibilities. From my perspective, he needs to focus on the project, not on a bunch of generic objectives."

Listening to the three professionals banter back and forth about objectives was tiring! I let the conversation continue for over ten minutes. I thought it was important for them to let out any frustrations they had about objectives. There is no doubt that they saw little benefit in setting objectives at this point in their crisis. I suggested that they get up and stretch for a few minutes and think about what they had discussed and then we would sit down and either define objectives or move on to the next process.

> *OS Phase* **Avoidance**
> **STRATEGY 8**
>
> *For a project to be successful, the project manager must keep everyone's attention on the project's objectives. Objectives are more than a list of hopes and dreams. They represent what's important. Remember also, that as an element of scope, objectives will take time and cost money to achieve.*

# CHAPTER 9
# Objectives Burnout

Why do so many professionals brush off the *objectives* gathering process as a waste of time? If the definition of *objectives* development is a *process* to define success parameters of a project, what in our nature as humans causes us to be so complacent? Do we not like to have someone measure us? When we take the time to develop *objectives*, why do we often set them on the shelf until we hit the **OS Phase** before we think about them again?

These questions are part of the mystery of human behavior. Maybe we are overwhelmed with the intrusion of *objectives* in our lives. Starting with our childhood and continuing to our adult life, we have *objectives* for everything. Our grades in school measure our performance; we join the business world and find that again we have to meet corporate financial *objectives*, quality *objectives*, safety *objectives*, contracting *objectives*, hiring *objectives*.

*Objectives* surround us everywhere we turn.

Maybe we have too many consultants that work with company executives to establish these long lists of organizational *objectives*. Whatever the reason, many professionals are suffering from *objectives* burnout.

Project managers cry out, "Please let me manage this project on my own without having to be beat up with some stupid *objectives*."

We have to get the work done…enough with the *objectives*…they're impossible anyhow and no one really cares.

Maybe our *objective* would be to have no *objectives*…sounds good…but not today.

Just when we thought there was a chance to escape the world of *objectives*, we're reminded of the age-old guidance to have SMART *objectives* (Specific, Measurable, Attainable, Realistic, Time Bound), but today I don't feel so SMART.

Today I feel really dumb!

Sometimes a break is the best strategy to get everybody's mind clear. Sometimes it isn't!

Based on the scowls growing on Alice and Bruce's facial expressions, it didn't take long to realize that the break didn't work as well as I had hoped. Just as soon as we sat down, I turned to Troy, since his expression wasn't so sour looking. I hoped that he had something upbeat to share to get the group back on a positive track. I wasn't disappointed as Troy took the floor to speak.

"I agree with both you and Bruce and I was serious about my yo-yo comment," Troy said, speaking to Alice. "But the fact that we have missed both objectives we listed on the flip chart and we did so without any advanced warning leads me to believe our current process for working with objectives is flawed. I, for one, want to be successful. If we provide a new date next week and then miss it, our careers are over! That fact alone gives me some pause to listen to this discussion. Maybe we've all missed something in the past when it comes to how we use objectives."

Taking that opportunity to get the discussion back on a solid footing, I suggested that we all work together to brainstorm a list of objectives for the balance of the project. My plan would depend upon how serious they would be in the objectives gathering process. To avoid any bias or groupthink actions by Bruce or Alice, I asked each to write their objectives on separate sheets of paper and turn them into me as they completed them.

This anonymous brainstorming technique, sometimes referred to as the "Delphi" technique, is great because it keeps one person from dominating the process. Another advantage of the technique is that it allows everyone to write at the same time. This works extraordinarily well when you have many participants and want to keep them all engaged as much as possible.

The session began and ended on a very positive note. No one complained! That was amazing!

Alice took the lead as facilitator and began copying the suggested objectives onto the flip chart. Several of the brainstormed items were redundant and after some fine-tuning, we ended up with four objectives for the project.

Even with Troy's support throughout the brainstorming effort and Alice's willingness to facilitate the session, not everything went smoothly. The biggest problem was the reluctance by Alice and Bruce to give enough relevance to objectives. They kept falling back to the point that getting started on the project activities (on the adjacent whiteboard from Friday evening) was the most important step and that objectives were not really a necessity and could wait.

It was easy to understand their opinion of the objectives setting process. So many managers today will have seemingly endless numbers of objectives passed down to them from senior management. In many cases, the objectives are nothing more than some target value that a consultant said was achievable.

If everyone raises the bar and makes it happen, then life will be good. A sad reality is the fact that most projects start the same way. The team dedicates a little "happy" time to developing objectives and then everyone is anxious to move on to the real work on the project.

The objectives are set on the shelf for executive management's use if they ever ask for them, but that's about it. Fill in the box on the form and move on.

It was hard to read their faces as to whether or not the group was buying into the process of objective setting. In an attempt to demonstrate relevance, I asked everyone to think of any analogy pertaining to objectives in their personal lives. Troy was first to take the floor and speak.

As he began, Alice finished writing the objectives on the flip chart (Chart 9 - 1), sat down, and gave him her full attention.

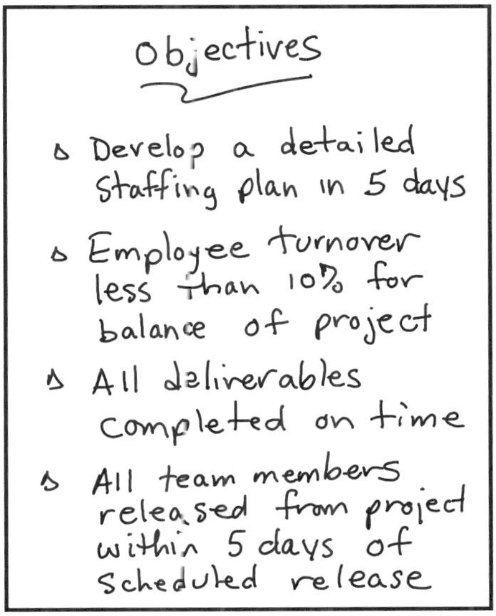

Objectives
- Develop a detailed staffing plan in 5 days
- Employee turnover less than 10% for balance of project
- All deliverables completed on time
- All team members released from project within 5 days of scheduled release

**Chart 9 - 1**

In a clear slow voice and with everyone listening, Troy began to share his thoughts. "When we went on break earlier, I spent a few minutes thinking about the objectives setting process. From my experience, objectives are usually committed to at the time they're first developed. As we laughed about earlier, the team members will each hold both arms high in the air and do the wave or some other excited utterance.

"It was no different on our project. Everyone was excited with the process, but it didn't take much time for the thrill to disappear. In fact, I don't ever recall talking about the objectives again until after our initial session with the investors and executive committee. As crazy as it seems now, during the course of the project no one really cared.

"When I took a few minutes to think about why this happens, I immediately thought of an example of objectives in my personal life. It really bothers me that we were so complacent and I wanted to see if it was just me or not."

With passion in his voice, Troy began his story. "I'm not sure if everyone will agree, but I liken New Year's resolutions to objectives we set for each upcoming year. They feel good at the time. Sometimes we are so excited about them we announce them to all of our friends, but if we don't put a system in place to achieve the resolutions, we might not make it more than a couple of days or weeks before we miss and then walk away from the resolutions completely. If we do this enough times, we don't even bother to take the time to create them anymore. The correlation between resolutions and objectives is uncanny."

By this time, everyone was listening carefully to Troy. He was describing something that everyone in the room had experienced. I wasn't alone in my curiosity of his personal example.

Bruce enjoyed Troy's analogy and even added his own related comments. "When you think about the New Year's resolutions, they're usually positive actions we want to take. Many resolutions, like losing weight, starting an exercise program, or stopping bad habits, would have real benefit to us personally, but we don't take them seriously once the excitement of New Year's wears off."

Concluding, Bruce said, "When you think about it, why even set objectives if we know up front that we'll probably miss them anyhow? It seems like Troy demonstrated why we don't need to do so many. Time spent on setting objectives is time lost on the project itself."

With all three in agreement, and with that agreement reflecting poorly on the objective setting process, I stood up, went to the flip chart with the Stupid Triangle drawn on it, and then spoke. "You are all correct. If you have no intentions of trying to meet the objectives on the other flip chart, then our effort here discussing them is wasted."

Troy answered, "I don't think we said that we weren't going to try to meet the objectives. We will try, but if we don't we can't worry about it."

"I agree with Troy," Bruce added, "but we should still target the cost and time objectives. Those are very important."

"Hold that thought for a minute," I said. "Let's look at the Stupid Triangle and see what it tells us about objectives."

Turning to the group, I asked, "Who can tell me where scope comes from?"

Puzzled looks prevailed, but Bruce answered quickly, "From the requirements that we talked about earlier."

Without disagreeing, I repeated what we had discussed early about requirements. "True, but I thought we decided that the scope of the project was bigger than just requirements."

I asked again, "Where does scope come from?"

The room was silent.

Before I let them get anymore frustrated, I added the word stakeholders to the Avoidance Triangle drawing (Chart 9 - 2) and described the relationship shown on the Avoidance Triangle. "Scope comes from stakeholders, who represent anyone associated with or affected by the project. Additionally, stakeholders will set more parameters for defining scope, more than just requirements. They will define our

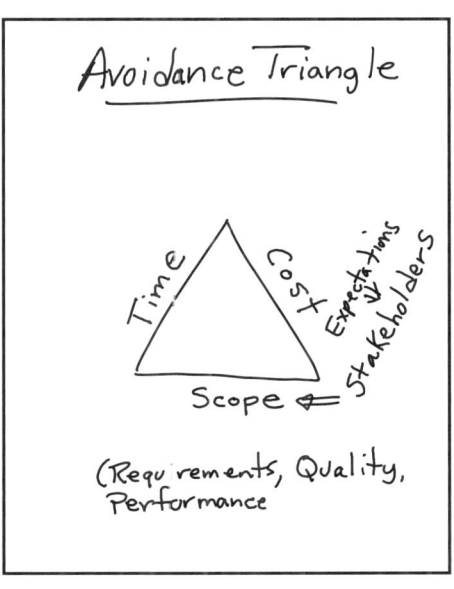

**Chart 9 - 2**

quality goals, the product description itself, and the performance and technology expectations."

Seeing that everyone was listening intently, I continued to define the relationship of objectives to the Avoidance Triangle. "Stakeholders have desires and needs that translate into scope. What we have to make sure of is that we capture the needs of the stakeholders in the project's Stupid Triangle. If we forget any scope, we will have concerns with meeting our time and cost targets."

It was fun to see Alice's mind churning with the discussion of stakeholders. She put her thoughts into words while standing, and then pacing, as she spoke. "When you look at what we're talking about as far as stakeholders are concerned, what each of us has experienced is the reality that each stakeholder has very specific expectations and we have to manage those expectations. If we don't manage the expectations early in the project and if the expectations are still there at the end of the project, then the project will be considered a failure by at least that stakeholder. There will be at least one stakeholder that isn't pleased and will be frustrated."

Troy explained his understanding of the concept by taking us back to the New Year's resolution example that he used earlier. Everyone agreed on the definition of the key stakeholder in that case; the person making the New Year's resolution. If they ended up missing the resolution, they might be the only person affected, but it was nonetheless still sad. The New Year's resolution was some type of hope or desired outcome during the next year. When the person setting the resolution doesn't achieve the outcome, frustration sets in, often influencing other items as the person begins to lose focus.

Alice was first to comment on Troy's analogy. "That has to be the most depressing comparison I have ever heard. I never realized the impact on myself when I make resolutions and then don't keep them. I don't know about everyone else, but I'll never be the same. I may never make a New Year's resolution again."

Alice's comments brought a sober tone to the group until she couldn't help herself and started to laugh aloud.

As if directed by an orchestra conductor, everyone broke into laughter at the same time. Alice's levity provided a much needed tension relief to the group as they continued to laugh and joke back and forth about previous New Year's resolutions for several minutes.

After the laughter in the room calmed down, I directed everyone's attention back to the listing of objectives where we then examined each to see who the person was that would want that expectation. We even discussed the chances of not meeting the expectations. As it turned out, several of the seven original objectives dropped off the list due to the lack of an identifiable stakeholder or interest and a couple of others surfaced, bringing the total to nine objectives.

It was interesting to see how easy it was to develop meaningful objectives. All we had to do was first identify the stakeholders on the project and then analyze what they had already pointed out was their expectation from the project.

After staring at the list of nine objectives for a couple of minutes, Bruce added, "Now I see where we are going. For each of these objectives, we need to make sure that we have adequate time and technique to accomplish or satisfy each one."

With an obvious level of excitement in my voice, I added, "Exactly! Wherever there is an objective there is something we will have to do to meet the objective. Since it will take time or effort, we call that something scope or stuff, if you prefer!"

Alice added, "So until we have a solid understanding of the objectives, we really won't know what the scope of the project consists of?"

"That's right," I spoke with a lot of excitement as I added the new term and underlined it on the sheet hanging on the wall with the Avoidance Triangle depicted (Chart 9 - 3). "If we don't know the objec-

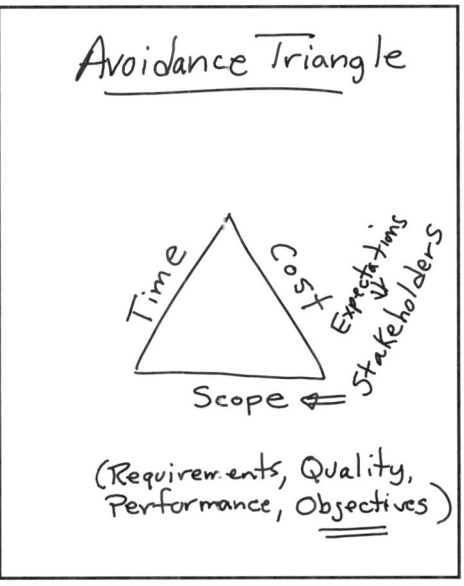

**Chart 9 - 3**

tives of the project, how on earth could we ever be sure we had the proper scope for the project?"

Continuing, I added, "This doesn't mean that we can't continue to drive the project towards completion. After all, the project started without working objectives and made a lot of progress before their absence impacted anything. What we need to remember is that we do not want to hit the OS Phase again. In order to be successful in avoiding OS Phase 2, we need to be very diligent in looking at all scope-related aspects of the project."

I then had them sit down where they all could see the project issues list from the night before, the list of deliverables, and the list of objectives. What surfaced quickly was the correlation between the lists. The importance of defining objectives and deliverables was evident to all.

Troy summed it up beautifully by concluding, "It seems pretty obvious that if we want to avoid the OS Phase we need to understand what the project is all about. After thinking about deliverables and objectives, they both describe the basis of the project. Speeding out of the gate to get going without understanding where we are headed isn't a good option. If we had performed this exercise in the beginning of the project and then validated it along the way, the OS Phase might not have happened. We have to make sure we don't do it again!"

"That's an understatement," Alice interjected. "We have to get it right this time."

"Hopefully, with our new appreciation of the importance of deliverables and objectives we'll be able to define the stuff," Bruce said with a smile. "Once we get the scope defined, we'll have a solid grasp of the time and cost. This should be all we need to get going again full steam."

Being careful not to lose the enthusiasm of the group, I added, "Now that you understand the significance of scope and the purpose of

> ***OS Phase* Avoidance STRATEGY 9**
>
> *The Avoidance Triangle is a simple, but effective tool for reminding us of the importance of scope and the relationship between objectives and stakeholders.*

deliverables and objectives, you should be excited to know that we are almost there. But, no matter how you look at things, objectives management might be the most important process for the project manager to focus on."

"Let's take a five-minute stretch break and come back and start to look at the processes you will need to put in place to make all of this stuff work so that you are able to get the project back on track."

## CHAPTER 10
## Finding the Magic Pill

It is almost impossible to read any newspaper or business journal without seeing details about another major project in trouble!

We keep repeating the same mistakes.

We have to do something!

What's the answer?

The good news is that we live in a world that offers fixes. The bad news is that these quick fixes never really work the way we intend. The good news is that there is another quick fix to implement if the first quick fix failed to improve the situation. The bad news is that this quick fix won't work either.

All it seems to take anymore to fix a problem is a credit card and a call to a toll-free number. It's easy to order the secret formula to help a person lose weight, stop smoking, build their physiques, or as we are interested in, improve their project management performance.

Each advertisement bursts at the seams with pictures of beautiful people caught up in the sheer joy of using the various products.

Isn't life great!

Sarcasm aside, the irony is that with a little self-control and a realistic plan of attack, we can solve any problem that confronts us without the need for a magic pill.

It's hard to accept at first, but, more often than not, the best project management tools are simple *processes*. Remember, *processes* originated centuries ago with projects performed years before there were computers or the Internet. We should define each process first. Then, and only then, we should consider how to support them with current-day technology.

> To avoid the **OS Phase** we just need to use *processes* that focus on development of the *scope* for the project, manage *roles* and *responsibilities*, and anticipate and mitigate *risks*.
>
> With the same level of insight when we finally acknowledge the fact that to lose weight we have to exercise and eat fewer calories, we should also recognize the simplicity and importance of managing these three project management processes.
>
> If we focus on these processes and don't let go until they are performed properly, we can't lose. Ever!

Everyone enjoyed the chance to stretch, but they were also eager to get back to the effort. Without wasting any time, I began summarizing the discussion we just completed. "We all made it through some of the tough parts of the project management process. Understanding the concepts of the Stupid Triangle, deliverables, and objectives is not difficult, but it is ahhhh…."

"Annoying?" Bruce interjected, quickly followed by laughter from everyone.

"That's not the word I was thinking of, but it'll work," I added. "You apparently understand these concepts. Now let's see how they all fit together."

"Promises, promises," Alice added. "If I see anything else that we forgot to do on this project, I'm going to get real depressed."

"I hope you are going to tell us where we need to go from this point," Troy commented.

Getting back in the lecture mode, I went to the Avoidance Triangle chart again (Chart 10-1). "Now let's consider the

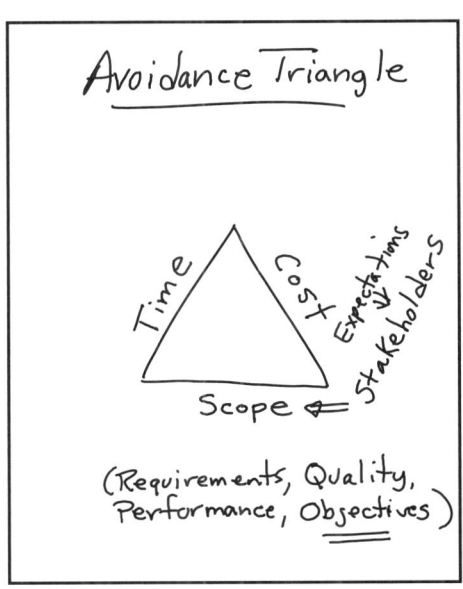

**Chart 10-1**

significance of the triangle. As I mentioned earlier, it's easy to be convinced that given the proper scope, most project managers have the skill to apply a realistic schedule and appropriate cost estimate.

"Personally, it's impossible for me to think of any aspect of a project without getting the mental image of the Avoidance Triangle or, as Bruce now likes to call it, the Stupid Triangle.

Speaking with what must have seemed to everyone as a broken record, I continued. "The problem is the concern of getting all the right scope."

Turning to the group, I asked, "Why do I keep drawing this Stupid Triangle?"

"Because you're strange!" someone shouted.

"Besides that," I smiled. "What value does this Stupid Triangle add to our considerations of the project?"

Troy took the floor and provided an excellent summary of what we had discussed so far. "If the project manager fails to remember these relationships, then they are crippled from the get-go. The unfortunate reality is that it's easy to beat down soft targets for time and costs due to their lack of detail. When the balance of the scope finally surfaces, reality sets in and life isn't good. The path to the OS Phase is firmly set in place."

Bruce's pre-meeting anxiety was surfacing again. After a few steps pacing along the wall, he stopped and said, "I understand the importance of what we've talked about so far. But we need some solid strategies real soon or we'll be hosed when Monday arrives."

"Bruce, you are learning about a lot of concepts and terms. I haven't introduced the term hosed yet, but it sounds like you already know about it."

Laughing with the others Alice added, "We use that term a lot around here, usually in a joking manner. Unfortunately, this project's situation is not funny anymore. We have some real big concerns to deal with before Monday."

With as much empathy as I could muster at this point in time, I responded, "Adding a little levity to a bad situation might actually help out. We have to make sure that we don't let the stress of everything limit our ability to think through possible solutions."

"I think we're all ready for the next step!" Alice added.

Taking her lead, I asked them to try to be patient for at least twenty more minutes while we walked through a little background related to where we were going next.

Everyone nodded in agreement, but I knew that twenty minutes would quickly disappear.

I began to describe the Avoidance Model that I now use religiously on every project I encounter. The model's derivation started several years ago when I came to the realization that the same project management approaches were failing on each project I reviewed. The most fascinating aspect of the observation was the realization that the problem projects had completely different products, but the same project management processes were broken. Failures were on projects for software development, design/construction, and manufacturing. After stepping back and looking at the root causes, some simple process problems surfaced.

The first problem area was the impact of the complexity of the project management related tools and procedures that were put in place. On top of that, it seemed as if everyone or every organization was trying to outdo the other. It was very hard to repeat successes or to roll out project management across any enterprise because of the varied and unique approaches.

These different approaches made everything complicated for anybody from the outside looking in at the project. What I found was that once you peeled back the onion and looked beyond the complex processes, their problems were the same as others I had encountered. That led me to recognize that their problem was nothing out of the ordinary.

Here's the answer. With experience, we recognize the real magic pill or solution to project management concerns is actually simple. In order to make sure that everything proceeds smoothly we needed to define the process for managing the stuff.

All three were listening intently as I went to the front of the conference room and commented, "We will begin our effort by reviewing the scope management processes."

I then drew a process flow-type of figure at the top of the flip chart (Chart 10 - 2) and started to speak as I was writing the word "scope" on the chart. *"Scope...we need to have a well-understood and documented process for capturing and managing all project scope, and we need to have assurance that the status of the scope within that process is current, correct, and complete."*

I continued my explanation by giving a generic example of what I was trying to demonstrate on the chart. "On any project, as short as one day in duration or as extensive as ten years, we need to first assess if there is a good scope management process in place and then we need to evaluate the performance of the scope management activities.

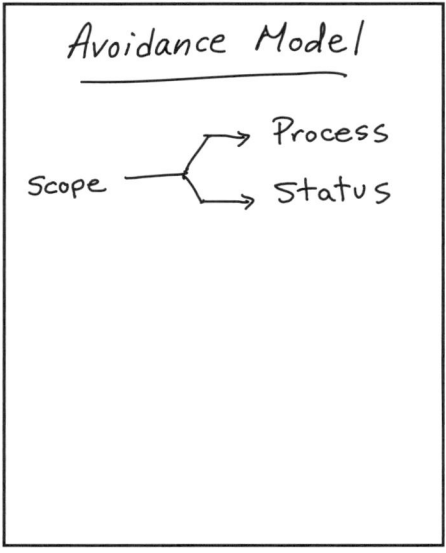

**Chart 10 - 2**

"Most projects that hit the OS Phase don't have a sound scope management process.

"Team members will argue this point for quite awhile, but most will change their mind when we introduce them to the real definition of scope as shown by the Stupid Triangle.

"The Stupid Triangle is rigid in its depiction of the relationship between scope, time, and cost. If scope isn't managed well it's difficult to understand how the time and cost could end up anywhere close to what we wanted unless by sheer coincidence or luck."

"Have you ever seen a failed project that had a good scope management process?" Troy asked as a very pertinent question.

Turning to Troy I smiled, because I hadn't really thought about the question before. "I've never thought about it from that perspective, but thinking about it a little, I've rarely ever seen a good scope management process on any project. That fact alone answers the question; that is a big NO!

"Putting together the perfect model seemed simple to me," I said, while continuing with more comments about the importance of scope.

"We have to select a process methodology for identifying and managing scope. There is no other choice! Looking back at our definition of scope, it consists of the efforts and steps that take time and money/resources necessary to accomplish the ultimate deliverable, which is to say, the product. With the power of computer systems and databases, this should be rather straightforward."

Alice's facial expression told me that the light went on in her head as she commented, "I'm not saying that I didn't understand the significance of scope before, but I think it's finally sunk in that it's not even the importance of scope, but it's the importance of having a scope management process!"

"That's right, the key word is process," I responded. "As a consultant, my life became much easier when I started looking at project management in process terms. Remember, when I'm working on a project that hit the OS Phase, my complete understanding of what the technical details are will most likely be lacking. At the same time, it's still possible to review whether or not the scope is in fact being managed properly. That knowledge will lead to the ultimate solution, usually one that's not dealing with technical concerns."

"You're right," Troy added. "When you consider the number of projects that occur everyday, it just doesn't make sense that we have to manage them all differently. What we need is a process where every project we work on manages the scope in the same way."

Everyone was now listening intently, and Troy asked another question. "I've listened to the discussion, but I would be surprised if the concept of focusing on scope wasn't already a high priority for most project managers. After thinking about the Stupid Triangle, it is clear that if you manage scope, everything else should follow. Why would anybody disagree with this basic reality?"

"Let's let Bruce answer that question," I responded.

"Our reality was much different," Bruce stated in a defensive manner. "When we started our project, the only discussion point was that we had to meet the March completion date and we better get it done in the allocated budget because there would only be one trip to the bank. We all thought we knew what the scope was, although we didn't think of it that way. We developed a schedule and the activities on the schedule represented what we had to complete."

For the first time, Bruce was recognizing flaws in the project initiation processes. He continued by saying, "What I'm realizing now is that we should have focused on the scope first and then worked the schedule and validated the budget allocation. We did it backwards. However, most importantly, we didn't have a scope management process per se. By default we may have kept track a little, but I know we never drew the triangle; I mean the Stupid Triangle."

Everyone laughed.

"What's next?" Troy asked eagerly. "Your twenty minutes are almost up."

Thinking to myself, I wondered if the project might have turned out differently if Troy had been so attentive of time. Well, that's a thought best kept to oneself!

Responding to his challenge, I summarized the discussion thus far. "Actually we've worked our way through some of the scope processes, those for identifying deliverables and objectives. We will have many uses for those listings you developed earlier and now the lists will help to serve as a foundation for the project. What we need to do is see if there are any other ways we can squeeze out some more scope."

"Where do stakeholders fit into the picture?" Alice asked, explaining that I had promised them a discussion on stakeholders.

"Excellent question, Alice!" I responded. "When we think about what else must be in place for us to succeed on the project, the next feature that surfaces is the area tied to stakeholders, that of Roles and Responsibilities."

Continuing with this thought, I said, "Scope is essential, but we also need to know who is doing the work and what they are actually doing." The second area of emphasis was now clearly set as I drew it on the flip chart (Chart

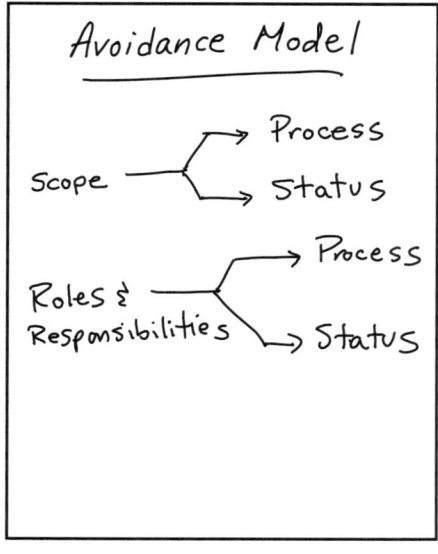

**Chart 10 - 3**

10 - 3) and repeated the same statement used for describing Scope. *"Roles and Responsibilities...we need to have a well-understood and documented process for capturing and managing all project roles and responsibilities, and we need to have assurance that the status of the roles and responsibilities within that process is current, correct, and complete."*

"How could anyone even think about proceeding with a project without knowing the scope along with details of who will participate in the project and perform the work?" Alice asked with a smile. "We need to know who the Subject Matter Experts are. We need to know who has to review and approve completed work on the project. Any time we define scope, we need to understand all of the interactions between the stakeholders."

"Excellent! Too many times we see that roles and responsibilities are taken too lightly," I responded. "Serious consequences happen when project managers don't pay attention to this key process area.

"What's also important to understand is how the model depicts a need for a process and an understanding of the status. The model is exactly how I sketched it out on a piece of paper the first time. The requirement for a process and status were subliminal links to previous organizational roles, subject to frequent audits by outside organizations. In those situations, it was always important to have a procedure or process in place to assure compliance with the standards and regulations, and then we had to demonstrate that the staff actually used them; thus the need for status."

Troy summarized the discussion from his perspective. "Ironically, nothing in the model so far is anything we shouldn't have known, but the way it's presented really brings the message and connection home to me this morning."

"Great observation," I responded with a wide grin. "There is little chance that anyone could invent anything new in the project management arena, but a little shuffling of the terms and concepts might help everyone understand them better."

I went on to set up an important example to reinforce these process concepts. "Now let me describe a scenario to you all and see what you think as we move to the next area."

I started by asking them to imagine an organization that specializes in a certain type of project. "One team has successfully completed six different installations of a similar project with each of the six projects going exceptionally well. In every case, the scope management processes were well defined and followed. All roles and responsibilities were well defined and followed. The customer was very pleased with the results and life was good.

"Now the same customer wants the seventh project, identical to the first six. The scope is, therefore, well-known and the scope management processes are still well defined. The same team will work on the seventh project. The customer is the same and is excited about the prospect of this latest initiative. Everything is wonderful. Everything is set up like a textbook case.

"Now the key question," I spoke with a grin. "What should the project manager do from this point forward?"

There were several responses from the trio, but none caught the point until Alice joked, "Maybe the project manager should go read a book or play some golf.

"Alice, you've got it!" I shouted. "Playing golf is the right answer. With everything in place and no concerns, what else would a project manager possibly need to do?"

"We have just described the perfect project," I continued, emphasizing the word 'perfect.' "When describing this scenario in classes or seminars, I always ask the obvious follow-up question. 'How many of you have experienced the perfect project?' "

After a lot of laughter, everyone agreed that the perfect project is not common.

"Most of the time, instead of having perfect projects, we encounter projects where there are significant concerns with having an unbalanced triangle, or there are roles and responsibilities that are unclear or are not being honored."

I went back to the flip chart and then kept on with the process discussion. "An incredible aspect of looking at scope and roles and responsibilities is that these two areas represent the facet of the project the project manager has the ability to hold firm, and, in practice, must hold firm. Think about it. If the project manager is able to manage the scope and has a firm grasp on all role and responsibility assignments, the project manager's life will be fantastic."

Speaking with a smile, Bruce added, "Since my life wasn't fantastic, at least during the past couple of weeks, then it must be time to admit that our project wasn't a perfect project."

"Okay, now let's see what it will take to make your world a little better," I responded while smiling to acknowledge Bruce's comment. "Now that we all know what the perfect world is like, we need to jump back to reality. With any project, there will be some uncertainty. Without falling to a helpless state or a state of mass confusion that afflicts many projects, the project manager should begin to evaluate those things that are affecting scope management and role and responsibility assignments and flag them.

"In reality, we have one additional process that we have to concern ourselves with on projects, to deal with the imperfect concerns. This third and final aspect that we need to pay attention to is Risk," I said, while adding the third process area to the flip chart (Chart 10 - 4) and continuing with my discussion. "*Risk...we need to have a well-understood and documented process for capturing and managing all project risks, and we need to have assurance that the status of the risks within that process is current, correct, and complete.*"

"The risk management process represents the third, and perhaps the most important, tool for avoiding the OS Phase," I said, while pointing to the Avoidance Model on the flip chart. "Risk management is vital to overall project success. The strategy behind the emphasis on risk is straightforward. Scope and roles are in place, or at least they should be. Project uncertainty, in the

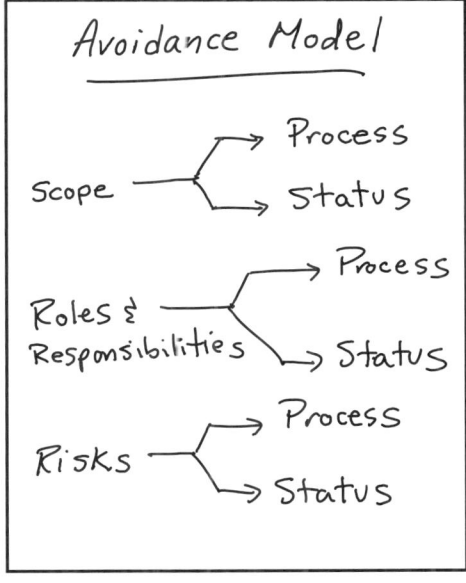

**Chart 10 - 4**

form of risks, is softer and more difficult to nail down. Risks must be managed or they will manage us!"

Continuing to describe this latest addition to our process assessment, I turned to Bruce to make sure he understood the relationship of the three process areas. "As with the other key processes, our choice of risk management techniques must be simple and easy to understand. If we can accomplish our effort with that stipulation, risk management will provide an excellent tool for success."

At this point, I decided to direct the discussion at Bruce with full force. "Bruce, let's not mince words. If you manage scope and roles, and keep your attention on project <u>risks</u>, you will have the best chance possible of avoiding the OS Phase. That's a reality!"

"That may be reality, but that's not my world," Bruce spoke defensively. "We have to deal with our situation, not a textbook project like the one you're referring to in this example."

Unlike Bruce, both Troy and Alice appeared to appreciate the Avoidance Model. Their support would have to be good enough for now. Given time, Bruce may realize the significance of risk. It's possible that he might soon appreciate how it could have helped him to avoid the OS Phase. Unfortunately, time was not something anyone had an abundance of at the given time. It looked like it was time to switch gears for a few minutes and get Bruce recalibrated on how he should manage performance reporting for the balance of the project.

My twenty minutes were up so we decided to move to the next area of discussion. Just as we were about to start, Bruce got a phone call and had to step out of the conference room. After he was out of hearing range, Alice apologized for Bruce's behavior. She felt that his actions were possibly his way of taking an offensive position instead of letting himself be pinned in the corner for the problems on the project.

Understanding both her frustration and concern, I acknowledged his comments and concluded that trying to get Bruce back to a positive mood was going to be a challenge, but that was okay. Whenever anyone is caught up in defending their actions, it would be surprising if they weren't defensive. This same scenario plays out all too often with all of my clients. It is important initially to let everyone defend their existing world.

Troy joined the discussion by adding an excellent comment. "We have to remember that Bruce and others like him believe they've done everything right. Their world is always different from the perfect world. In Bruce's case, we will have to use his emotions to help him understand and validate the third process. Without a little help, he just won't buy into the concept that his key role is to focus on risk management."

Bruce returned in a few minutes. He had received a call from Barry, a senior member of the executive committee. Barry wanted some heads-up on the details for Monday's meeting. For the first time this morning, Bruce realized that Monday was going to be a serious event and the usual exaggerated performance briefing wasn't going to work.

> ***OS Phase* Avoidance**
> **STRATEGY 10**
>
> *Projects do not fail. Processes fail. It is vital to ensure all scope, roles, and risk processes are adequately defined and working before initiating any project.*

# CHAPTER 11
# It's Customary to Say Everything is Fine!

How is it possible for projects to get in so much trouble before anyone at the executive level is aware?

It's actually quite amazing when you consider how many times it happens daily. The ability of projects to continue unabated, while tens of millions of dollars in overruns are accumulating and the corporate office is unaware, almost seems impossible. Reality and headlines, however, describe circumstances where it happens, and happens often!

Every day the public invests in publicly traded companies without a clue that they are spending money on hundred million dollar projects without so much as even a basic method to ensure prudent behavior. Accounting scandals worldwide have revealed an extraordinarily complex set of deceptive practices and *processes*. Regulations will curb the magnitude of abuse for a while, until another crisis changes priorities.

Where do the problems start?

Amazingly, the performance reporting *process* is the culprit. Whether formal or informal, this seemingly routine *process* is not working. Its primary purpose is to take an accounting of accomplishments and a comparison of performance against the baseline plan and then pass the information upward to senior reporting levels.

As simple as this step or *process* sounds, this is where a big problem surfaces. Something as routine and simple as performance reporting can get out of control with little effort, sometimes intentionally, and other times not.

As a *process*, performance reporting has many weak steps, and a common culprit is the embellishment and reporting of "percentage complete" and "progress to date!" As humans, we want to avoid rocking the boat more than necessary. It is common for

> project managers to provide performance more in line with where the project should be versus where the project actually is at the time. The tendency is to report too much from the very beginning. The thought or hope is that it will be easy to make it up down the road, something that of course never happens.
>
> It is human nature to exaggerate accomplishments to date. Few project managers or line managers have made it through their career without embellishing the performance of some effort they were working on. We don't want to confuse exaggerated reporting with someone having a positive outlook on everything. Optimism is a great trait for a project manager and should be encouraged.
>
> Blind optimism and avoidance of reality are precursors to the **OS Phase**.
>
> You must avoid both!

Since Bruce brought up the subject of exaggerated performance reporting, it seemed like a good time to discuss how that particular process works on the project.

With everyone gathered again around the table, I turned to Troy and asked, "You mentioned earlier that your project was reported as 95 percent complete last month. How do you feel now about that percentage? Do you still think 95 percent is accurate?"

Pondering slightly at the question, Troy replied in a thoughtful tone, "It's odd, but the percentage complete doesn't really mean much at this point. We need the project completed. That's what's important now, not just some percentage. In fact, the more I think about it, the more trivial it becomes in my mind."

Troy's comments charged Alice up and she continued with Troy's theme. "After reflecting on the past two days, it's clear that our focus the last six months on the project's percentage complete value actually may have caused us to become complacent.

"It's so ironic, because the first question out of anyone's mouth on the executive committee always relates to a magical performance metric or measurement. We became so narrowly focused on this number, and we lost sight that it didn't really predict anything. We discovered Friday that this measure didn't mean much at all."

Troy finished the thought by concluding, "We were both devastated yesterday when we received the real status."

Bruce, the source of the percentage complete reports, stared out the window of the conference room and sat quietly, without reaction for the first time this morning.

"There should have been warnings that the project was in trouble," Troy added. "Why weren't there any warnings?"

"What we found yesterday came as a major surprise," Alice said, "I agree with Troy. If we only had gotten some type of warning, it would be much easier to deal with today. If the performance metrics we were using for the status review meetings didn't tell us what was going on, you should have warned us yourself, Bruce."

Jumping quickly into the discussion to divert any verbal confrontation between Alice and Bruce, I latched onto her last comment and decided to become a little more direct with my questions. "I heard what you just said and I believe you, but…"

"But, there's always a but with your questions," Alice said, smiling again.

With care not to let this moment pass, I responded with a smile to acknowledge Alice's candor, but continued the intensity of the questioning. "But, if you were in fact told by Bruce three or four weeks ago that the project was in trouble and you were also told by Bruce that the project wouldn't meet the planned close-out date scheduled for this week, what would you have done at that point?"

"Don't even bother to answer, Alice," Bruce interjected as he broke his long silence. "All hell would have broken loose! This is precisely why most people hide a lot of information around here. If anyone ever has a problem, the management team either comes with long stares and subtle threats or they conduct a pep rally where we're challenged or otherwise convinced that we can get over the bar, even though the bar is so high now that it's out of sight. I guess I mistakenly thought I could turn the project around, but I was wrong."

"Way wrong!" Troy said, with a hint of sarcasm in his voice.

This time Bruce was not going to lose the floor and he continued with his explanation. "Anytime you even hint that something is in trouble in this organization, everyone starts to micromanage the person with the bad news and nobody ever fixes anything. I may complain about what we're doing here this morning, but honestly, this is the first time I've ever seen somebody that wanted to fix our problems. If you all hadn't met at the airport, you both would be in Dallas plotting my demise."

Bruce was gaining momentum and said something that caused everyone to pause for a moment. Standing and looking directly at Troy and Alice, he said, "When I sit back and think about it, I did hide the true status of the project from everybody. I knew what I was doing at the time and I'm not ashamed of it!"

"Why did you do that?" Alice asked.

"Because you and the other members of the executive committee can't handle the truth!" Bruce shouted with an intensity not seen up to this moment, while maintaining a serious tone to his voice.

With a slight snicker growing on Bruce's serious facial expression, it was clear that he was venting some steam that had built up during the course of the project. It was obvious in his expression that he was relieved to get his feelings out in the open.

In an indirect way of admitting that she didn't take offense at his comments, Alice responded in a light-hearted tone directed at Bruce, "Whoa, you're starting to sound like Jack Nicholson."

At this time, I recounted one of my favorite Dilbert cartoons.

Everyone laughed at the cartoon and even gave real names to the cartoon characters sitting around the table.

Realizing that it was not the time to point fingers, everyone accepted Bruce's comments, even Bruce himself, and it was time to move on. With an unexpected acknowledgment from Bruce, it seemed appropriate to understand the performance-reporting shortcoming. It had taken several hours this morning to convert Bruce into the process side of project management, and it seemed by his actions that he was getting interested in finding out more about the OS Phase.

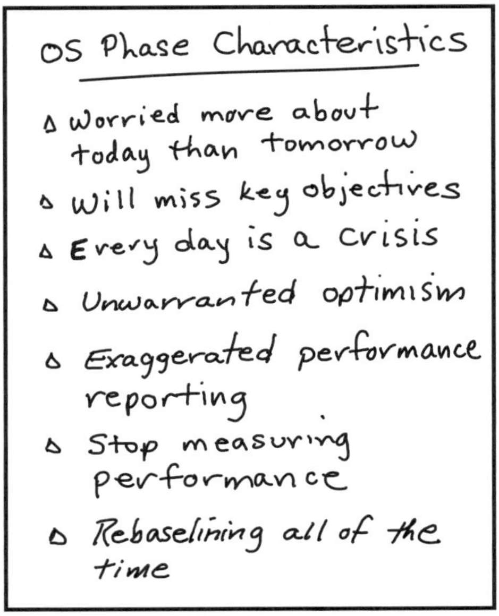

I acknowledged Bruce's comment about the *shoot the messenger* environment. I then stood back and began capturing OS Phase characteristics or precursors on two flip charts (Charts 11 – 1a and 1b). We then began to relate them specifically to the current situation.

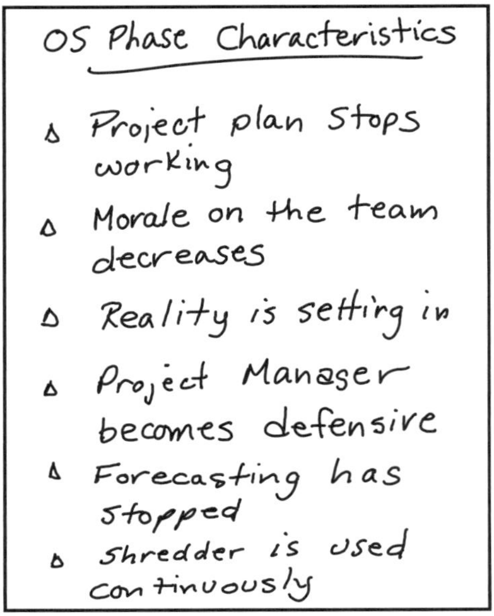

After listening with a strong interest, Bruce added the classic, and unknown to him, standard comment on troubled projects. "Please tell me that the reporting deficiencies I'm guilty of aren't unique."

Smiling, I answered with a reassuring tone in my voice. "It is completely too common and often dismissed as a routine expectation. The important

**OS Phase Characteristics**
- Worried more about today than tomorrow
- Will miss key objectives
- Every day is a crisis
- Unwarranted optimism
- Exaggerated performance reporting
- Stop measuring performance
- Rebaselining all of the time

**Chart 11 - 1a**

**OS Phase Characteristics**
- Project plan stops working
- Morale on the team decreases
- Reality is setting in
- Project Manager becomes defensive
- Forecasting has stopped
- Shredder is used continuously

**Chart 11 - 1b**

thing is to find the underlying reason for exaggerating progress before we judge. If the reporting fails because of flawed processes and the project manager takes the high road, fix the process and move on. It doesn't appear that this is a case of deliberate deception with criminal implications."

"Hold on a minute," Bruce said, while rising straight up in his chair and pointing a finger in my direction. "The conversation is starting to get a little off track. We are all working our tails off to get the project completed. I appreciate your comment that we haven't done anything criminal, but just the fact that you brought that up in the conversation is troubling."

"I agree with Bruce," Alice added, while staring hard in my direction. "Where are you coming from with that comment?"

"It appears that I have your attention," I said, with a less serious tone in my voice. "We tend to trivialize performance reporting and never get too uptight when it's exaggerated, but in the cases where a subcontractor claims progress payments that aren't earned, it could easily be considered fraud."

"Think about it," I said, while moving my eyes back and forth between the three managers. "If a subcontractor succeeded with a similar deception, and received payments for work not completed, it could become a serious legal concern. In the same regard, your investors on the project might be concerned about what happened and could enforce remedies included in their funding documents because the project missed a target date. Any action, of course, is based on there being a mention of it in the contract documents."

Bruce was starting to look depressed so I turned to him and tried to give him some reassurance. "More than likely, any action on the investor's part would be against the company, and not necessarily against you, Bruce. The rationale in your situation was wrong, but most people would support the position that you were confident that you could get it done and that you were overwhelmed and unable to distinguish the repercussions of your actions. Now to your question about how common it is that faulty reporting occurs; the number of times it occurs would be staggering if it were even possible to determine that value. Project managers manage the news for a lot of reasons, not the least of which is the perception that it's a lot easier to get beaten up once at the end of the job when you don't make it, than to get beaten up every week when the project manager tries to provide a realistic target."

Listening to every word now, Alice turned to me and asked, "Do you mean to say that what we've seen here is common? Because I don't buy that! I've worked on projects most of my career and have never purposely reported false progress! I can't believe that I'm in the minority."

After Alice finished, Troy added his two cents. "I don't think we have to say whether or not we've exaggerated progress on projects or anything for that matter. Project management is all about dealing with humans and as was said earlier, humans have a basic desire to please. How they do that varies with each person. We will never know how many people exaggerate what they report; it's probably not everyone in the world, but it's certainly more than just Bruce.

"It's becoming common knowledge that an unbelievable number of professionals have falsified or exaggerated their resumes; Sunny Bates of Sunny Bates Associates in New York City was quoted May 23, 2006, in Forbes.com that the estimate is a staggering value of 40 percent of the work force. It's difficult for me to think that anyone capable of that would hold the line when it came down to reporting performance of a project. It happens, and in our case it happened on our project, and now we need to deal with it."

Leveraging off Troy's comment, I added a very biased and undocumented opinion. "Troy did a great job describing reality. If indeed every project manager in the world updated their reported progress to where they really were with their project's performance, the decline in overall performance on a global basis would be significant. It's sad, but most executives want to think that everything is wonderful. Going back to Bruce's rendition of Jack Nicholson, a lot of organizations would not like to admit it, but there might be executives out there that, if given the reality of where they are, couldn't handle the truth. The reality of faulty reporting is with us every day. How we deal with it is what separates us from others. No matter how you interpret what was just said, the reality is that it happens. And when it does, faulty performance reporting becomes a classic entrance into the OS Phase."

Turning back to me, while still shaking her head side to side, Alice was eager to add her own opinion of my comment. "I still don't agree with your opinion of the magnitude of the problem, but we'll never have the data to prove it one way or the other, so it is moot. As we've seen, though, on the project, it's impossible to ignore the impact of the accumulation of embellished performance reporting. There is no doubt that this problem could easily lead to any project's collapse if not discovered in time. As we experienced here, the project hits the OS Phase, then the project manager acknowledges for the first time that the project isn't as far along as once reported. I guess the ability to resolve the problem varies from project to project. Hopefully we can deal with it on ours."

"It's impossible to guarantee anything," I responded. "But if we can repair the broken processes and can establish a realistic target that everyone will buy into, your project is definitely doable. In fact, I'm so confident that you all can turn this project around, before I leave I'd like to see how to sign up for a trip to the Grand Canyon."

The last comment helped to break the growing tension in the room. We were now dealing with some difficult concerns, and keeping a lightened mood would be more productive in the end.

After a slight pause, I picked up where I left off. "As depressing as the OS Phase may seem, it is actually quite common in every business sector. It seems that every day, or maybe every week, we hear about a major corporation filing for bankruptcy. Those companies have hit a specific type of financial OS Phase. The OS Phase isn't just for projects, but the symptoms and solutions are the same. When you read the newspapers and journals, you will read about projects around the world that hit the OS Phase every minute of every day. That's what keeps me so busy. It is such a shame, though, because it is avoidable. By rights, I should be unemployed."

"You said it's avoidable," Bruce commented. "How could we do it differently? I never stopped working on the project. It might be an underestimate to say that many members of the team and I spent 12-16 hours each day working on details. There just weren't anymore hours in the day."

"First of all, that's too many hours to be working," I said with a sympathetic ear. "With that type of effort you're more likely to burn out than you are to finish the project."

"Where were you a couple months ago?" Bruce asked with a smile. "It seemed that management didn't think we were working hard enough if we didn't put in a lot of overtime."

Noticing Alice and Troy's obvious silence, I wouldn't be surprised to find out that they were part of those encouraging the overtime usage. I added my opinion regarding the overtime concern. "I don't want to get side-tracked away from the performance reporting concerns, but I don't want the overtime problem to be lost either. When you look at overtime on a project, think for a few minutes as to whether it is a cause or an effect of poor performance. It's an interesting question, actually what many call a conundrum. Think about that one for a while."

"I don't remember when the overtime started," Troy interjected, "but it should have been a signal that the project was not on schedule or had some kind of concerns. When you think about the Stupid Triangle, you realize that unplanned overtime starts a ripple effect."

Turning to Alice and Bruce, he continued by asking, "How did the executive committee miss that connection? Who was pushing for the overtime?"

Both shrugged their shoulders and winced. It wasn't important to the discussion, but, in the future, I don't believe that a request to add overtime will surface without someone challenging it. All three got the message loud and clear. Using a lot of overtime is usually a sign that a project is in trouble. If it isn't in trouble yet, given enough overtime and eventual team member burnout, it will be!

Although overtime use is an important part of most regular performance reporting processes, it was important to get everyone back into discussing and understanding the support system and processes for project performance reporting. It was vital that we deal with process problems before moving any further along. The erroneous performance reported by Bruce wouldn't have happened if proper processes were in place.

A critical element of any project management performance reporting initiative is the type of support systems or processes available for the project manager.

# IT'S CUSTOMARY TO SAY EVERYTHING IS FINE! 87

To make sure that everyone was on the same page with terminology, I went to the flip chart and drew a simple overview of the controlling systems that are frequently in place within companies (Chart 11 - 2).

Bruce was the first to ask a question. "Are we talking about computerized systems for all of these processes?"

"They don't have to be computerized," I answered, "but nowadays they usually are automated.

"The computerized portion of these systems is called the Project Management Information System or PMIS. The term Management Control System or MCS describes the total package, including not only the computerized aspects but also the processes themselves.

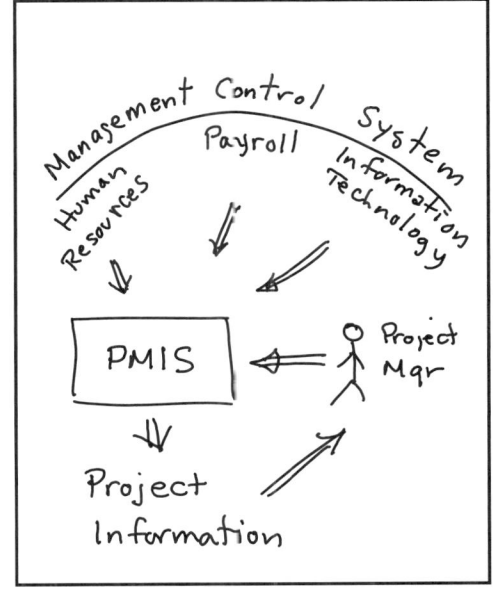

**Chart 11 - 2**

"It is entirely possible for a small organization to have a Management Control System that is very effective, but is considered informal because it doesn't have the sophistication of the additional Project Management Information System."

Turning to Bruce I asked, "Do you have any computerized management information systems to help you manage the data associated with the project?"

Shaking his head in a depressing back and forth nod, Bruce answered, "We have computer systems that are supposed to support the project, but when you sit back and look at how long we spend inputting and correcting the data, sometimes it seems that all we do is feed them…and feed them…and feed them some more. Sometimes I feel as if I'm chained to the computer and, unfortunately, in the end, the computer does very little to help me manage the project."

Jumping on this point, Troy joined in to ride on the all too common Management Control System excuse train. "As a company, we've invested a lot of money and development time putting in place our management control and scheduling tools. Even though Bruce's point is well-taken, it's hard to believe that we could have done any better."

Responding to Troy's comment about the Project Management Information System, I made some general comments so as not to drift too far from the discussion of how the project ended up in the OS Phase. "Many people think the way to avoid problems on a project is to buy or build fancy computerized tools. While it's no doubt that they can help, project management is not about computers, it is 98 percent about dealing with humans. You can never take the human out of the equation. Unfortunately, the high-tech environment is so dominant in organizations now that many project managers wrap themselves up in the tools and in the processes for feeding these automated systems. It's not uncommon for a project manager to think that the main purpose of project management is to feed the computer. When this happens, the project manager quickly loses sight of the overall project effort. Without warning, the OS Phase happens.

"It would be great if we could throw all of our computers out the window, but that would only make things more difficult. It is important to remember that the computer is a tool, not the process."

"If we can't get rid of those evil computers, then what should we do next?" Alice asked, while understanding for the first time that I wouldn't have taken the time on a Saturday morning to help them if there wasn't a get-well possibility. "We've learned that our performance reporting processes are flawed, we've failed by working too much overtime, and now we find out that Bruce is spending the lion's share of his day updating computer systems. These new problem areas don't even include the reality that our project's objectives and deliverables were less than adequate and, as a result, our ability to forecast an accurate total cost and completion date is flawed, at best."

Although it was quite a sobering description of where the project was, Alice nailed it! There were problems with most of the project management processes used to date. Not just one or two, but actually every process had concerns, and these were only the processes we'd looked at so far.

With everyone waiting for the answer to Alice's question, I said, "The details of what we do next are right here in front of us and I predict that everyone will survive the meeting on Monday, so patience on everyone's part will be the best strategy. But before we jump into the solution, we need to make sure we understand all of the attributes of the OS Phase. We have to ensure that the team avoids the OS Phase in the future after the project is back on track, and, realistically, you can't avoid what you don't understand!"

"Alice is right, we've messed up a lot of processes and we need to fix them," Troy commented with an air of impatience. "But doesn't Bruce have to do something right now? The project is in the ditch and the project manager must get involved in righting the situation. That's his job."

"The point is hard to argue," I replied, while turning and responding directly back to Troy. "But now the time spent on any OS Phase remediation is time robbed from other important activities. Wasted time and misdirection of the project will now become a major contributor to the project's potentially fatal downward spiral. Even though you might be working hard on the details, the OS Phase itself is secretly increasing in magnitude as we sit here this morning."

The frustration of the three was growing again and understandably so. For the first time Saturday morning, all three were sitting quietly and seemed to be waiting for the next words of wisdom.

When looking for causes related to hitting the OS Phase, there are many that we will consider. Ironically, the performance reporting process we were discussing is a major contributor to the OS Phase. It is reasonable to conclude that if proper information were available to the management team, the OS Phase would not be a surprise.

The effectiveness of the Management Control System or, actually, the lack of effectiveness of the system, is one of the biggest contributors to the OS Phase.

"You need to explain what you mean by that comment," Troy said before I could respond voluntarily. "I understand what the Management Control System is, but I don't' understand how it leads to the OS Phase."

"Good point," I said. "Let me explain. First, ineffective reporting processes themselves do not affect the project, but instead, they mask the project's problems and prevent timely resolution. It's no wonder so many projects get in trouble before anyone knows about it. These deficiencies represent a fundamental failure in the ability to manage projects proactively and, more importantly, they demonstrate a complete breakdown in routine project performance reporting processes. This information void results from an ineffective Management Control System.

"Any senior executive should be horrified to discover a project in serious trouble when it's late in the project. In most cases it's too late to do anything. The executive can't change the situation but, instead, can only manage the news. If the Management Control System had worked properly, it's possible that preventive actions could have occurred earlier."

Alice now had a question. "When looking at project failures across different industries, what is the single biggest contributor to senior management's lack of timely information about these projects?"

Everyone was indeed interested in this response. We had talked about several project deficiencies but hadn't pinpointed any single problem. I hoped they wouldn't be disappointed when I sidestepped the answer. "There are many problems that lead to project failures. In most cases, the actual cause is different, although poor scope management processes, resources problems, and ignorance of risks usually head the list. The real concern, and it took me a long time to realize it, was the amount of time it took senior management to actually find out about the problem, whatever the problem was for the project. This goes back to the Management Control System deficiency."

Continuing with the same thought, I said, "After considering that problem and evaluating the process within numerous large companies, it was clear that corporate performance reporting methods in use today at many companies are worthless. They are too complex and too easily embellished. For many, the ability to mask problems is relatively easy. Problems are sugarcoated until it's too late to avoid significant project impacts. The occurrences of underreporting the seriousness of project problems happen frequently and often involve hundreds of millions of dollars."

# IT'S CUSTOMARY TO SAY EVERYTHING IS FINE! 91

Listening to every word, but questioning the conclusions, Alice asked a very reasonable question. "Your comments do make sense, but didn't many companies add enterprise-wide reporting systems called Enterprise Resource Planning (ERP) and other management systems so they could pass important data to executive levels?"

Responding, I said, "Yes, that was the plan, but it turned out that many of these systems were too complicated and difficult to use."

Nodding his head in agreement, Troy added some interesting comments. "From what I've read recently, the real irony is that many of the enterprise-wide software roll-outs that were embarked upon to implement these systems fell victim to the OS Phase themselves. It is impossible to tabulate the hundreds of millions of dollars of collective overrun on these ventures alone. Even worse, many companies are now questioning whether or not these systems even improved company performance."

Smiling at Bruce and Alice, I added to Troy's analysis of the business world. "His comments are right. The purpose of the computerized systems supporting project managers will be an important part of our future discussion. Right now we need to complete our specific discussion related to performance reporting. It is important that we understand what you might want to present to the executive committee Monday related to this area of the project. Without knowing all the members of the committee, it's clear to me that they will want to discuss the current problem in relation to what they thought the status was before the meeting. We'll take a few more minutes to talk about that area and then we'll take a much deserved break."

With non-verbal agreement from everyone, I took the floor and presented some comments related to performance reporting. "Project forecasts must be completed and submitted in a consistent and timely manner. The complexity of performance reporting in a corporation with thousands of projects in progress at any moment is staggering. Most organizational groups do not have a common reporting chain, so the differences and complexities are usually only apparent to outsiders looking in. We must be in a position to expect realistic forecasts from project managers, even if it's bad news. The processes that work for mega corporations and their countless projects should be the same processes used here for the handful of projects that might be occurring at any point in time. What's needed is a simple process that is reliable and resistant to embellishments and inaccurate assessments. It must work for small projects and even the largest projects ever attempted. It is often impossible to bring any sense to the volumes of data passed on to those in a management position for them to recognize eminent failure."

Turning to Bruce, I continued the discussion. "Performance reporting, as we know it today, takes up considerable time and resources and has limited value. Instead, a project manager should be able to press a button and create the monthly performance report. The data should be in the system and the report format should already be in place."

Bruce acknowledged the suggestion and commented, "It's easy to stand here now and agree, but the reality of putting that type of process in place is much different. It's hard enough just to find the data, let alone make sure it's accurate and timely."

Bruce's comment was on point and needed attention before we went much further.

Alice began to chuckle to herself. When Troy asked what was amusing her, she described an advertisement she recently saw in a project management magazine. "A software company, trying to join the Project Management Information System provider market, advertised as a good thing that they have over 100 different management reports available from their project management software programs. Wow! Think about it, why would anyone want 100 different management reports? Is this really a 'good thing'?"

Troy was grinning with Alice and said, "Wouldn't it be better to advertise that they had a computerized system that managed the data so efficiently that they've created and are providing 'one' report that captures all key elements of a project's performance?"

The comment and his enthusiasm ended with Alice and Troy exchanging a high-five slap of the hands.

With a smile, Bruce shouted out the answer to Alice's question. "Unfortunately, simple won't sell; simple just doesn't sell!"

Everyone agreed with Bruce's conclusion, as well as a suggestion that everyone take a short break to stretch.

# IT'S CUSTOMARY TO SAY EVERYTHING IS FINE!

> ***OS Phase* Avoidance STRATEGY 11**
>
> *Care should be taken to ensure that time spent on performance reporting isn't wasted. Project team members need to report progress when it occurs and should submit forecasts on a regular basis. It's important to design a performance reporting process that is simple.*

As we walked from the conference room, it was clear that the energy level was increasing. Without exception, everyone realized that their problems today weren't the fault of any one person, but instead a complete breakdown in the project's Management Control System processes and a lack of support from the automated Project Management Information System.

# Avoiding
# the OS Phase®

CHAPTER 12
# The Relentless Pursuit of Scope

Up to this point we've discussed the importance of managing the *stuff*, or *scope*. We evaluated the relevance of ***deliverables*** and ***objectives*** to the *scope* definition ***process*** and we took a minor glance at how to report this information to management. We also sat back and recognized the relevance of managing projects from the *scope, roles*, and *risk* perspective. Now it is time to drill down and look at specific ***processes*** to support each of the *scope*, *roles*, and *risk* initiatives.

No matter how you define the project, you will be doing something to achieve some type of end-result. The something you are "doing" is where we want to put the focus. This ***something*** is what we call *scope*.

*Scope* is everything. If you must develop requirements for the project, they are *scope*. If you have to develop procedures or ***processes*** to support the project, the development is part of the *scope*. Considering the laws of physics, for every action there is an equal and opposite reaction. The same holds true for *scope*. There is an element of *scope* contributing to any resource requirement or time expenditure.

*Scope* is the foundation of the project. With thorough *scope* definition and relentless *scope* management, other critical aspects of the project will fall into place.

*Scope* development is not free. It will take quite some time to derive the adequate level of *scope*. Unfortunately, our first observation is that the necessary cost or effort to pursue the *scope* at the beginning of a project is not consistent with the minor allotment for this portion of the project.

This must change!

Emphasis on the importance of up front efforts is necessary to avoid the much greater costs incurred with hitting the ***OS Phase***.

> The importance of doing it right the first time is an understatement. Across the world, at every company, in every home, the time and money lost on projects hitting the *OS Phase* is staggering. The project manager must be able to develop *scope* even if the company culture doesn't support it.

**I** restarted the discussion by bringing everyone back from the discussion of performance measurement and performance reporting to the basic nature of the scope management process. "We mentioned earlier the importance of managing the stuff or, as we call it, the scope. We all agreed that scope management was crucial for avoiding the OS Phase. We discussed several philosophical aspects of project management, but now we need to move away from that world for a while and utilize a simplistic but thorough process or tool for actually managing the scope of the project."

After getting positive nods from everyone, I went again to the front of the conference room and approached the Avoidance Triangle drawn on the flip chart. I pointed to the bottom portion of the triangle (Chart 12 - 1), the scope portion and then spoke. "In order to fully understand the extent of the scope of any project, it is necessary to investigate all of the parameters that tie to scope, no matter how remote. Remember, our definition of scope is anything that takes time or costs money. This, then, requires that we look for the anything. which includes everything in every way possible! This is not and can never be a trivial effort!"

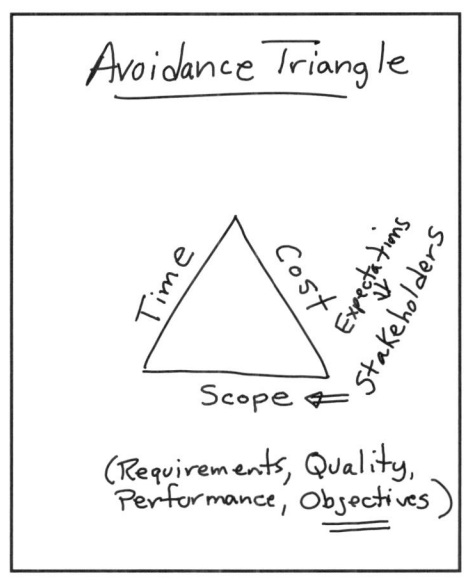

**Chart 12 - 1**

Turning to Bruce I asked a question that, although simple on the surface, becomes very difficult for anyone to answer when you look back at our definition of scope. "Bruce, here's an important question. How does your project team actually manage the scope of the project? I know we've talked about how important it is to manage scope, now I need to know what scope management process you use on the project."

I then drew a box around the word *process* on the earlier chart we had hung on the wall

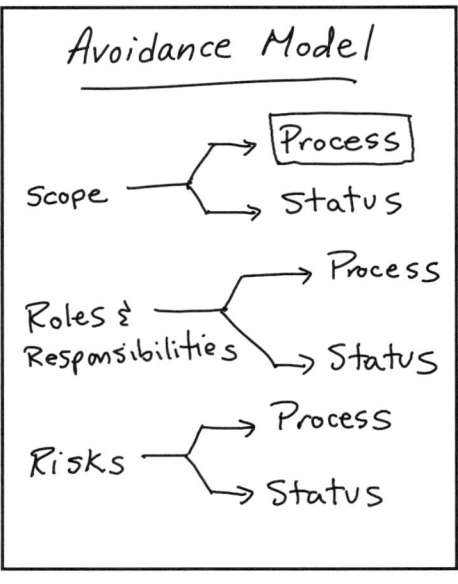

**Chart 12 - 2**

(Chart 12 - 2). Using the classic broken-record technique, I repeated the same comment made when first describing this Avoidance Model. "Remember, we said for scope that we need to have a well-understood and documented process and we need to have a clear understanding of the status of all related management processes. This will never change!"

Bruce's puzzled look and next question were all too familiar. "What do you mean by the word scope? You keep saying scope and I don't think we're talking about the same thing."

At this point, a feeling of déjà vu becomes overwhelming and a natural reaction is to start fussing at Bruce because we've already discussed the subject at length. We spent almost an hour defining the word he didn't know the meaning of an hour later. I used to wonder if it was my approach or if it was a general lack of understanding of what scope really means. But time after time, just when I think everyone understands the scope processes, the opposite realization strikes again, evidence that we've only begun the new learning process.

Actually, what I've realized is that an un-learning process is required first. We have to unlearn years or even a career of using key

# THE RELENTLESS PURSUIT OF SCOPE 99

project management processes ineffectively. This is often not a pretty picture and is not easy to do!

With a subtle, but deliberate smack on the back of his head, I got Bruce's attention and asked. "Bruce, do you remember how we presented scope as anything that took time or effort?"

"Yes, but that was an hour ago. A lot of things have changed since then," Bruce said, cracking a smile. "The definitions we are discussing here make so much sense at the time, but I keep reverting back to how we used to do things on the project or, I guess, how we planned on doing things."

"This change in how we use the word scope is a significant modification to our thought processes," Alice added. "We've always made it very clear to our customers in the company what we were trying to achieve. I guess we thought of that as scope and then moved on. You keep bringing us back to process and that's not consistent with our mind-set up to this point."

Joining into the discussion, Troy asked Bruce to read the project's description. "What Bruce will read is what we've thought of as scope. This description is the basis for our project and was accepted by the executive committee as the gospel."

Bruce then read from the project's management summary.

***The Mountain Adventure Initiative is a multifaceted collaborative integration of processes using a complex supply-chain methodology linked to the interactive and quick response elements of the Internet.***

Alice added, "That's the *scope* as we see it."

"Wow!" I exclaimed with a less than professional response. "Somewhere in the midst of these buzz words you failed to mention the fact that your team didn't have a clue to what they were doing. Even though I can see how the committee might get excited about your project from that description, you haven't answered the basic scope question."

I challenged them again, "How do you manage scope? How do you manage the necessary work required to complete the project? What process do you use? Do you have a project management tool that supports scope development?"

Troy slid the project's requirement document across the table towards my direction. "Here's the scope, if that's what you want. But I'm not sure what you're going to do with it."

Laughing, Alice said, "Maybe he would like it better if it was shaped in the form of a triangle."

It was hard to keep a straight face after Alice's comment, so I smiled while acknowledging her and then went back to a more serious mode. "Hey, the requirements document looks great and would look even better if it were shaped as a triangle, but the document is NOT a process. I want someone to describe a process, specifically the process for managing scope!"

Knowing that more frustration was imminent and seeing no response on the tip of anyone's tongue, I continued with the broken-record technique. "Yes, I've heard what you said, now what I want to know is how, not what, but how you are managing, tracking, and monitoring this thing called scope."

Picking up the requirements document I said, "Troy, as we said earlier, the requirements are very important, but they don't represent all of the scope. Requirements documents focus on conditions that have to be met in order to complete the project, but the requirements or specifications don't even come close to defining all of the work that has to be completed. Requirements documents are a *thing*. I asked someone to describe a process or tool for managing scope.

"Once we review how you are managing scope then we can determine if you have a complete grasp of all of the scope."

Alice and Troy seemed to be getting noticeably frustrated with me again. They were becoming irritated at my comments about what they *weren't* doing. The reality is that no one enjoys criticism, and that was what I was directing at them in the form of an unrelenting barrage of questions.

There was no way to sugarcoat the questions related to scope management that we made up to this point, but, in order to avoid a mutiny, I slowed things down a bit and began to retrace our steps.

After removing the Avoidance Triangle from the flip chart and hanging it on the wall, I went back to the flip chart and wrote several bullets under the scope heading (Chart 12 - 3).

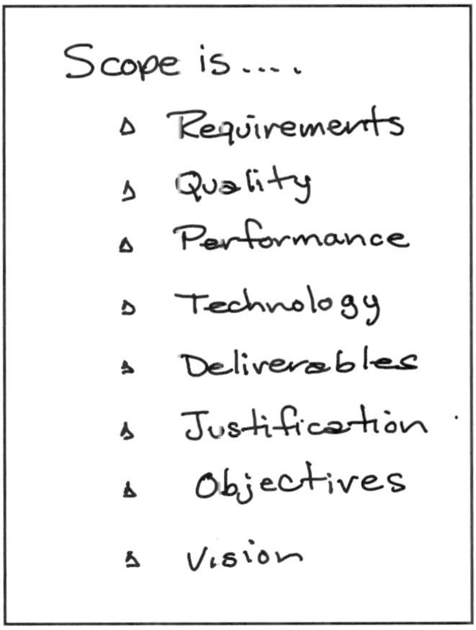

With everyone focusing at the list, I said, "Scope is derived from any one or all of these items or categories. In fact, there may be others in addition to these."

Bruce returned to his cynical tone and spoke out, "Just how would you expect any one of us to look at those items and then end up with anything that even remotely looked like a definition of the scope of our project? Several of these items actually overlap or are subsets of other ones."

"That's a perfect question, Bruce. Thanks for reminding us why we are usually so poor at identifying the scope on our projects. We don't do it well because it is confusing to know how or where to start. That's why it's common to gravitate to the requirements document. The list of requirements represents something we can get our arms around without much difficulty. It has substance and we can document and manage each item."

Alice was again looking like she was really connecting with the discussion. She added what will turn out to be several profound observations. "Wait a minute. This is perfect. When we talked about the Stupid Triangle earlier, we all agreed that if you knew the scope, the time and cost were easy to manage. I shook my head in agreement at the time, but now I really understand why that statement is true. As you described scope with the various bullets, it is obvious that finding the stuff, as we called it earlier, is indeed difficult. However, once it's found and documented, the schedule aspects and cost aspects are much easier to derive. Scope is, in fact, the ultimate driver on the Stupid Triangle."

Alice then looked around the room at everyone and concluded, "If we do a poor job identifying the scope, it only stands to reason that the time and cost forecasts will be nebulous and subject to significant

Scope is ....
- Requirements
- Quality
- Performance
- Technology
- Deliverables
- Justification
- Objectives
- Vision

**Chart 12 - 3**

movement once we discover what they really should be for the project. This, of course, is not until after the real scope is discovered, often not until the project hits the OS Phase."

Troy was fully engaged in Alice's description of the processes leading up to and including the OS Phase. "Alice, I hope you can remember that speech for Monday morning. I'm not kidding. I think that we should consider soon what we are going to announce at the meeting and I'm beginning to agree that delivering a new forecast without looking at the entire scope could be fatal. We need something along the theme you just presented."

Everyone nodded in agreement. Alice was pleased at Troy's endorsement.

Bruce seemed eager to move forward and started by asking a question related to the bulleted listing on the flip chart. "With the listing of scope related features so scattered, where should a project manager start? I think we're all anxious to see how we should attack the project from the scope perspective, but again that listing is confusing, not to mention exhausting!"

Alice added another profound comment. "The confusion of the list and the sheer overpowering nature of scope itself is probably why most project managers avoid the hassle. It's easier to just price out what we know and worry about the rest later!"

"Perfect comment, Alice," I added. "It's a clear behavioral concern that we all have a tendency to procrastinate on things we don't understand or we think are too confusing."

"Project management falls into that category, especially the confusing part," Troy added jokingly, as everyone broke the tension with laughter.

"Now that we understand that we have to do something, let's get over this fear of the list and see what we can do to straighten out the processes a little," I commented, while simultaneously tearing the bulleted listing off the flip chart and hanging it next to the Avoidance Triangle on the wall.

I then turned to the group and asked, "Would everyone agree that scope has to be something tangible? Something we can write down and document?"

"Yes." The response was unanimous.

"Good! Now let's look at a simple tool we can use to capture and store the details of the project scope," I replied affirmatively. "What we want to use is a tool called a Work Breakdown Structure or WBS for short."

"No way!" Bruce said, jumping to his feet. "The Work Breakdown Structure is not a tool you use to manage a project. They are only useful for formal presentations or for the accountants to keep track of spending on the project. You simply can't use a WBS for what we've been talking about this morning."

Interrupting Bruce's rebuttal, Troy challenged his comment, "Wait a minute, Bruce, we absolutely presented a WBS when we first proposed the project. In fact, I clearly recall someone saying that we would use it to manage the project."

"I don't think that commitment had anything to do with managing the project work itself," Bruce responded. "Our intent was to use it to only keep track of our expenditures and progress as appropriate."

Turning to Alice, Bruce asked, "Isn't our accounting system broken down in a WBS format?"

Responding quickly, Alice said, "Yes, the project does have a WBS format for collecting costs. I've personally never thought about it in terms of managing something as complex as scope and I don't think anybody else does either."

Bruce jumped back into the conversation by first agreeing with Alice and then adding his own thoughts. "That's right. We use the WBS to capture costs and to make sure we capture all aspects of the project, but I definitely do not use the WBS to manage the project's day-to-day work. It's been nothing more than an accounting system to me. Actually, the WBS is a pain in the butt most of the time, now that I really think about it."

Alice smiled at Bruce's comment and went on to say, "That's right, Bruce. We used the WBS to beat you up all of the time. I'm not surprised that you don't like the WBS much, if at all."

Bruce's negative comments about the WBS, along with Alice's comment, were sinking in to everyone. My first suggestion for a tool had taken a major hit right out of the gate, again, that déjà vu feeling!

As upsetting as their reaction was, it's actually a common reaction.

Most project managers are not very enthusiastic about using a WBS. The problem is the perception that it looks too much like some bureaucratic work requirement, not necessarily a project management tool.

Bruce summarized everyone's feelings by saying, "You're going to have to present a compelling, persuasive argument to get me to change my opinion of the WBS, at least in the way we use it on our project. I can't envision how scope itself would be even remotely linked to a WBS."

Surprisingly, their comments were similar to mine not too long ago. For years, I used a WBS more from a compliant perspective than as something I thought would help me out on a project. There are few project management texts or courses that don't include the WBS in their material, but most don't obsess over it.

In an effort to calm the mood, I asked Bruce to go to the board and draw the WBS for the project. His smile said a lot. He didn't have a clue what the WBS looked like. I then turned and asked Troy and Alice to draw it. There were more blank stares!

I took this opportunity to say that they weren't unique in their use and knowledge of the WBS. Most project managers look at the WBS as a process that each must be compliant with, but that's all. I've referred to this type of behavior already as "compliant behavior." Someone will do something because they "have to," not because they "want to," but definitely not because they feel that it adds value.

Compliant behavior is common on projects and within organizations as a whole, and it is rather difficult to change or correct. Once someone feels that a task doesn't really help them but they have to do it, they will generally become negative any time the item is discussed. Today was no exception!

In order to modify compliant behavior, it is important for them to understand it. I started the discussion of compliant behavior and then provided several examples:

- *It is much easier to convince someone to wear a seat belt by showing them the results, as horrific as they are, so that they*

*"want" to wear the belt. Instead, law enforcement puts many in a position of wearing a seat belt only because they have to in order to avoid getting a ticket.*
- *Advertisers convince car owners that they want to change the oil in their vehicles by providing a vision of what happens when they don't change oil on a regular basis. The "pay me now" or "pay me later" slogan conveys this technique.*

Troy clearly understood the approach I was taking. He listened to the examples and then finished defining the concept. "In marketing, there are two strategies for selling products, *push them on the consumer* by hard sales or indirectly convince the customer they want the product, thus creating a *pull from the consumer*. The pull is the best choice by far, but in many application areas, it will often take more time than the push process."

"That was a great description of our own marketing choices," Alice said in a convincing tone. "On our project, we recognized the importance of creating the pull, but that was going to take too long. The marketing group decided that a full scale advertising blitz would be required to initially get our customers in the door."

Following Alice and Troy's comments, I went on to tie this concept to the WBS. "Transferring these same concepts to corporate organizations is straightforward. From a people perspective, it is the highest priority to get everyone to do what is best for the organization, but we typically don't feel we have enough time to convince everyone, so we push processes or rules on them instead by creating lengthy procedures or compliancy documents. Unfortunately, behavioral tendencies will drive many to rebel against items or processes pushed upon them. In the case of the project team, the WBS meets all of the compliant behavior criteria. Once a process is designated as required, with no perceived value added by those tasked with using the tool, it's tough to change that feeling."

Adding to her earlier comments, Alice said, "Don't misunderstand what we're saying; compliant behavior is often successful in that it accomplishes the bottom line objective. The problem is the general lack of support by those that have to comply. Relating this to the project, it's easy to see that if our team has too many rules to follow, what you call compliant requirements, then project team members might spend too much of their time complaining about the rules instead of working on important project processes. Compliant behavior is not preferred and is certainly not always effective."

It was fun listening to Alice describe so succinctly the same words that I use day in and day out to convince teams to look for processes that work and avoid the implications of compliant behavior. Now that she was on board, the problem now was to get the other two tired professionals in the room to modify their opinion of the WBS, including how they felt about the WBS development process itself.

I started my spiel the same way I've had to do so many times before, by first providing the textbook definitions of the term WBS and then getting everyone to look at the project using the WBS perspective.

After lengthy and sometimes heated discussions, we ended up with a WBS (Chart 12 - 4).

After sitting back and reflecting on the completed WBS, it became apparent that a big concern was whether the project as we were discussing it was one big project or actually three smaller projects. As crazy as the suggestion was, that the overall project consisted of three smaller projects, we had to deal with the concern before continuing.

Bruce wrote the three smaller projects on the flip chart (Chart 12 - 5).

During the process of developing the WBS, it became apparent to everyone that there was a lot of confusion between activities related to the project and ongoing operational activities after the adventure

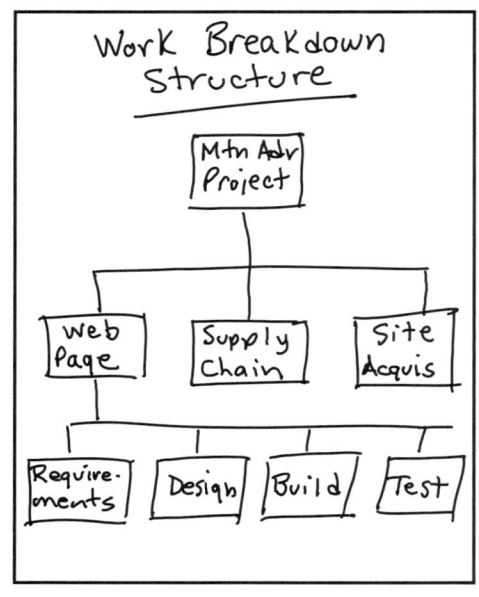

**Chart 12 - 4**

# THE RELENTLESS PURSUIT OF SCOPE

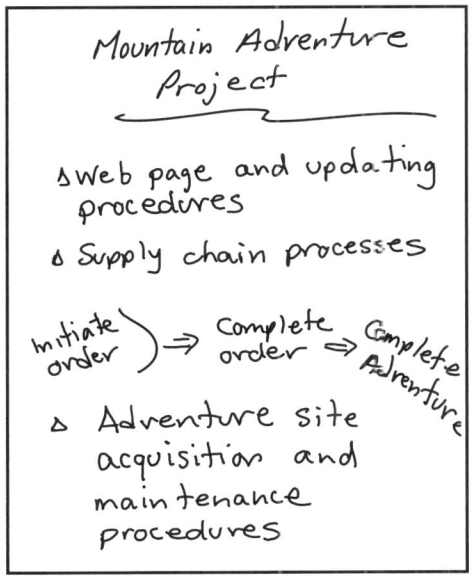

**Chart 12 - 5**

sites became operational. The handoffs weren't clear and, in fact, roles and responsibilities for operations weren't even finalized at this point.

Although we're not working on the details of the roles and responsibilities at this moment, it is clear that there will be significant concerns when we do discuss that facet of the project. Bruce was focusing on getting the project completed. Unfortunately, the effect of the transitions from project work to operations was starting to create problems that were taking a lot of Bruce's time.

Although it's too early to say for sure, I wouldn't be surprised if the OS Phase wasn't triggered by the surfacing of these concerns.

In order to keep everyone engaged, I began to ask questions while presenting and discussing the WBS. Troy was cast the first inquiry. "Troy, do you remember our definition of a deliverable?"

Troy answered quickly and confidently, "I don't remember the text book answer, but I recall that deliverables represent something you deliver to an interested stakeholder. You told us that deliverables were a thing. I remember Bruce's sarcastic comments when you introduced the word *thing*."

Everyone laughed and Troy continued, "The most important characteristic I remember was the concept that when we complete all of the deliverables, the project is completed. We developed a listing of deliverables on the board."

"Super!" I said, while trying to allow time for Troy's comments to sink into everyone's mind. "Now keeping that definition in mind, how does it relate to the WBS, which is defined as a hierarchy of the project's deliverables?"

Bruce was first to answer. "It tells me that the deliverables on our list should be evident on our WBS and vice versa. At first glance, there is some match, but not as much as I would have expected."

Returning the comment, as a question to Bruce, I asked, "Which is better defined, the deliverables list or the WBS?"

"Actually, they're both....how do you term it...hosed!" Bruce said with a smile.

I went on to explain that this observation is common. On projects of this magnitude, it is difficult at first to get everyone on the same page. It's so easy to focus only on the project's end date and target budget. We are often so overwhelmed with what we're calling the scope management processes that we complete deliverables listings and WBS references as compliant actions only. Most often they are completely different and no one even notices!

I described what happens when we drill down the branches of the WBS. The result will be increasing detail related to the higher-level deliverable. Eventually we will break the work down to a level where we can manage the effort effectively. The Work Package is the lowest level deliverable. This term is consistent with most project management texts and instructions. The Work Package will be broken into the activities necessary to complete the Work Package itself.

The activities then represent actions to perform and the Work Package represents the actual deliverables to be completed. When we stop looking at the WBS as a compliant tool and start to consider it a scope management process, our thought processes will undergo a major overhaul.

Alice indicated that she had a question, so we gave her the floor. "I like what I'm seeing with the WBS. The way we're looking at it this morning is helping me to understand the scope, but what about how we're using it on the project to tie to our accounting system? So far, you haven't mentioned any linkage to budgets or expenditures. Am I missing something?"

"Actually, Alice, you keep working as the master of ceremony, describing each new area of discussion," I said. "If it weren't for your lead-ins I'd have a difficult time keeping Bruce and Troy focused."

Alice took the compliment graciously. Her comment had the effect of lightening up the mood in the room enough to where I felt we could finish this subject before taking another break. I took the opportunity to explain an important benefit of the WBS. "As it turns out, Alice, the linkages of scope to cost and also time occur with the WBS. We usually draw the lowest level activity as a rectangle or as a schedule time-line; we could instead draw it as a little triangle, a little Stupid Triangle! Then since each higher level combines the deliverable elements of the items below, we could draw summary triangles to the point where we eventually draw the top-level box as a triangle.

"In my world, the WBS is drawn with triangles, not rectangles," I said, while drawing triangles over the rectangles on the flip chart (Chart 12 - 6). "I showed them as rectangles first so that you could see the correlation to what most textbooks reference, but now I want you to see the significance of recognizing the relationship to time and cost. As it turns out, the WBS is where the Stupid Triangle is actually formed."

"So what we should be doing is identifying deliverables, putting them in a Work Breakdown Structure, and assigning time and cost to each as we list them?" Alice asked.

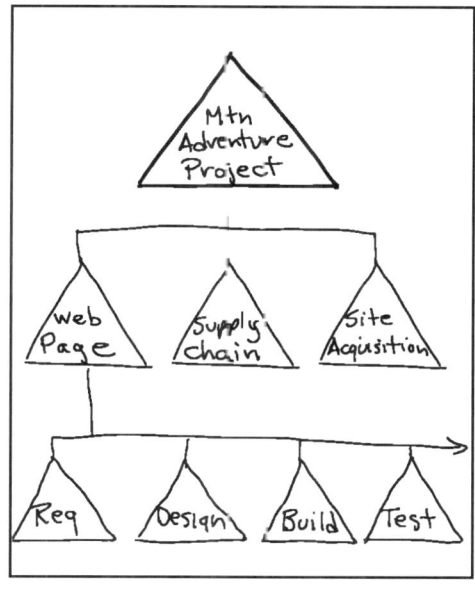

**Chart 12 - 6**

My sense was that she was just confirming a thought and not actually asking a question.

"Will you hold it against me if I say you are wrong with your statement?" I said, without being critical. "You're into the discussion so much now that I hesitate to challenge your comment, but we don't want to do what you just spoke about."

I took this time to describe the importance of identifying the scope first, all of the scope! Only after you identify all of the scope do you develop the schedule for the activities, and only after the schedule is finished do we estimate and integrate the cost for each item. The process of developing project scope, time, and cost baselines is a sequential process. We must know what we're doing first, then we look at the best sequence for each work item. Then and only then do we estimate the associated cost, based on the scope and time you have identified.

The process of identifying the scope side of the Avoidance Triangle completely before assessing the time and so on is definitely contrary to many existing standard practices. Most project managers or anyone using a WBS will identify each item, seek the corresponding time and cost elements at the same time, just as Alice described.

Bruce was obviously having difficulties with this statement so he jumped in to ask a rather pointed question. "Why in the world would anyone wait for all of the scope definition to put time and cost into the WBS? That seems to be backward of any logical process. It would seem much more efficient to sit down once at the computer and enter all of the relevant data and then go from there. If at that time you know dates and durations, why wouldn't you go ahead and put them into the database or scheduling software?"

"From purely a process perspective, both you and Alice are absolutely correct in your thinking," I responded. "Inputting the data all at once would seem to be the most efficient process. Our goal, though, is to be as thorough with the scope discovery processes as possible. From a behavioral perspective, we might have a tendency to feel too much of a sense of accomplishment or completion when we put scope, time, and cost into the file. That false sense might lead us to be less diligent or relentless in our pursuit of all of the scope. We have to both understand and then manage the behavior if we want to avoid the OS Phase."

Everyone seemed to understand the point except Troy, who asked, "Are you saying that if your boss or customer gives you a date and time for your project that you shouldn't put them in the schedule system at this time?"

"That's exactly what I'm saying! To put them in now would bias any relevant analysis you might do of the complete project scope. Think about it. When your sponsor or customer gives you a project or contract to perform, they will provide a scope statement of some kind, a due date and budget. From those three items, only two are absolute and they are…?"

"Time and budget…" Alice answered quickly.

"Perfect!" I exclaimed. "Now, if you fall into the trap of force-fitting the project to those fixed elements, then you will be inclined to overlook scope. At this point, you will probably be trying to eliminate some of the scope because as it stands, the time and budget are extremely optimistic. To look for more scope at this point seems futile. As a result, the bottom line is that the relentless pursuit of scope isn't attempted."

Continuing, I went back to the relationship of behavior to these processes. "Human behavior affects 98 percent of all project management processes. Understanding behavior and understanding how it might affect your project is vital. When the scope of the project already exceeds reasonable estimates for the associated time and budget allocations, behavioral tendencies will lead us away from new discovery. The scope is there, we just don't seek it out because we can't handle any more. We don't want to know the truth, because as Bruce so eloquently said earlier, we can't handle the truth! Later in the project, when the scope actually surfaces, we cry foul and blame the problems on something we call scope creep, like it's a disease and we're a victim!"

With everyone's attention guaranteed at this point, I continued with the same level of intensity. "If the amount of scope creep is substantial, then a visit to the OS Phase is likely. No one is saying that the discovery of scope in the beginning of the project will be easy, but it must be done regardless."

Bruce listened intently but was not completely convinced with my explanation. He asked, "Where is it written that this is the proper technique? I don't recall ever reading anywhere in a book or manual to capture scope first before even considering time or cost."

I returned his comment with a smile and confirming nod, "Your memory is perfect. This is not a common recommendation. If any text did suggest a process to complete the scope first, I'm sure they didn't imply it to the extent of what we're suggesting here.

"The reason for the comment is purely behavioral in nature," I continued. "The best way to get unbiased information is to avoid getting involved with all three sides of the Avoidance Triangle from the beginning. For the most part, there aren't any hard and fast rules, just some pointers that you will probably appreciate after you've had a chance to think them through."

Letting what was just said sink in for a few moments, I looked for everyone's attention before presenting a little performance briefing of our own. "Speaking of the triangle, I was given two hours to introduce you to a simple, but complete, way to view project management. The two hours are up and now we need to see where we go from here."

"You rat!" Bruce said in an excited tone. "You knew when you said you promised the two-hour limit to the lecture that we would not let you stop at that point, didn't you?"

Smiling, I responded to Bruce's semi-compliment. "You caught me, Bruce, guilty as charged! Getting professionals to change years, or even their entire career, of ways of thinking and doing things is not easy. Your patience is not overly abundant, especially considering what is in front of each of you. Listening to a lecture on what you should have done takes a lot of patience on your part."

Alice took the lead and said, "We've learned a lot of how we need to look at scope; now we need to look at the other execution steps related to the project. We weren't executing what we thought we had to do, let alone the fact that we didn't have all of the stuff identified. I think we still have a big problem related to actual execution processes, not just scope management."

Responding to Alice in as positive a manner as possible, I said, "Execution is important and it's clear the project has problems in this area. We will address those processes as well. I do want you to keep in mind that if we complete the planning processes properly, then the execution processes proceed smoothly as long as we manage the risk and performance reporting properly, as well. Finding and categorizing all the scope in the beginning of the project is a critical part of planning, and failure to capture all of the scope, as we've seen, was a problem; the ripple effect on execution is significant. Unfortunately, if it's not in our face, we blame the problems on other processes."

Quiet during most of the discussion, Troy added his thoughts, which demonstrated that his silence was not an indication of boredom or confusion, but instead one of quiet reasoning and thought. "Based on what we've discussed, I agree on the importance of finding the complete scope before a project proceeds too far down the road. In reality, for the balance of our project we won't have a clue what the remaining scope of the project is until we start taking a hard look at it from every angle. It's really easy to think of scope as the set of requirements or specifications for the project. This is totally incorrect. The final product and the requirements that get us that product are certainly part of the scope, but only part of it. Scope includes meetings that we attend. Scope includes the meeting to discuss what scope represents to us. It is everything. If each element of scope is linked to time and effort as shown by the Avoidance Triangle, then scope is the most important thing we need to accomplish!"

It was amazing to hear the passion in Troy's voice and see it in the emotional movements of his hands. Alice and Bruce listened intently and then complimented Troy on his summary. There were still some important implementation concerns as they related to the scope management processes, but those must wait until we look at the other supporting processes for the project. Overdosing on scope at this time would be counterproductive.

Before embarking into a new subject, we all took a short stretch break. This time the buzz in the hallway was different. It was too early to tell if everyone was comfortable and understood the processes of scope management. It would be obvious soon enough!

> *OS Phase* **Avoidance STRATEGY 12**
>
> *Definition of deliverables and objectives is important for defining project scope. The WBS is the "tool" used for actually managing the scope. Design the WBS template so that it is applicable for all company projects and it is capable of capturing all of the scope for each project.*

# CHAPTER 13
# Defining Roles and Responsibilities

A basic *process* often overlooked or attempted with only a half-hearted effort is the assignment of *roles* and *responsibilities* for a project. This omission is a strange occurrence, because when asked, nearly every professional will agree that this is an important step, especially for high priority assignments.

Think about it. If you absolutely had to get something done, wouldn't the designation of who was going to perform the *scope* be important? If your project or effort was necessary to save the world, wouldn't you be thorough when making sure that everybody knew their *roles* and *responsibilities* before the project began? The answer is easy, *absolutely yes!*

Why then do we fail to do it every day of the week on projects?

It just doesn't make sense!

In many cases, we document assignments only as a compliant step, not something considered helpful to the project manager. This is amazing! The mystery that many project managers fail to realize is the relationship of *role* and *responsibility* assignments to the all-important pursuit of *scope*. This *process* will ultimately contribute to how long the project will take as well as determining how much effort it will take or how much it will cost.

Thinking back to the *Avoidance Triangle*, we must never forget that *scope* represents the project. *Scope* represents everything that takes time or effort. *Role* and *responsibility* assignments are vital, then, for identifying who is accountable for every element of the *scope*. Only the person doing the work is best suited to provide the cost and time estimates.

Without a defined *process*, the project manager is doing these actions either much too informally or in the worse case possible, not at all. In either of these scenarios, the path to the *OS Phase*

# DEFINING ROLES AND RESPONSIBILITIES

> will be set in place and then the only person identified as responsible for the project's failure is the project manager.
>
> Defining actual *roles* and *responsibilities* and getting necessary commitment is a hot issue in most companies. Seems simple, but in reality it is complicated getting adults to agree. The combative attitude of those that want to be responsible for everything discourages most project managers.
>
> It's a crazy world.

When we discussed roles and responsibilities in terms of the project management Avoidance Model, it was clear that without knowing who performed the scope we would be vulnerable to eventually hitting the OS Phase. What we need to discuss now is the degree of detail necessary for managing the roles and responsibilities and what tool the team could use to capture the information.

Troy seemed eager to begin the discussion of roles and responsibilities. His comments thus far demonstrated his understanding of organizational behavior. "When we reflect back to the statistics referenced earlier this morning, that project management is 98 percent dealing with humans, we understand the significance of behavior. To influence this behavior, we need a tool that communicates to the team. Satisfying this need is not negotiable. Good communication is vital. It's the only way humans know what to do."

"Well, I'm glad we're finally finished talking about scope," Bruce interjected, with a relieved tone to his often-frustrated voice. "I agree that scope is important, but I'm exhausted with all of our discussion about it this morning. The subject of roles and responsibilities is so much more appropriate."

"Let's not leave scope in the dust," Alice said in a serious tone. "A scope management process must be put in place immediately. Then we need to assess the supporting processes. The emphasis on scope has actually helped me to realize the significance of roles and responsibilities. After you go through the intense effort to figure out what has to be completed, we just won't want to stop there. Knowing who will do the scope seems to be a natural transition. It will be more important than ever before."

Addressing the importance of managing roles and responsibilities to the group would be a little easier than our discussion of scope. Since none of the three had ever mentioned any process or tool, I expected that roles and responsibility management would need attention, as well.

I turned to Troy and asked, "What process does the team use to manage work assignments and other roles and responsibilities?"

With a little uncertainty in his voice, Troy provided the expected response. "I guess I've never really thought about it before. From what I observed, everyone had job descriptions and knew what they were supposed to do and if they forgot, Bruce made a point of reminding them."

Everyone laughed at the comment about Bruce, and then Troy continued, "We never really worried about having anything on paper regarding roles. Everyone knew for the most part what their jobs were and that seemed sufficient. Now I'm afraid you're going to tell us that it wasn't enough."

Before I could answer Troy's comment, Bruce took his all too familiar defensive stand and challenged what Troy had said. "Wait a minute! We had names for all of the work entered in our schedule software program. We noted every resource assignment, whether or not anyone agreed that the resources would be available. I think we had roles and responsibilities covered. We knew what everyone was doing."

With a good view of the whiteboard from where I was standing and seeing the answer to my upcoming question already in view, I asked Bruce another rhetorical question. "So out of all those problems you came up with last night and have written on the whiteboard, none of those had anything to do with someone supporting the project that might have misunderstood or ignored their assigned roles?"

"I didn't say we were perfect," Bruce answered with a combination of frustration and uncertainty in his voice. "At the end we did have some concerns with resources. One of our biggest problems was when we realized that the person who actually developed some of our

# DEFINING ROLES AND RESPONSIBILITIES 117

key software modules was the only person that knew what was done and he left unexpectedly two weeks ago."

Alice jumped in and beat me to the same question. "Why wasn't the documentation for that system adequate to answer questions without the developer?"

"That's where the problem occurred. We didn't have any documentation whatsoever," Bruce responded defensively. "We didn't have finalization of the documentation as an activity on the schedule. It seemed like something we could do after the system was operational."

The example provided by Bruce fell right into the argument with roles and responsibilities and their ultimate tie to scope. It turns out that the documentation of the systems wasn't identified on any schedule or list. In fact, to the developer's defense, when he left he may not have realized he was deficient on anything.

"Did you have a roles or responsibilities listing or chart that the team used other than the resource references on the schedule?" Troy asked.

"No! I'm not sure what the big deal is anyway," Bruce said defensively, "I told you before that roles and responsibilities weren't a problem. What happened to us was the addition of items at the end of the project that we didn't expect. It had nothing to do with roles."

With care not to alienate Bruce, I kept the pressure on, just enough to avoid it seeming like an interrogation. "Where did you track roles and responsibilities for scope that were not listed on the schedule?"

Bruce snapped back with a typical blunt answer. "Nowhere. In fact, that question doesn't make any sense. If it's not on the schedule it couldn't have any roles assigned to it. Remember, we use the scheduling tool to track resources."

"Looking back at the developer that left two weeks ago, do you have any way to identify what exactly that person was responsible for completing or supporting? Obviously you're looking for an expert in that area to take the person's place," I stated, while looking directly at Bruce and continuing to hammer home the importance of roles and responsibilities management. "What about the efforts of the home office staff and management, like Alice and Troy? Are they on the resources listing? Are they responsible for document approvals? Is there any chance that one of them is a Subject Matter Expert in the area where you lost some of your key resources?"

Bruce had a puzzled look. "What do you mean document approvals and Subject Matter Experts? Our resource listing identified who was going to do the work. That's what the system is designed to support. You're talking about something that's totally outside the realm of project management. If you want to know the details you're talking about, you need to contact human resources or the team member's official manager."

Realizing that Bruce's defensive wall had risen and his interest in listening to the discussion was gone, I suggested a five-minute break to catch our breath. It was clear that Bruce was frustrated with the discussion. On his way out of the conference room, he made a phone call on his mobile phone. Something about the discussion of **roles** must have triggered the call.

I think he just demonstrated the tool he used on his project.

\* \* \*

When everyone returned to the conference room, I displayed my version of a Responsibility Assignment Matrix or RAM on my laptop (Exhibit 13 - A). They would have to crowd around the screen, but since we hadn't arranged anything else, that was as good as it was going to get.

The example Responsibility Assignment Matrix that we looked at was simply a matrix displayed with a spreadsheet format. Going down the left hand side of the spreadsheet, scope items were listed and across the top there was a place to identify the person related to the project, any persons that could be an approver or a Subject Matter Expert, or anything relevant to the project.

Alice was focusing on the laptop's screen, squinting to see the various role and responsibility assignment designations allocated to each of the persons on the matrix. Intrigued with what she was looking at, she asked, "Why are there so many codes? I'm used to a very simple RACI chart with four different types of role assignments

## DEFINING ROLES AND RESPONSIBILITIES

### Responsibility Assignment Matrix

| | President | Vice President | Functional Manager A | Functional Manager B | Functional Manager C | Functional Manager D | Functional Lead A - 1 | Functional Lead A - 2 | Functional Lead A - 3 | Functional Lead B - 1 | Sales Manager | Plant Manager | Engineering Manager | Architect / Engineer (A/E) | Equip Manufacturer | Project Manager A | Project Manager B | Employee A - 2 | Employee A - 3 | Employee A - 4 | Employee A - 5 | Employee A - 6 | Employee A - 7 | Employee B - 1 | Employee B - 2 | Employee B - 3 | Employee B - 4 | Employee B - 5 | Employee C - 1 | Vendor A | Vendor B |
|---|---|---|---|---|---|---|---|---|---|---|---|---|---|---|---|---|---|---|---|---|---|---|---|---|---|---|---|---|---|---|---|
| Work Package 1 | A | C | | C | | | R | R | R | D | D | | | | BC | | P | | S | I | I | I | I | | I | I | | | I | | |
| Work Package 2 | | | | | | C | C | I | D | D | D | D | A | | | | | | | | | | | P | SB | R | R | R | | R | R |
| Activity 1 | | | | | | | | | | | | | | | | | | | | | | | | | | | | | | | |
| Activity 2 | | | | | | | | | | | | | | | | | | | | | | | | | | | | | | | |
| Process 1 | | | | | | | | | | | | | | | | | | | | | | | | | | | | | | | |
| Process 2 | | | | | | | | | | | | | | | | | | | | | | | | | | | | | | | |

Suggested Symbols

- P = Primary preparer (single point of accountability for the entire activity)
- S = Primary support to preparer (unlimited)
- I = Provides input to preparer(s) (unlimited)
- E = Subject Matter Expert (unlimited)
- L = Lessons Learned Contributor (unlimited)
- B = Backup to primary preparer - P (unlimited)
- R = Responsible for reviewing completed product (review only - no signature)
- C = Responsible for reviewing completed product and concurring by signature
- A = Responsible for acceptance / approval of completed product (only 1 permitted)
- D = Receives a distribution copy of completed product (unlimited)

**Exhibit 13 - A**

(Responsibility, Authority, Consult, Inform). This looks like a crossword puzzle."

Bruce laughed at the comment, and then added his own joke, "I keep looking for a Stupid Triangle, but all I see is a bunch of scrambled letters."

"I can see that if it's not shaped like a triangle, it's impossible for you to understand it," I said, looking back at Bruce with a smile.

Continuing, with everyone engaged, I moved again to the flip chart and began writing some letter codes and their definitions.

As I wrote each term on the flip chart, I explained what the specific role or responsibility code represented. "There's nothing special about the letter. Any code could work. What's important is the definition."

I continued to describe the terms while I wrote each definition out on the flip chart (Chart 13 -1). "In the case of 'P', the Primary Preparer is the person held singly accountable for getting the task completed, no matter what! This might be the most important term because I believe that if there isn't a person assigned and held accountable for each element of work, it won't get done. I also do not believe in having more than one person accountable. I appreciate that a project is a team and each work item will often have a team involved with completing the work, but the buck has to stop somewhere. There must be one and only one person accountable. That person is whom I will be directing my attention to as the project manager. The remaining role and responsibility codes are most often for the benefit of the Primary Preparer."

"Is it possible to be both the 'S' and the 'P'?" Troy asked, while being engrossed in the discussion.

> Responsibility Assignment Matrix
>
> P – Primary Preparer with Complete accountability (1 person maximum)
>
> S – Support to Preparer (could be several people)

**Chart 13 - 1**

"Absolutely," I responded. "It is very common for the same person to have more than one role on a particular work task or process. In fact, many times project managers themselves are overloaded with too many assignments and the matrix illustrates that completely. The assignments of a Primary Preparer and the person(s) in support of the Primary Preparer are at the top of the list because they will drive the completion of the task or process. The 'S' represents anyone actually working on the task. It is possible to be accountable for getting the task completed without actually working on it yourself."

"Wow," Bruce exclaimed. "If there was a matrix for the project, the column under my name would just be a solid black line because there would be so many letters crammed into each box."

"Bruce, just think about it…" Alice said, joining in to the fast moving conversation, "…the Responsibility Assignment Matrix is something a project manager shouldn't be without. Why would you ever want to hide or keep that information a secret?"

"I'm glad you all are developing the same passion I have for a Responsibility Assignment Matrix," I added. "It's hard to imagine not having one for everything."

# DEFINING ROLES AND RESPONSIBILITIES

"That reminds me," Alice added, "you keep saying that you're identifying roles and responsibilities for tasks or processes. What do you mean by processes? Are you referring to project processes, or what?"

"I should have clarified some elements of the matrix earlier," I responded with an apologetic tone and a big smile. "The left hand column represents scope, anything you have to perform on a project, the same as what we've been talking about all morning, which might also include organizational or project-based support processes."

"What's an example of a support process you're referring to?" Bruce asked.

Thinking aloud for a minute or two, I provided a couple of examples and jotted them down on the flip chart (Chart 13 - 2).

"In the case of the payroll process, the project might not be processing the payroll for the team; the company's payroll group completes that process for everyone in the company. It might be important to understand roles and responsibilities of that process for the instances you have to interface with the payroll group to clarify the accuracy and timing of actual cost hours and costs to the project.

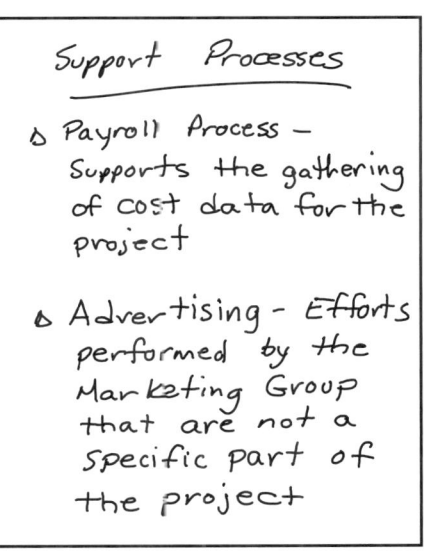

**Chart 13 - 2**

"I pulled the advertising function out of thin air. Does anybody agree with me on that choice? Or do you have another suggestion?" I asked.

"You must be reading our minds," Alice quipped and then continued, "Troy and I have to review what Bruce is doing with the project and make sure marketing is in sync. That's not an easy task, but it has to be done every status period. This is especially valid now because the marketing group is already working on the next version of this system. They like to advertise and set impossible dates for implementations."

"Don't hold back, Alice," I said with a smile.

"Actually they had a lot to do with getting us in trouble on this project," Bruce added. "I'm not going to make any excuses. We didn't keep track of scope the way we should have at any time on the project, but in the beginning that was due to the massive push by that group to get going."

"It seems so long ago," Alice added, "but I remember the meetings, one after another, chanting that if we don't start we won't ever finish. When I think about it now, that was about the stupidest statement I've ever heard! They would say it every time we met."

"You would almost feel as if you were sabotaging the project if you sat for even a moment to reflect on where we were going with the project," Bruce said, while shaking his head in a negative direction. "All we had the first couple of months were cheer leading or pep rally sessions. It got to the point that some of us were going to bring pom-poms so we could start jumping and dancing around in the conference rooms."

"You're giving me a real bad vision in my brain, Bruce," I commented with a smile. "Let's try to get that picture out of our minds and look at the rest of the codes for the matrix. Hopefully you'll agree that a little more detail on roles and responsibilities for the project from this point forward will help make sure everyone is focused."

Going back to the flip chart, I added four additional codes to evaluate for any task or process (Chart 13 - 3).

I went through each of these items and explained their significance. The 'I' for those supplying

```
RAM Codes

I - Provides input
    to Preparer

E - Subject Matter
    Expert (SME)

L - Lessons Learned
    Contributor

B - Backup to
    Preparer
```

**Chart 13 - 3**

input seems unimportant, but could actually prove vital in assuring that everyone knows what steps or processes they have to support with information. It's not necessary to drill real low with this assignment. The purpose is to expose the most important handoffs.

The 'E' for Subject Matter Expert is my most recent addition. It's turning out that many projects are getting in trouble because the institutional knowledge within the performing organization or even the customer's organization isn't there anymore. When a project team is performing any kind of modification to an existing system, whether it's a software program or a sophisticated manufacturing or production system, the original designers or owners are now long gone.

The role of a Subject Matter Expert might be vital on a project, but if we wait until we realize we need one, it might be difficult to deal with in a short notice time period. Alice added their concern with needing someone really experienced in supply chain design and rollout. This wasn't discovered until deep into the project. It seems odd that the subject didn't surface earlier, but that's not uncommon on large, complex projects when we don't take the time to look at these roles and responsibilities up front.

The 'L', representing Lessons Learned Contributor, causes many odd looks. We all know what lessons learned are for a project, the captured detail of previous initiatives, but why on earth would you want to know who a lessons learned contributor is when you start a new project. It's funny, but as soon as someone asks me that question, their eyes show that they, in fact, know the answer already. It's a cinch that the project manager will benefit by knowing what someone else has experienced doing the same work process.

For most of the things that we work on, we are enough of an expert or are experienced enough to get it done. In some cases, though, it would really pay benefits to check with someone else that had good or even bad experiences doing the same thing. The 'L' isn't the most important role and responsibility assignment, but it does bear consideration.

As I was explaining the process of the matrix, Alice asked a question that everybody was probably pondering also. "Do we have to assign every one of these codes to every work task and process?"

"Great question," I responded, and then sat down to explain some important considerations about the Responsibility Assignment Matrix. "We've talked about compliant actions and why they are a bad idea. I feel the same way about the Responsibility Assignment Matrix. If you don't have one at all, I'll definitely want to see something close to it or you won't be able to convince me you are managing roles and responsibilities. Nevertheless, using every code for every item would usually be overdoing it quite a bit. Being excessively compliant is not an approach I would recommend either. However, by the time we finish reviewing these codes, we will end up with a couple that you will want for every item. They will be the exception rather than the rule."

Continuing, I said, "If we don't have a Subject Matter Expert, we're not going to shut down the project and wait for one to show up, but if you realize that having a Subject Matter Expert is important and you can't find one…"

"…then you have a Risk!" Troy shouted.

"…or, you're hosed!" Bruce shouted louder.

"…and you'll end up in the OS Phase!" Alice said, bringing everyone to laughter.

"Bingo!" I said, jumping from my seat and giving them each a high-five in acknowledgment of their comments.

With a proud look on my face, I again recognized their comments. "This morning we've discussed a lot of new items. If you can just remember the Stupid Triangle and the relationship between Scope / Roles / Risk, then I'll know you're on the right track to get everything back under control. Your ability to succeed will be based on a confidence that you understand what has to be done and you understand what will happen if you are haphazard in your approach."

In a reassuring voice, I brought them back to their reality. "You can't avoid the OS Phase on your project, because you're in the OS Phase right now, but if you move forward with these thoughts, you'll avoid it the second time."

"Is it common for a project to hit the OS Phase more than once?" Troy asked, hoping the answer would be NO.

There was an obvious interest in my response, so I tried to be as succinct as possible. "I don't have statistics, but if you ask most project

# DEFINING ROLES AND RESPONSIBILITIES 125

managers or team members that have had the OS Phase experience, they also had a second visit. In fact, most would suggest the second visit came quickly after the first and was even worse. The second OS Phase experience could easily be the death knell for a project."

Alice smiled and added, "From what I've read in the newspaper, I guess the Big Dig in Boston hit the OS Phase quarterly!"

"That's a great example," I responded. "That project is a classic example of the OS Phase. As a multi-billion dollar construction effort to build underground highways within the existing Boston infrastructure, it was a massive undertaking. This project doesn't compare in scale to the Big Dig. Based on its size alone, I'm sure it was considered to be a 'special project,' a project not needing the type of tools we've talked about."

"You can just hear them now …" Troy interjected, "we can't possibly use a Responsibility Assignment Matrix because it would be too complicated and unmanageable. We'll keep track of roles and responsibilities in a 'special way,' not sure what that is, but we'll do something."

Everyone laughed at Troy's impersonation of the roles and responsibilities discussion. Without knowing the details, it's unfair to say how they managed their stuff and roles, but when you run over budget in the billions, it's fair to say that there were problems.

Bruce was careful not to miss any of the discussion of the OS Phase. After a few minutes of reflective thought, he commented with an important observation, one I hoped he truly believed. "I guess if you trick yourself the first time into thinking you've fixed everything, it surfaces real quick that you did the same thing as you did in the beginning of the project, that is jumping back on the project without really understanding what you had left to do."

"I'm glad you're the one that made that comment, Bruce," Alice responded. "You've been a little skeptical today about the discussion and I'm convinced we need to do an about face or we're going down the tubes again."

"And as we said earlier," Troy added, "if we hit the OS Phase the second time, the next corrective action plan might be with another team of leaders."

They all seemed to be mulling Troy's words over in their heads. No one argued. It was a good time to catch our breath so I stood and announced, "Okay, let's take a break for a few minutes, freshen our drinks, grab some fruit or a pastry. When we return, we'll go over the rest of the responsibility codes and then move into the details of what we need to actually manage the risks that fall out of our scope and roles investigations."

With no arguments at the suggestion, everyone moved quickly, indicating that they would be ready to start back very soon.

> ***OS Phase* Avoidance STRATEGY 13**
>
> *Ninety-eight percent of project management is dealing with people. Until we identify and link all of the stakeholders to the scope, nothing meaningful will happen on the project or any supporting process.*

CHAPTER 14

# Who Do I Really Work For?

Depending on the size or nature of the project, the project manager could have many reporting relationships. From sponsors to customers, regulators, and special interest groups, it is possible to have so many relationships it's hard to keep up with them on a real-time basis. The Responsibility Assignment Matrix or RAM provides a simplistic tool for identifying and managing the *roles* of all team members, even those we have to suck up to on an occasional basis. It is important for everyone to understand every *role* on the project. When used effectively, a RAM will assist the project manager with communication of all stakeholder expectations.

Managers and customers are important to identify. They may not do work specifically on the project, but their connection to the project is vital if we are to satisfy the ***Avoidance Triangle's*** need to have persons assigned to any step that takes time or effort. Failure to identify key reporting and communication relationships could easily jeopardize the successful timely completion of the project.

The RAM is a simple tool. It is easy to use it to create sign-off documents based on designated names. A RAM provides validation of *scope* when looking at project handoffs. As you make assignments, it becomes clear that more *scope* could actually exist.

Changes to RAM assignments must be agreed to by "both" parties. The project manager should not make unilateral changes to project assignments without agreement of the affected person, even when directed by a Sponsor or Customer. As project manager, you should resist the tendency to accept ***responsibility*** if someone gives you an assignment without discussing it with you first.

The RAM process is a real checks and balances system with the ***scope*** management element of the project. If you find anything that has a ***responsibility***, then it must in turn be ***scope***.

Think about it.

We returned from the break in what seemed like only a few minutes. It was now time to introduce more aspects of managing roles and responsibilities. The enthusiasm of the group moved up a notch with the earlier discussion. It was important to make sure they knew what tools they should use after I left their sphere of influence. Too often, roles and responsibilities initiatives fail if attention wanes, even a little.

I started the session with a request for questions or comments from what we had talked about earlier. Alice didn't waste any time jumping back into the discussion.

"Don't the project management software programs manage resources for the project manager?" she asked.

The response was easy. "They only manage or identify the actual person doing the work, the role we have referred to as the 'S,' or support to the preparer. The software tools generally do not identify the support personnel, such as any Subject Matter Expert or any person or persons providing input and so on. Ironically, it often turns out that the most important resource is not the actual individual doing the work, the 'S,' but in fact is the person supporting the effort. It's difficult to find these individuals and it's just as difficult getting them to commit to any level of support. Without their involvement, the project manager can end up without the expertise to get the work done efficiently. That shortcoming can turn out to be very limiting, depending on the nature of the project."

Entering into the discussion, Troy asked, "Why not use a RACI diagram that we talked about earlier and not the RAM which seems more complicated? I remember that tool from a project management article. They would identify responsibilities, authorities, support, inform and consulting roles or something like what we've talked about this morning."

"You're right, these tools are very popular in project management circles, and many large projects have some rather complex documents with that information listed," I said, affirming the idea as something to consider later.

"Have you ever seen them in use?" Bruce asked, while still leafing through the project management text from the conference room shelf to find an example.

I answered, "They're used frequently, but their impact is minimal. The team will prepare the RACI chart, almost as a compliant act, then have several meetings to discuss it, and then they put it up on the wall or in a plan of some kind and then…"

Interrupting before I could finish the sentence, Alice said, "…nothing…and then absolutely nothing happens after that point!"

Continuing with her thoughts, Alice stood and went to the flip chart. "I remember using these on projects several years ago. We sat down, went through the main scope items one by one and then assigned those routine codes. If I remember correctly, we never even presented the list to everyone named on the list. It was as if we were doing one of those compliant acts you've talked about this morning. There wasn't much enthusiasm about the process, just a lot of effort putting it together."

"You mean you didn't do anything else with the identified roles?" Troy asked. "Did you tie them to the schedule or anything like that?"

"What we did was brag about them and show them to our sponsors or management teams and then we filed them away," Alice said bluntly. "In fact, the thoughts in my mind about that worthless experience are causing some concern on where we are going. I realize that the Responsibility Assignment Matrix we're looking at this morning is different from the basic RACI charts, but won't the results still be the same?"

"I agree," Troy added. "I can't imagine any benefit of doing a matrix at this moment. We have some pretty important concerns to deal with and the more I think about this, the more it reminds me of busy work."

"Amen!" Bruce chimed in. "The last thing we need to be doing now is busy work. We don't have time for that kind of stuff, especially before Monday."

"I'm having a bad feeling about all of this," Alice continued, without even acknowledging Bruce's comment.

"Let's stop for a minute." I spoke, trying to interrupt the surge of negativism towards the responsibility assignment process.

Turning to Bruce, I asked, "Just how do you get someone to do something on the project? Do you sit and hope they know what to do? Do you expect them to read your mind?"

Bruce was not enjoying the sarcasm, but he did see where I was going with the comments as he responded, "We give each team member a listing of tasks they are responsible for and then they proceed to do those items."

"Is there any confusion as to what they need to do?"

"Of course there is. That's partly why we are in trouble," Troy injected. "Several team members apparently misunderstood their responsibilities and a couple actually forgot what they were responsible for performing."

"We need to remember a basic characteristic of humans," I spoke, while panning the room and making sure all three were listening. "In general they will not do anything until someone communicates with them. Stated another way, when we think about communication, we sometimes take it lightly, when, in fact, it is absolutely necessary in order to get anything done. One of the greatest benefits of the Responsibility Assignment Matrix is the way it communicates with each team member. You basically identify the work that needs to be completed and then go from there."

With great interest in the bantering back and forth between Bruce and me, Alice joined in and changed the discussion as she walked up to the wall and stood next to the Avoidance Model diagram (Chart 14 - 1). "This is great to hear. When we talked about the Avoidance Model of scope / roles / risks, the relationship of roles fit well, but I didn't realize the significance until we went through this last ordeal looking at scope. In fact, now I understand what you meant when you said that once you find the scope and then get agreement to the roles, you have all you need to be successful."

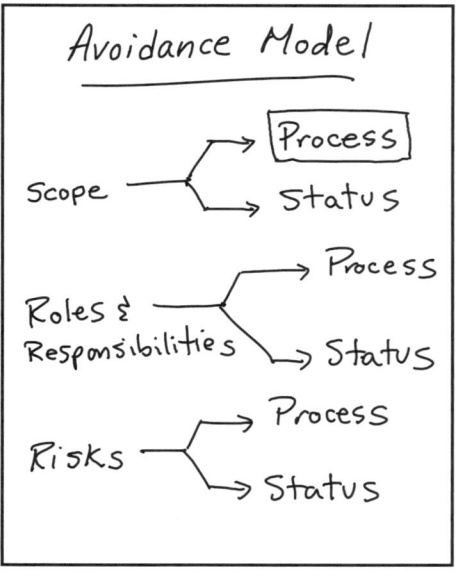

**Chart 14 - 1**

Building on Alice's comment, I said, "I'm not saying that you should have done anything differently; I just wondered if you worried about those things. You see, that type of work activity is present, and as we said earlier, the project management software programs don't consider these categories of items."

"But they still have to be done. They're part of the Stupid Triangle," Alice interjected abruptly. "When you think about it, there are a lot of roles that might be missed."

"Speaking of that," Troy interjected, "what about codes for reviewing or approving items? What are the best options for the Responsibility Assignment Matrix?"

"Great question," I responded, while moving back to the flip chart. "There are several codes that I prefer to use for those categories. In fact, this is where I differ from most practitioners. This area must be covered well," I said, while writing the next three codes on the chart (Chart 14 - 2).

It was obvious from everyone's look that there was a little confusion with these new designations. Most often, the "A" is assumed for a high-level approval, where in fact we're looking for someone to "Accept" the work task. The basic qualification for an "A" is that the person with that designation must actually review the completed work item. This is not a rubber stamp approval and the designee is generally not a senior-level person.

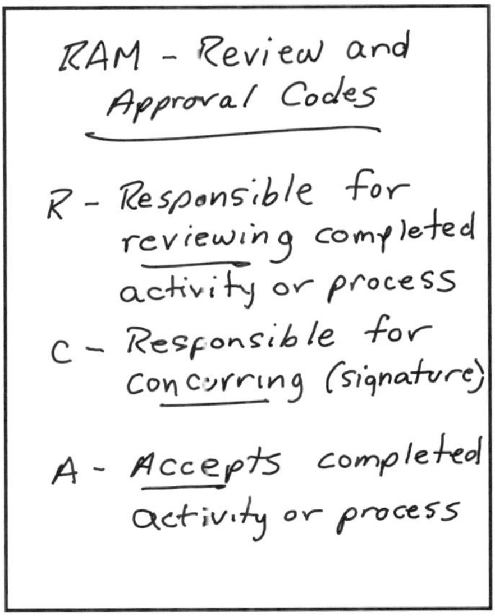

Alice spoke first. "I'm not following what you're saying. Given your definition, what would be the purpose for the Acceptor designation? Who would the Acceptor normally be?"

"That is the great unanswered question," I responded. "I found out by accident once that we were issuing substantial contract

RAM – Review and Approval Codes

R – Responsible for reviewing completed activity or process

C – Responsible for concurring (signature)

A – Accepts completed activity or process

**Chart 14 - 2**

documents that no one actually reviewed in their entirety for accuracy. Different people read sections they were interested in, but not the whole document. A common problem with the Reviewer and Concur designations is that many involved assume that someone else actually looked at the details. After all, it's not uncommon for managers to feel they are too important or too busy to read the twenty-eight pages of a contract being readied for issuance. And then...."

Interrupting, Troy finished the thought. "...it turned out that no one ever looked at the document. The Acceptor designation is the person you want to be responsible for reviewing and accepting the task as being in compliance with requirements."

"Great observation," I responded and continued. "What we find out is that in too many cases the project manager is considered to be the Acceptor. That seemingly small assignment will make the project manager's involvement difficult at best."

Alice sat back, shook her head, and spoke softly. "I just remembered that one of the main purposes of our trip up here was to clarify the roles and responsibilities for project completion activities and turnover. Now that I think back to yesterday, I don't recall even discussing roles. That's amazing. Because if we never closed on who was going to do what for the balance of this project, what on earth did we do for eight hours?"

Turning to Bruce and Troy, she continued by asking, "Do either of you remember anything we did when it came to assigning roles for the balance of work?"

"I'm getting depressed," Troy responded. "We were so focused on the delay itself that we never really looked at the real elements of the failure. If we hadn't had this discussion today we would have gone down the same path for the second time."

"That's right," Bruce added, "we got so sidetracked with the actual time delay and how we were going to break the news, I personally forgot all about getting the proper plan in place for the balance of the project. As I'm sitting here listening to this discussion, I basically took on everything from this point forward and I just can't succeed if that's the case."

Turning back to Troy and Alice, I said, "Help me to understand. You thought the project was near completion and you made a trip here to finalize the testing and transfer activities, including defining those responsible for each?"

"Yes," Alice responded, "but everything is different now. What we expected to hear at the meeting didn't happen and what we thought we were going to do after hearing the news is now being changed, which in the case of the latter is good!"

Speaking for the trio, Troy said, "What we need to do now is understand the timing and processes related to assigning roles and responsibilities."

Even though the comment was credible, everyone knew my response before I even started talking. To help with the response, I drew a small Responsibility Assignment Matrix on a clean flip chart page (Chart 14 - 3) and said, "Capturing roles and responsibilities is impossible if you don't have a handle on the scope. Since we have agreed to put a WBS type process in place for the scope, then the assignment process for each corresponding role and responsibility is made a little easier."

In order to demonstrate that the concept of process was integral to their complete understanding of the OS Phase, I drew a simple process flow on the flip chart (Chart 14 - 4) for explanation. The flow chart depicted a process with several steps that created some type of data, like employee name.

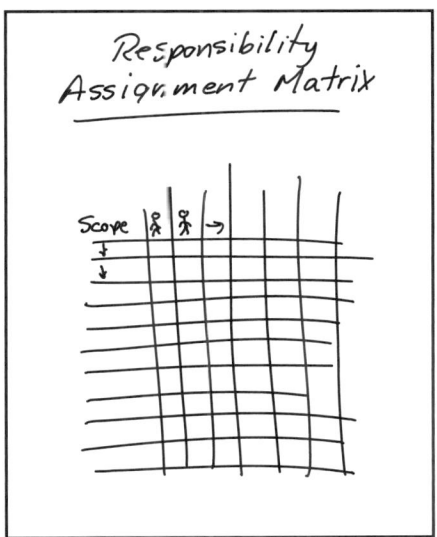

**Chart 14 - 3**

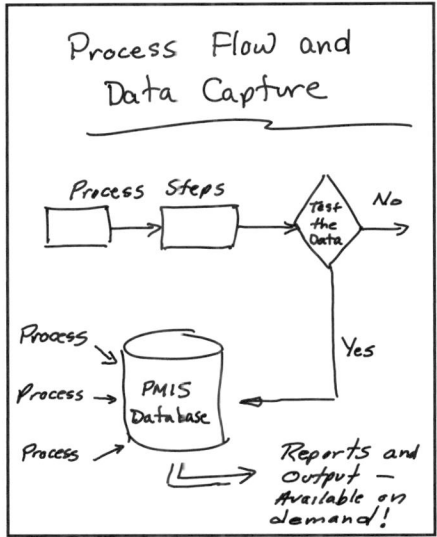

**Chart 14 - 4**

After testing the data for specific attributes, the flow chart showed the evaluation step for the data item prior to inclusion into a database (db). The database is the repository for other data and then will be the source for reports.

With everyone's attention, I went on to say, "The use of spreadsheets or database management software makes the necessary processes manageable. An important aspect, though, is to keep the processes simple. If everything gets complicated, then many will avoid it and real time benefits will be lost. We need a database where information is stored, using a defined process where the project data is simple to gather and then equally simple to retrieve. A spreadsheet makes a very simple database to use and to describe to others."

Bruce seemed to be in agreement with the discussion, but showed some skepticism by commenting, "This process is great on paper! Actually implementing this process is a little more difficult than you've depicted. Getting anyone to commit to doing work is so painstaking that sometimes it's easier to do the work yourself."

"That's right," Alice added. "At our project meeting on Friday there wasn't a big showing of hands volunteering to get this project completed. As we said before, when a project is in trouble, no one wants to have their name linked to the sinking ship."

"This brings up an important point," Troy said, while agreeing completely with Bruce and Alice's comments. "It's one thing to be a consultant and describe the perfect world, but then you get on a plane and leave town. We're left with a process that never works as easily as it did when you presented it to us."

Everyone added a noticeable chuckle to Troy's comment.

Continuing, Troy added, "These comments are not intended to be derogatory, but instead are realistic. You've described a process for roles and responsibilities, but how do you actually make it work? How do we use this process to avoid the OS Phase again?"

"Let's jump out of the textbook case for a few minutes and get into our real world situation," Bruce said with a determined tone. "We have a lot of problems to face, and I'm not certain that the rest of the team understands the magnitude of the problems and specifically where they fit into the solutions."

Listening to their comments, it was apparent that everyone agreed that project management concepts would work, but there was some growing concern about whether they would work on this project, considering the current situation.

At this time, I went back and re-emphasized the relationship of the Avoidance Model (Chart 14 - 5). For this project, or any other for that matter, the first step is establishment of the scope management processes and then definition of the scope. The second step is to establish a viable process for managing roles and responsibilities. What everyone had forgotten was the third process, the identification of risks for the project. The risk process provides the mechanism to identify areas where inadequacies with the scope and roles processes exist.

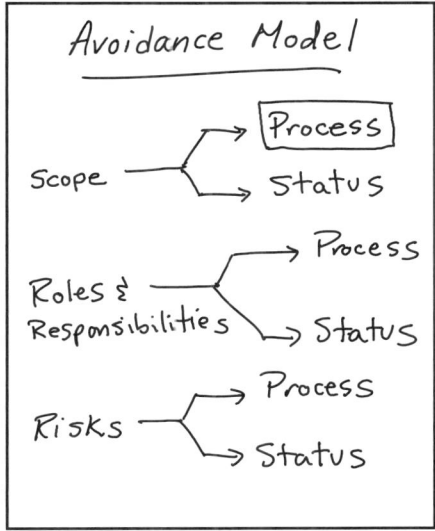

**Chart 14 -5**

Reminding everyone again of our previous discussion of the magic pill, or by its formal name, the Avoidance Model, I said, "Risk management will be the process for managing those things that just don't seem to be working as well as they should in order to support the project. We don't want to agonize over every little detail. If we have a problem, add it to the risk listing and then take it from there… as deemed appropriate."

Alice was totally engaged in the conversation. Sitting back and reflecting on the complete discussion, she added, "As simple as the Avoidance Model seems, it is vital for understanding the dynamics of a project. We need to get the process in place for scope, and roles, and then use a risk management process to support any deficiencies. It's so simple when you just sit back and reflect on it."

Troy then added some additional insight. "You can identify any number of scope items floating out there in front of you, but until you assign these scope items to someone, nothing will get done."

"Excellent," I added with reassurance. "The process is so thorough and linked together. When it comes to scope definition, the roles process is a major contributor.

Think about it. As soon as you assign a person to that task, sit back and watch what happens. Primarily, a major jolt to the scope baseline occurs. The person assigned to the scope element will start to think about how the work progresses and will realize that the allocation of time and cost is inadequate. By assigning roles and responsibilities, we actually start squeezing out more hidden scope."

"Scope that was there all the time but stuff we just didn't know about yet!" Bruce added with great enthusiasm. "Actually, you've convinced me that scope is the center of any project. Everything, that is to say, all other project management stuff, links to the scope. Everything derives from scope."

"That's interesting," Troy added, validating this new thought in his mind before speaking. "Now that you mention it, there are a lot of times at the end of a project where it's extremely difficult to get anyone to take the responsibility for certain items."

"Troy, that's a perfect example. No one wants to take charge of an activity if it appears the budget for time, cost, or both are inadequate. This is especially true when everyone knows that the project itself is overspent or late."

In order to have any degree of certainty that the team would move forward using the roles and responsibilities processes we discussed, I suggested that we brainstorm the advantages of the Responsibility Assignment Matrix. This was part of a subliminal process to get each of the three team members to feel strong and certain about the process before they met with the executive committee on Monday.

> RAM Advantages
> 
> △ Helps to clarify two-boss syndrome
> △ Reduces uncertainty about assignments ⇒ reducing or avoiding arguments
> △ Provides necessary detail without being too complex
> △ Provides a validation system for controlling project costs

**Chart 14 - 6a**

### Chart 14 - 6b

**RAM Advantages**

- Supports organizational transitions
- Uses colorful designations or shading to depict areas where roles are still soft or unknown
  ⟹ provides a great visual for a boss, sponsor, or customer
- Could be used to create a sign-off document

### Chart 14 - 6c

**RAM Advantages**

- Provides a communication tool where everyone can see their own roles and the roles of others
- Prevents ownership creep... doing the work of others to get the job done
- Clarifies complete expectations and understandings of roles and responsibilities

### Chart 14 - 6d

**RAM Advantages**

- When performing major acquisitions a RAM is essential for assuring everyone knows what responsibilities and authorities are for each process and step
- Designates non-project projects/processes that non-designated personnel are working on

### Chart 14 - 6e

**RAM Advantages**

- Drives out hidden scope.. becomes a significant scope management tool
- Requests management approval of the RAM to demonstrate commitment
- Ensures that all stakeholders are considered
- Supports identification of roles and responsibilities for functional managers regarding personnel actions

Going around the table, we each added one item to the list as to the benefits of the Responsibility Assignment Matrix. Troy stood by the flip chart and captured the following items on several sheets (Chart 14 – 6 a, b, c, d, and e).

After putting down the marker, he looked over at Bruce and said aloud what was on everybody else's mind. "As I was writing this list, it was hard to imagine why we wouldn't use a Responsibility Assignment Matrix immediately."

Bruce and Alice agreed that the Responsibility Assignment Matrix has significant advantages and agreed on the importance of developing the matrix early in a project. In the case of their project, it's not too late, but the earlier they develop the Responsibility Assignment Matrix, the less bickering there will be about roles midway into the project. We must never forget the real costs and delays incurred from time spent on organizational concerns. Proper use of the Responsibility Assignment Matrix will help to avoid or reduce conflicts.

Taking advantage of the interest in the subject of roles, I took a few minutes to summarize the processes again. "Let's go back to our Avoidance Model. Any time there are problems with scope or roles, you must consider adding a commensurate risk. We need to identify roles and responsibilities at the very beginning of the project, NOW!

"If we have a conflict where a necessary person is not available to perform the described role, then we need to add a risk. What we know is that we must identify the roles and responsibilities of all stakeholders."

Shaking her head in negative salute to the process, Alice began to have second thoughts and brought everyone back to a different reality. "I agree that stakeholders should be identified, but the more I envision the Responsibility Assignment Matrix, the more I realize that the sheer magnitude of doing it seems overwhelming. Isn't it possible to just get started and then figure those details out later? I'm just not sure that our culture will support this effort quickly enough."

Understanding where Alice was coming from and appreciating that Bruce and Troy might be thinking the same thing, I responded. "If you don't take the time to understand roles and responsibilities, there is not much use of continuing on with the project. In all fairness, we complete projects every day without formally identifying roles and responsibilities, but you can rest assured that a process existed to manage the roles, either informally or by constant pestering. Your project has a problem with role definition and to ignore that deficiency will not make it go away. We must understand that work just doesn't get completed if we don't link the work or scope to the human that will perform the action."

Continuing I said, "Remember, if we have concerns with roles and responsibilities, then we will have risk and potentially extra scope. The extra scope will take time and or cost money. If we don't manage the roles and responsibilities aspects, we can never be certain that our predictions for the project are even close to being accurate."

"How deep should I define these roles?" Bruce asked. "We don't have much time before we have to hit the ground running."

Responding to his concerns, I said, "At this stage of the project, it is vital to have a clear understanding of roles and responsibilities for all current project activities and especially the future operational and support processes that will be integral to the rollout into the real-time market environment. Assigning detailed coding designations for each activity or process is only necessary if there are concerns for that particular item. It must be assessed activity by activity."

Continuing, I concluded with a very important observation. "It's often said that we don't have time to identify roles and responsibilities, especially for large projects. It's great to do, but we just don't have time. The reality is that you can't afford not to take the time. Remember, the roles, like the scope, are there whether we identify them or not."

With still a degree of skepticism, Troy asked, "What keeps us from going through all of the effort to identify and assign roles and responsibilities only to find that they are ignored or aren't kept current?"

"There's a real possibility that the whole process will fail," I spoke in response. "If the management team doesn't take the process seriously, then the roles will change and the Responsibility Assignment Matrix will be outdated in short order. You have to be careful and don't just make it something you hand out or hang on a wall and then only use for reference. The real benefit of the Responsibility Assignment Matrix is not as an informational document, but as an action document, a tool that keeps everyone on their toes. It should be displayed where everyone can see it and it should be referenced any time a question of roles and responsibilities is brought up in conversation, and, most importantly, it must be updated whenever changes are made."

Bruce seemed to be in agreement with the need to solidify and manage roles for the remaining work. Turning to Alice, Bruce commented in an almost questioning voice. "The Responsibility Assignment Matrix looks like something we could really benefit from if we used it. It would be great for providing to each of the team members information on who is doing what. We just need management's support to make it work."

"Absolutely, you need their support," I added. "But remember, start small and simple. Don't get bogged down by the Responsibility Assignment Matrix development process. Use the details that you gather related to the remaining scope and tie roles to those work items. It's important to remember that we might want to list all personnel across the top of the Responsibility Assignment Matrix even though they have limited involvement because they can still create scope. Use the "D" on a Responsibility Assignment Matrix to identify those that "need" the completed product for that particular element of scope or process. In some cases, that might be their only involvement. Use an "I" to represent those that provide information, but again that might involve only limited involvement. Remember, these activities are in fact as much a part of the project scope as anything else you capture."

Out of the three, Alice seemed to be the most moved by the discussion of roles and responsibilities. She turned to Bruce and Troy and presented her summary thoughts aloud. "We need to all look at the benefit of having a Responsibility Assignment Matrix. The Work Breakdown Structure, or work element, links to those team members involved with the project and then connects their names to what they will be doing. If everything goes well, the process of completing the Responsibility Assignment Matrix will actually identify more scope and triangles. When we look at all of the players on each work item, we might realize that having or not having a Subject Matter Expert might actually take time or cost money, so then what they do is actually scope. Before today, I would never have considered hours or costs related to some of these support functions. They're pretty important when you think about it. It will be interesting to do an accounting when we're finished with assigning roles to the scope, and catalog scope that surfaced as a result of this effort. I'll be willing to bet that we will end up with many extra hours that we never anticipated."

"Now you know why this process is so vital," I interjected to reinforce the importance of this process in their minds.

Concluding her discussion, Alice addressed Bruce specifically. "As far as management support, I now realize where we've been going this morning. We need to use our meeting on Monday not as a meeting to dump empty promises on the executive committee again, but instead to get them to understand the processes we need in place to get the project finished. We need to make sure we get the management support from them at that time."

Troy was nodding his head in approval, and then added, "...and wherever we discuss a process in the meeting, we need to assign the roles and responsibilities right at that time."

---

*OS Phase* **Avoidance**
**STRATEGY 14**

*The quiet delay on many projects is the time lost in completing management reviews and approvals. Identify all review and approvals on the Responsibility Assignment Matrix. Negotiate up front the degree of these reviews in order to minimize delays. If adequate time isn't included in the schedule for reviews, the time required must be included in the forecast.*

# CHAPTER 15
# Risk…The 4-Letter Word That Scares the Bajeepers Out of Executive Management

When done properly, the project manager nails down *scope* and *roles* as the first order of business. If life is good and everything goes well, and there are no *risks* with the project, all the project manager has to do is stand out of the way and watch the project happen. If everything goes exceptionally well, then maybe a few rounds of golf will be possible.

Unfortunately, that type of situation is rare and most often the project manager has many *risks* to deal with every day. Even worse, we have to recognize that *risks* are dynamic, often shifting as the phases of the project proceed and as we elaborate more of the *scope* details.

To succeed, the project manager has to "challenge" stakeholders to come clean on *scope* and *risk*. If anyone sidesteps this process, the triangle will grow larger later in the project when the damage will be most detrimental. It is important to emphasize that determination of *scope* and *risk* for a project are vital steps to perform now, not when it's too late!

An important benefit of identifying *risk* up front is its contribution to defining the amount of project management effort needed for a project. The greater the *risk*, the more we need project management *processes* in place and the more we need an experienced project manager.

Project managers become *risk* managers after a project begins the execution phase. If there are no *risks* identified on the project, then there is actually very little for the project manager to work on.

Life would be boring!

Bring it on!

The discussion of roles and responsibilities ended on a good note. It's hard to tell whether everyone agreed with all of the coding suggestions of detailed roles and responsibilities, but at least they now have them in their minds. In practice, it isn't important what codes you use, it's just important that the team use some type of action oriented coding structure and use it everyday. Our earlier discussion alone should serve as a good reference point whenever anyone on the team begins the process of defining roles and responsibilities on the remaining elements of the project as well as on future projects.

It was now time to support Bruce, Alice, and Troy in the identification of the key risks. In order to get everyone to commit to a risk assessment, I began the discussion by promising that I would stay to the end of the day and help them if they worked diligently to identify the top ten risks for the project.

I hardly finished my comment when Bruce responded with his predictable sarcasm, "Does this mean that if we don't agree to review *risks* you will go away?"

"No, it means that I will just take you aside and give you some special one-on-one attention," I quipped back, while the others were still laughing at his comment. "We all know that you're enjoying the discussion."

After receiving an affirmative smile from everyone regarding my willingness to stay with them, I continued by introducing more background related to risk management. "The difference between the successful execution of a project and the failures we often read about in business magazines is how the teams managed risks associated with their projects. When assessing failed projects similar to yours, interviews with project team members revealed a profound mystery. Even though it was common to discuss and manage risks on each project, it was a disorganized effort. Project managers performed risk management because it seemed like the thing to do, but in most cases, the team's processes did not consist of a single comprehensive listing of all project risks and their attributes. Risk reduction and management processes were haphazard at best."

They all agreed that their project was no exception.

Pausing for a moment with my explanations, I hoped that one of them would get the discussion moving in a positive direction without anymore prodding from me.

I didn't have to wait long for Troy to start the ball rolling.

"If I understand our agenda for the Monday meeting, we need to bring the management team up to speed on what has happened and what our strategy is for getting back on track," he said, while looking for a confirmation from Alice and Bruce. "The meeting on Monday would seem, then, to be the best time to present and discuss any risks we identify today, or is that too much detail for that type of meeting?"

Responding to the group as a whole, I turned to Troy and spoke with as much empathy as I could muster. "You'll have to answer that question because I've never met the audience you will be facing. I can only suggest that you go to the meeting without pointing fingers, without making excuses, and without extensive detail, because none of those three items belongs in an executive committee meeting of any kind."

Alice was intrigued and quickly stepped to the flip chart and jotted down the three items (Chart 15 - 1). In order to solidify the point, she repeated them, categorized each, and then, while talking aloud, tied them to the risk management process from her perspective. "Finger pointing without a mirror wouldn't be accurate and nobody likes the whining that is associated with excuses. As far as details, we just won't have the necessary details by Monday. Risks, on the other hand, will provide a good basis for highlighting project concerns and proposed actions at the meeting, so talking about risks now would be a good idea."

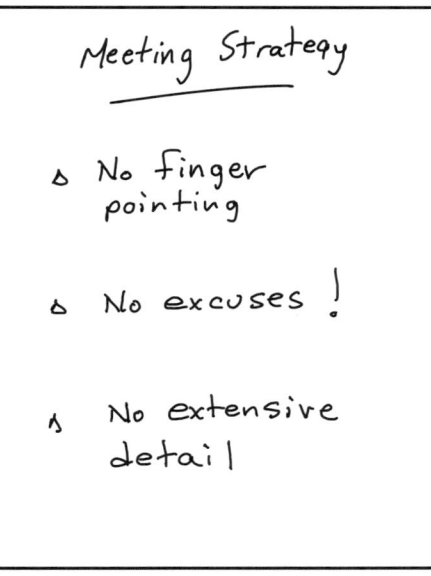

**Chart 15 - 1**

"Leveraging off of what you just said — if we do in fact discuss risks on Monday, we can't forget to give them some sense that we know what to do with them this time!" Troy added with an unusual sarcastic twist to his voice. "This meeting will be all about building confidence in our ability to avoid the OS Phase the second time and that will be a hard sell."

"That point brings up a pertinent question about the meeting agenda for Monday," Bruce said, while making sure everyone was listening and at the same time pointing to the various flip chart sheets hanging on the walls of the conference room. "Are we going to talk about the OS Phase and Stupid Triangle? Or are we just going to present how we're going to manage the Scope / Roles / Risks?"

Alice jumped in and responded to the question. "Without a doubt, we need to make sure we do it right this time. It's difficult to know what best to start with, but I suggest we tell them we hit the OS Phase. That discussion alone will create its own agenda. We have to convince the executive committee that the problem is real and is not fixable by a lot of finger pointing and chanting."

"That should work well!" Bruce said, with a mix of sarcasm and jovial bluntness.

"I can see it now," Alice said, while raising both her hands above her head. "They'll raise the bar on you, Bruce, and you'll be real motivated from that point on."

Everyone laughed at Alice's antics.

Troy enjoyed the visual of Alice jumping up with both hands reaching towards the ceiling, but then brought everyone back down to the real world by adding his thoughts. "Along with the reality of hitting the OS Phase, and our recommendation, we must convince them that we have a grasp of the scope of the remaining effort. The beauty of what we've talked about today is the natural way it should fit into any discussion related to the project. Now that we've been introduced to the Stupid Triangle it would be almost impossible to discuss scope without bringing it into the discussion. So to answer your question, Bruce, we need to be prepared to present the OS Phase, Stupid Triangle, Scope, Roles, and Risks."

Bruce let the comment sink in, and then asked, "How are we going to present risk? I'm not sure they will buy into the concept the way we have discussed it this morning. The executive committee has always presented itself as a group of risk seekers, even though they often talk out of both sides of their mouth when it comes to risk. I'm just not certain we can introduce our way of looking at risk without some sort of criticism popping up."

Alice understood the concern with risks and suggested a good way to present the subject to them. "If we can convince the executive committee that scope is anything taking time or effort, then we could leverage off of that definition and present risk as a subset of scope based on the correlation that if a bad risk happens, it will take time and effort to deal with it."

Bruce laughed and added, "That makes risk kind of like want-to-be scope!"

"Yeah," Troy added, "and we don't want-it-to-be!"

Bruce's confidence was showing. His understanding of the relationship of risk surfaced with some minor changes to the flip chart depiction of the Stupid Triangle and with his subsequent comments (Chart 15 - 2). "When we graphically add Risk to the Scope area of the Stupid Triangle, it's easy to see a rationale for adding a contingency reserve or some type of contingency to be used if a risk happens. After some more thought, it then seems almost intuitive that the way we identify risk is much the same way we look for scope and vice versa. If we can convince ourselves of the relevance of managing scope in a formal way, then it goes without saying that risk will need the same treatment."

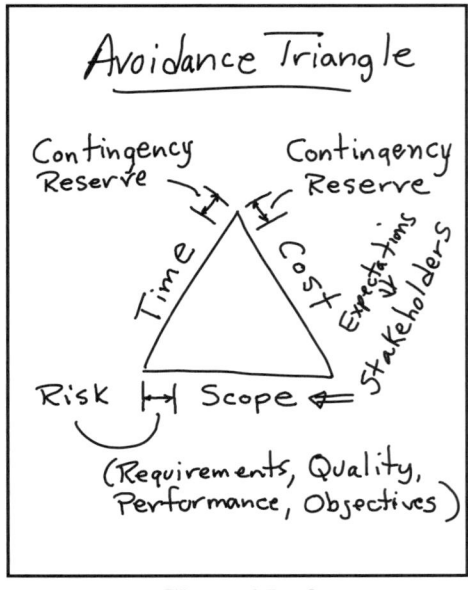

**Chart 15 - 2**

Alice was listening to every word spoken by Bruce and seemed almost hypnotized by his depiction of risk on the Stupid Triangle. When Bruce stepped back from the flip chart, she jumped up, took his place at the flip chart, and let us know what was on her mind. "What Bruce just described is profound. For my entire professional career, risk management processes were so obscure in my mind that I accepted them without any fanfare. I tried to ignore them if I could get away with it. Sadly, I don't think I'm alone in feeling this way. There's such a tendency to avoid having to deal with risks. You know, out of sight, out of mind, until of course the risks pop up at the worst time and the project ends up hitting the OS Phase."

"And then everyone asks…What happened?" Troy added.

"That's right. They should have known the OS Phase was coming, because they should have been looking at risks," Alice continued. "Whether you want to recognize a risk or not, it's there. And it will take time and effort to resolve it, just like the Stupid Triangle depicts after Bruce's addition."

After listening to Alice's thoughts, Bruce, with a noticeable passion in his voice, joined back in with some more relevant considerations. "It seems very clear that the size of any contingency reserve for time or cost should be based on the size and magnitude of risks; so instead of just guessing at contingency levels…."

"…or ignoring them all together," Troy interjected as laughter filled the room.

"That's right," Bruce acknowledged to Troy's humorous but realistic comment. "Ignoring contingencies and not including them in any project's baseline would be saying that there are no risks. And that my friends, when you really understand risks, would be extraordinarily optimistic."

The enthusiasm towards the risk discussion was important for putting everyone at ease for planning Monday's discussion. For the first time it seemed that everyone in the room had a vision of how they should proceed. Although it was a little early to be certain about the agenda at this time, I wanted them to understand the importance of getting the facts on the table and providing the simplest and most credible answer possible. Their proposal must be concise this time if they want a second chance to finish the project. In order for their proposal to have any degree of accuracy, they all needed to understand the importance of risk management.

Still engaged with the risk management concept as she stated earlier, Alice got our attention again and added more to her earlier thoughts. "Risk is fascinating because it looks at the dynamics of a project. Previously, the sheer fright of risks caused our project team and even the executive committee to shun them. What I've realized now is that when you don't worry about risks, life is so much simpler until, well you know…."

Everyone laughed at the comment and then Troy repeated a common cliché, "Yeah, life is simple when we sit in the dark. After all, ignorance is bliss!"

Bruce continued the discussion by getting all of us up to speed with the risk management processes used so far on the project. "If we're going to talk about risk, you need to understand that we actually thought about risks when we started the project."

It was hard for him to make this statement with a straight face. "That's right, we thought about risks when we started the project. If I recall correctly, we thought about them for about fifteen minutes and then moved on to other project steps. I know we won't make the same mistake this time, at least I hope we won't. After all, if there is no uncertainty, then we do not need an experienced project manager. The lack of uncertainty implies that all scope is known and all roles and responsibilities are identified and agreed to by everyone."

Bruce's revived attitude toward risks was encouraging. In order to get the process of risk discovery working properly, we turned the meeting away from processes per se and instead looked specifically at potential risks.

Troy suggested that we brainstorm around the table and see what risks surfaced. This simple technique resulted quickly in fourteen risks written on the whiteboard. The process worked well, but the results represented items that were scattered all over the project.

After studying the risks for a few minutes, Troy asked an extremely pertinent question, "Wouldn't it be better to group these items into similar categories? The way they're listed it's hard to really focus on them. In fact, the list looks kind of familiar, doesn't it, Bruce?"

Bruce smiled and responded, "The process of finding risks initially was also done by brainstorming and actually ended up with some of the same items. They didn't help before, and I'm not sure they'll help now. I'm not sure that I feel very good about what we've done on this brainstorming effort."

"Let's not react too much. There's nothing wrong with using a brainstorming process," I said assuredly. "Brainstorming helps to capture those items that are on our mind at the moment, but the process could be improved if we organized the process by brainstorming by category or project element. Whatever we do, avoid taking the risk identification process too lightly."

I went to the flip chart and wrote several standard categories (Chart 15 - 3).

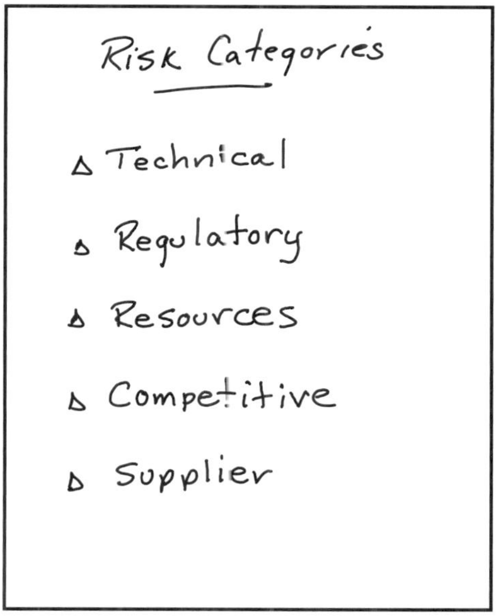

"There are many more categories than I've listed, but these are the most common that we can run into on projects," I said, while waiting for everyone to internalize the concept.

"What do you mean by the Resource category?" Troy asked, while continuing with a follow-up question. "Do you mean that the project doesn't have enough resources or that the resources aren't skilled adequately?"

Risk Categories

△ Technical

△ Regulatory

△ Resources

△ Competitive

△ Supplier

**Chart 15 - 3**

"Risks related to resources will fall in many sub-categories," I responded, "including the two you mentioned and several others.

"One very big risk is the concern that the team won't follow the roles and responsibilities designated on the Responsibility Assignment Matrix. This becomes a real problem if the team member is matrixed to the project. A recent experience really drove this point home for me.

"While sitting in the lobby of the Mission Inn in Riverside, California, I couldn't help but overhear a project manager speaking to an associate sitting on the adjacent couch. The project manager had just gotten off her mobile phone following a less than positive phone conversation. She was in the process of typing something in on her Blackberry® when she told her associate …

> *I'm in the process of sending an e-mail to go over his head. We've just missed the second deadline. The support we're getting from him is so disappointing. I just don't know what to do!*

"I really didn't mean to eavesdrop, but sometimes those speaking loudly and in a place where everyone can hear are crying out for help and don't really care who is listening."

Alice was following the story with a frustrated expression on her face. After shaking her head side to side, she provided the logical conclusion to the story. "That situation confronts all of us, sometimes almost weekly. Based on past experience, her situation will probably deteriorate even more and will end up consuming much of her time and emotional state. This is sad because the simplest approach would have been to identify the resource concern as a risk the first time it happened."

"That's right," Bruce added. "That situation happened a lot. I just let myself get frustrated, but never made much progress dealing with the problem. It's so natural now to think about this example as just a risk, something that we should consolidate with the other similar risks in the resources category"

"We're getting closer to where we want to be with the balance of the project," Alice commented. "I suggest that we take the risks we listed earlier and link them to the categories. We can then look for any gaps."

Before we could start with Alice's suggestion, Troy pointed to the list, turned around in his chair to Bruce and asked something that had been troubling him. "Isn't the risk related to not having adequate resources actually an assumption we listed when we started the project?"

"I'm not certain, but I think you're right," Bruce responded with adequate assurance in his voice. "In fact, several of these risks actually are similar to our project assumptions. From my perspective, it doesn't make much sense to track them as risks if they are already classified as assumptions."

"Actually, Bruce, you have it backwards," I responded. "The real question should be whether it makes sense to have assumptions on a project. When you think about what you just said, you validated that assumptions are unquantified risks and are most often identified early in the project and then put on the shelf for the remainder of the project. In practice, it is wise to avoid assumptions wherever possible. If we convert the assumptions to risks they are in your face all the time."

"In your face all the time?" Alice questioned by repeating my comment.

"That's right," I responded. "It is absolutely essential that when we look at risks we look at them all of the time. Although daily seems a bit excessive, I believe, at a minimum, the project manager should review risks with the team and upper management at least once a week. It's only when you are keenly aware of your risks that you have the ability to understand where the project is headed. If an assumption proves itself incorrect then the result is an impacted project baseline. This usually happens without much warning."

Based on a few questioning looks, I continued by providing an example of the difference between risks and assumptions. "If I am driving to the airport, I could assume that traffic will flow smoothly and there won't be any delays. However, if the assumption is incorrect, I might miss my flight. Instead, if I consider the assumption as a risk, then I might plan to leave earlier or I might want to have a map so I can take an alternate route. By considering traffic as a risk, I am more prepared to do something to mitigate the risk; whereas, with assumptions, we just stare at them at the beginning of the project and then we bury them on the shelf."

"It sounds like we could say that risk management is a sensitivity analysis on assumptions," Alice concluded confidently.

Eager to add his new thoughts, Troy said, "Now I get it. Wow! This is very important to understand. In fact, the more "mature" your scope is the less risk you have. If we don't do the scope and roles in a timely manner, Bruce will get involved in doing the scope and roles planning when he should instead be focusing on risk management. That type of distraction would lead the project back to the OS Phase."

The discussion of risk brought the team together and for the first time since I met them, the plan was clear and supported by everyone. Troy summarized it by saying, "Anything that does not fit into a simple execution pattern should be categorized as a risk. After making it this far, it's now important to recognize that Bruce's job as project manager is actually to manage project risk."

Turning to Bruce, he said emphatically, "If Bruce gets engrossed with items other than risk, it's safe to say that he is going to get bogged down with a level of detail that will eventually cause another failure, a return trip to the OS Phase!"

With some serious planning still on the immediate horizon, everyone stood and stretched. On his way out the door to the break room, Bruce etched his own personal emotions on the whiteboard.

---

**OS Phase Avoidance
STRATEGY 15**

*Manage risk processes with the same intensity that you place on the relentless pursuit and management of the scope and roles for the project.*

---

***Ignorance IS NOT bliss!***

Alice laughed when she saw the words of wisdom and suggested that we follow Bruce's lead and use the quote for the opening statement Monday morning!

## CHAPTER 16
## Exactly How Do You Plan to Execute the Project?

After the decision to proceed on a project, the most important first step is to develop a strategy for implementing sound project management *processes*. We need a plan to describe the project execution strategy with the primary focus of the plan on how to succeed and how to avoid the *OS Phase*.

As important as it is to create a plan before starting a project, it is often a big turnoff. Everyone wants to get started as fast as possible so they can show some real progress. After all, planning is something we can do when we have a little more time, say next week. Today we need to get moving!

Most want to do better, and most professionals agree on the need to plan, but, when discussing implementation of the project management methodology, there is a fear of having to perform too much planning. Why spend time thinking about how to proceed? This sounds too easy; after all, the project team is experienced. They already know what to do to get the project completed.

The rationale for initiating an aggressive start seems logical enough. Tied to the hasty start is the selection of a project manager who can hit the ground running. Whether they know where to go doesn't seem to be as important. To set this in motion, senior management develops a set of project management templates and supporting methodologies so that the project manager can comply with organizational requirements.

Alternatively, the other situation happens. The project manager wanders aimlessly looking for standards, only to find inconsistent or incomplete processes. The project manager must develop a plan, while simultaneously being beat on the head to get started on the real project.

It is easy to get a visual of the pep talk chanted by those wanting the project. "We must step up to the challenge on this one! If

> we don't get started immediately we'll lose the window of opportunity and will let everyone down!"
>
> The image of the perfect project manager is someone that has success-oriented instincts and can immediately demonstrate progress. The project manager is up against the wall. Dreading to say they can't do it, they proceed and the journey begins. Some are lucky and have everything fall in place, but most fail, and then blame it on the situation.

Now that everyone was back in the conference room following the quick break, interest in the upcoming meeting with the executive committee began to intensify.

"With regards to our meeting on Monday, what is the first step we need to perform in order to convince the executive committee that we have our act together?" Bruce asked, seeming to bounce possible answers around in his head as he asked the question.

"First, I expect that you'd better have your act together!" I said in a serious tone.

"Just like a consultant, restating the obvious and then charging us for the answer," Alice chuckled.

"I'm sorry; I don't remember giving you a bill yet!" I quipped back with a smile. "But please take my comment seriously. If you're going to convince anybody to let you finish the project, you need to have a plan, something that makes sense and is credible."

"If we give them a new date and budget, wouldn't that suffice?" Troy asked. "That's all they want to know, the date when the project will be completed and how much funding is required to complete it."

"I hope you're wrong," Alice commented. "Based on what we've been discussing over the past two days, if they only asked us for another forecast, then the other members of the executive committee are the problem, not us. If they are doing their job, they won't let us get by with just shoveling another set of numbers at them!"

"Way to go, Alice! Sounds like you've gotten serious about your position all of a sudden," Troy answered with enthusiasm. "Are you the same person that was strategizing with me on Friday about what budget forecast and completion date we should try to pass on without getting everyone too upset?"

Realizing that she was on the spot, Alice lightened the mood. "On Friday we didn't know that we had hit the OS Phase. We were just reacting the same way we always had in the past. You know, duck and cover!"

"And blame...." Troy added. "You forgot that on the way to the airport we were working on a rather extensive list of who we could blame. Actually, I think I've lost that list."

Everyone laughed at Troy's comment and we all realized the childish act of blaming others Unfortunately, casting blame is often a standard practice on projects.

"Wait a minute, everyone. Something isn't making sense," Bruce said, speaking in a serious tone. "When we talked about the Responsibility Assignment Matrix, the discussion was all about assigning someone to every work task and process. The purpose was to find every person that was accountable. What's the difference between doing that and assigning blame?"

Bruce brought up an interesting topic, one that Alice had thought about earlier.

"Let me answer that question," Alice said with confidence. "I believe that timing is a big factor. We were actually going to be filling out the Responsibility Assignment Matrix after the problem occurred. That is, look for who should have completed certain items and didn't. When you do a Responsibility Assignment Matrix, the intent is to complete it ahead of time, before the work is started."

Agreeing with Alice's comments, Troy then added, "Using the Responsibility Assignment Matrix we assign accountability, not blame. In a way they could be construed as the same, but the timing really is different."

"And so is the effect," Alice added. "When we assign accountability, the hope is that the blame process won't be necessary."

Alice's comment resulted in laughter by everyone. It was a good sign that all three were recognizing the advantage of a Responsibility Assignment Matrix.

"Let's get back now to the subject at hand," I said, trying to get attention back to the planning process. "Now that we just validated the benefit and process associated with the Responsibility Assignment Matrix, I'd like everyone to think again about what you might want to present on Monday."

"We don't want to make excuses," Bruce said, speaking as someone converted to a new way of looking at project management. "What we need to tell them is what we intend on doing to get the project back on track."

"We also need to commit to providing a new budget forecast and completion date, but not at the meeting," Alice added. "That is going to be difficult and may not go over well at all."

"You're right on that point, Alice," I added. "The executive committee will be looking for an answer, an answer of when the adventures can begin. I would expect that a marketing representative will be there and will want a date."

"That's right; the marketing manager is a gentleman named Rich and he is a member of the executive committee," Troy said, while beginning to tap the tabletop nervously and continuing with some discord. "If I were Rich, I would want that information also. I'm getting a bad feeling again. We're going to be destroyed if we don't give them some specifics."

"We're back to asking them to trust us," Bruce added, "and there's no reason to believe that they will trust us this time. In fact, I would be surprised if Rich isn't assigned as the project manager to finish the effort."

"Maybe we should come up with a date and budget even if it isn't well thought out, but just to have in our back pocket if we get cornered. Stupid Triangle or not, we need something," Troy insisted, while starting to pace the floor. "If we go in empty-handed we will be…"

"…hosed!" Bruce interjected, with the first lighthearted comment since this current discussion began. "There is no doubt about it, if we don't have a date, we will be hosed, and hosed in the worse possible way."

"Considering the fact you need to do something along these lines before the Monday meeting, it's about time that we discussed the first step to any project. This is true from day one of a brand new project or to the day we eventually recognize that major changes are needed, similar to what you are experiencing," I responded.

# EXACTLY HOW DO YOU PLAN TO EXECUTE THE PROJECT? 157

"This is where I really get confused," Bruce said, while opening Alice's project management textbook. "If I look in this book, it's not real clear what the first step actually is for a project. In fact, it seems that everyone has some special twist or step needed in the beginning of a project. It would seem that there should be more consistency in the guidance documents."

Agreeing with Bruce was necessary, but it was important not to dismiss what the textbooks suggest either. "The response to your question is mind boggling to the project manager. We have lengthy project management texts, complex articles, and numerous software systems from which to choose. Each system has its own magic pill! The confusion with so many remedies to choose from is discouraging to the project manager. The irony is that many of these books and software tools steer our focus away from the real concerns. Many of the proposed fixes are not even close to being practical in our environment."

Troy chimed in with a profound observation that demonstrated his growing understanding of the processes of project management. "What we need is a step or process that is consistently applied to each project. The plan of attack should not have to be different for each project. It should be the same for a new project or a project recovering from the OS Phase. Improving our project management processes shouldn't be a one-time shot. If we can't apply the new processes on future roll-outs, then it would be a significant waste of effort."

"Excellent," I responded. "The idea of repeatability is paramount. Now, let's look at the first step in our planning process. We must remember to do everything possible to keep the time and effort necessary for kicking off a project to a minimum; we can't afford a complex bureaucratic process."

Taking a position back at the flip chart, I began to describe a potential process (Chart 16 - 1). "What we need is a recovery plan that describes how Bruce and his team intend on executing the balance of the project."

For the first time, there was total silence among the three. They were either very confused or totally convinced. I was afraid to speculate which of these possibilities was correct.

Alice broke the silence first. "Let me understand what you're implying. The second bullet says that we need to define how we are going to manage each of the key project management focus areas, such as scope, time, cost, risk, and so on. Why is this important as the first step? It's going to take too much time to sit down and look at each of those processes. I think we all were expecting you to say that we needed to find the scope first."

After being just short of interrupting Alice in mid-sentence, Bruce added his similar comments. "Wait a minute. Alice is right. You said earlier that the absolute most important step we take on any project is to find the scope. Now you bring up a gigantic plan. Which is it?"

> Recovery Plan
> ▲ A narrative description of the project with emphasis on remaining scope
> ▲ A description of how Bruce and his team intend on executing the project, described in terms of the Project Management Focus Areas
> ▲ Details of the Project Management Focus Areas

**Chart 16 - 1**

Troy was listening to the bantering back and forth related to defining the remaining scope. His confidence and overall understanding were evident with his concise rationale for what was proposed. "I agree with you two that scope is important, but the first step shouldn't be to find the project's scope but instead to make certain that there is a process in place for defining what we need to do from this point on. It makes no sense to just jump in and hold a scope discovery party. Just a few minutes ago we did that with risks, and I think we all realized the fallacy with our processes. We were shooting from the hip and didn't think through any type of strategy or plan ahead of time. Based on the meeting that is on everyone's mind, I think it is vital that today we first define a process for obtaining the scope and once it's documented, define a process for controlling the scope. History on the project tells us that if you don't control scope, you will always be trying to hit a moving target. The best strategy would be to show up Monday with a plan, not with another set of objectives. New objectives just aren't enough."

"Yeah, Troy," Bruce commented with a sly grin. "We'll let you convince the executive committee that they don't need new objectives."

Everyone laughed, but realized that the task of explaining everything would be tough.

"That was a great summary, Troy," I responded, with emphasis to keep everyone focused on the new planning discussion. "There are many reasons to have a plan, not the least of which is to build confidence that the project team has a clue as to where they're proceeding. Without the support of management, it is difficult to get anything done in a timely fashion. The plan will help you get the support you need."

As I was presenting the idea of planning to everyone, it became apparent that Alice and Bruce would require a lot of persuasion regarding the importance and critical nature of planning. Agreement without commitment is important. It wouldn't be enough to have them agree on the need for a plan, they must feel so strong about it that they could convince any naysayer. So often, when we take the time to present how to perform project management processes correctly, everyone does the wave and chants in agreement but when they leave the session, they immediately revert back to their old ways.

If I were going to convince Alice and Bruce of the necessity of putting a plan in place, I would need to give them a sound reason. I decided to recap an experience from a training session that I had completed several years earlier.

With everybody calmed down and focused on listening, I began the story....

"As part of a three-day basic project management class, the group I was working with took a relevant case study from their own company and tied it in to the class material. The case study centered on a scenario where a junior-level project manager lead a project in which he actually had little technical expertise.

"The nature of the project was such that the project manager and team would require serious senior management support in order to be successful. I played the role as the owner of their company and the class members were each playing the role of the project manager.

Although I use this type of case study example often, it was particularly interesting with this company because of what was obviously a strained relationship between the owner of the company (my role) and the employees.

"Using the term 'strained' actually may be an understatement. I believe that most of the members of the class despised the owner of the company.

"As part of the exercise, we had a point where the class completed the initial planning process and were encouraged to obtain any needed clarifications from their sponsor or boss, based on our role assignments. Since I was playing the role of the company owner, and specifically project sponsor, questions started to fly, and fly furiously.

"The type of questions signified that all class members were letting go. It was as if they had an opportunity to say whatever they wanted to their boss without the risk of termination. It was hard to describe. Emotions were bursting out from everyone. I only regret that we hadn't videotaped the session.

"Midway through the question session, one member of the class stood up, leaned forward, raised his arm and finger, pointed directly towards me, and then let loose with his question, which came in a loud demanding voice. 'If you make me project manager of this project **WILL YOU GIVE ME THE AUTHORITY...THIS TIME...TO GET THE JOB DONE**?' Wow! There was no confusion about the question and it was abundantly clear that the concern of project manager authority was present in this organization.

"That in itself is not a surprise, because project manager authority-problems are common in most companies. What was special here was the intensity of the question, which really elevated in its significance from where I was standing.

"After the pointed and verbose question, everyone else in the class sat up in their seat and waited for the response....

"Without hesitation, but also without thinking too long on the answer, I stated, 'If you give me a good plan, I will give you all of the authority that you will ever need!' ...a good response that seemed to satisfy everyone. The class continued with many other pointed questions, each with an elevated level of intensity, but the direct response back on the authority concern quieted many in the group."

It wasn't until that evening that I realized the significance of the response given in the class. Give me a good plan and I'll give you authority. Hmmm! What a novel concept!

I went on to explain to Troy, Alice, and Bruce that the correlation between gaining authority and having a good plan was never so obvious. It's now impossible for me to think about authority and planning in the project environment without seeing them as linked with an unbreakable chain.

After finishing the details of the example that I provided, it was obvious that the example had interested all three. I turned and asked for comments.

Alice was first to speak. "That's a great example of why you need a project plan. I know that Bruce did not have a plan the way you are describing it, and I don't believe he had much authority either."

"You're right on both accounts, Alice," Bruce responded. "I didn't prepare a plan for the simple reason that no one asked me for one or at least not one the way we described it here. There was a lot of discussion about having a project plan, but I interpreted those requests as being for a schedule or Gantt chart, a plan for when we were going to do things."

"What about the authority problem? Was Alice correct with her comment that you didn't have much authority?" I asked.

Bruce sat back and spoke in his calmest voice of the morning. "Authority is a funny thing around here. Everyone talks as if you have lots of authority, but if you ever try to do even the simplest task and it steps on someone's toes, the authority halo tends to disappear."

Continuing before anyone could comment, Bruce said, "I am thinking very seriously about the Responsibility Assignment Matrix as a way to get the levels of authority out on the table and agreed to formally."

"Bruce, that's an excellent idea," I commented enthusiastically. "A solid use for the Responsibility Assignment Matrix is identification of authorities. The fact that you told us what you wanted to do demonstrates that you actually have a plan. The project planning process should be as simple as that."

"You mention that the Project Management Institute and other associations refer to the project plan as a necessary tool, but does every project manager really create what you're talking about?" Troy asked.

Without hesitation, I responded, "You guys are going to pin me in a corner and the answer is no. A large number of project managers either do not prepare a plan as we've described or they prepare one that's too complex. Overdoing a project plan might even be worse than not having one at all. A pathetic case is where a project team has an excellent project plan, but it was prepared only for show and then was put on the shelf when the project started."

Alice smiled, "Have you ever worked on a project where that occurred? Meaning that the team had a good plan, but they never used it?"

"Sad but true, the answer is yes." I responded. "It's amazing when you meet with the team and then plop the plan in the center of the table and watch the reactions. Unfortunately, as a consultant, this usually means I've worked myself out of a job."

"Interesting comment, but I've never seen a consultant work himself out of a job!" Troy said jokingly, as Bruce and Alice laughed.

After everyone calmed down, I went on to explain that as an outsider or consultant, my role was not to reinvent any process or reinvent the proverbial wheel, but instead to help the project team develop a plan for completing the project. If in fact the project team had already completed a comprehensive project plan, even though they never used it, my effort was small. Instead of creating something they already had, I focus on the 'why' of the planning process and then put my energies towards convincing them that they should implement the plan they already had prepared."

Reflecting on the current situation, Alice said, "It should be pretty easy to convince them since they're already in the OS Phase."

Bruce's pacing usually meant he was about to ask a question. He stopped while standing next to the schedule hanging on the wall and commented, "I understand now how you're defining a plan, but I don't think I'm alone when I call our project's schedule a plan as well. What's the right terminology?"

I answered Bruce's question as I approached him and the schedule. "You hit the nail on the head. I was just getting ready to address the terminology problem you described. Too many professionals call a project schedule a project plan. The plan that we are referring to now is much more than just the schedule. It's the description of how we are going to attack this project and it's organized to some degree in terms of the key project management focus areas. As we know, scheduling is only a part of the overall project plan. The title itself can lead to a lot of confusion and we can't afford for anybody to be confused, especially on Monday."

"What do you suggest we do to avoid the confusion?" Alice asked.

Bruce beat everyone to the punch again with his off-the-wall humor, "In order to ensure that no one confuses our plan with that of a schedule document, why don't we name it the OS Phase Avoidance Plan."

Alice smiled and said, "That's a lot of words to say at one time. But on a positive note, you would expect minimal questions as to the purpose of the plan."

"That's right," I said. "We might be just as comfortable, though, with a shorter version of the plan's name, so let's call it the Avoidance Plan. It's funny when you think about it. If you use the term Avoidance Plan for the first time to a group unfamiliar with the cynical OS Phase terminology, you will create a multitude of puzzled looks. Whenever someone asks what you are avoiding, you have the opening for the perfect response and a way to engage those interested in improving their overall performance. The answer seems almost too elementary. Before you start the project, develop a plan of attack."

"Based on the way you've described the Avoidance Plan, it shouldn't take much convincing to recognize how important a plan is for any project," Alice concluded. "But if we are going to make the Avoidance Plan work for us, we must work very hard to keep the plan simple.

Alice was again convincing herself about the relevancy of the Avoidance Plan. "Imagine, all we are asking for is a description of how the project manager and the team plans on executing the project as described in terms of Scope, Time, Cost, Human Resources, Risk, Quality, Communication, and Procurement. It is hard to imagine not doing this!"

Bruce turned to everyone in the room and stated, "I don't know about everybody else, but it would sure help me out if we were to develop the plan today. There's no better way to learn than to do. At least that's what I always say."

Developing a plan before Monday had a lot of merit. I suggested that we look at our strategy to manage scope first, since we'd talked about it so much. Later in the afternoon they could finish the other focus areas.

Addressing the three, I started the process for developing the Scope Management Plan element. "Before we go too far, I want to emphasize an important aspect of this planning process, which falls into a standard to adopt on every project. In the twenty-first century, we should treat project managers like adults. We should ask them to tell us what they intend on doing and then expect them to do it!"

"Gee, that's a novel concept," Alice said. "We're developing more and more problems in this area. Everyone wants independence but at the same time needs to have someone hold their hand. It's getting really old!"

"That's absolutely right!" Troy said with an excited tone in his voice. "We need a plan from Bruce and the team that we agree to and then we should hold them accountable for doing what they say they're going to do."

Bruce was quick to add his two-cents before Troy and Alice hurt themselves from doing the wave so many times. "I'm not agreeing to anything without first making sure that we have a shared vision on this puppy. Let's go ahead and develop the plan for Scope Management like we mentioned a few moments ago."

Bruce's request was legitimate, so, with everyone attentively looking at me for the first step, I asked Alice to take a marker and start taking notes on the flip chart, based on some questions I would ask the group.

Alice quickly grabbed the marker and was ready.

"There are several approaches we could take, but the easiest would be to title three different flip charts with the following: Technique, Deliverables, and Objectives.

# EXACTLY HOW DO YOU PLAN TO EXECUTE THE PROJECT? 165

With the three charts now taped to the whiteboard, side by side, I asked Troy and Bruce to take markers as well and to join Alice at the board.

It was important to keep the process simple. I asked each of them to write on the appropriate chart any ideas or techniques for managing the scope on the project (Chart 16 - 2). Next, they should each think about what the corresponding deliverables and objectives would be (Charts 16 – 3 and 4).

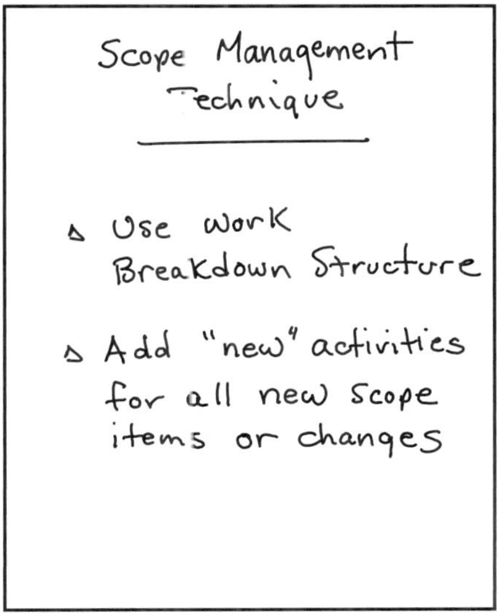

Troy was first to ask a question "Are these the deliverables and objectives for the project? I'm confused!"

It was obvious that Alice and Bruce were also waiting for the answer. "I want you to describe the deliverables and objectives just from

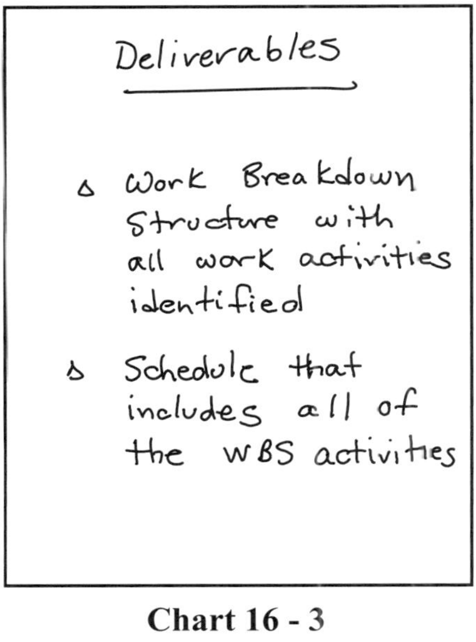

**Scope Management Technique**
- Use Work Breakdown Structure
- Add "new" activities for all new scope items or changes

**Chart 16 - 2**

**Deliverables**
- Work Breakdown Structure with all work activities identified
- Schedule that includes all of the WBS activities

**Chart 16 - 3**

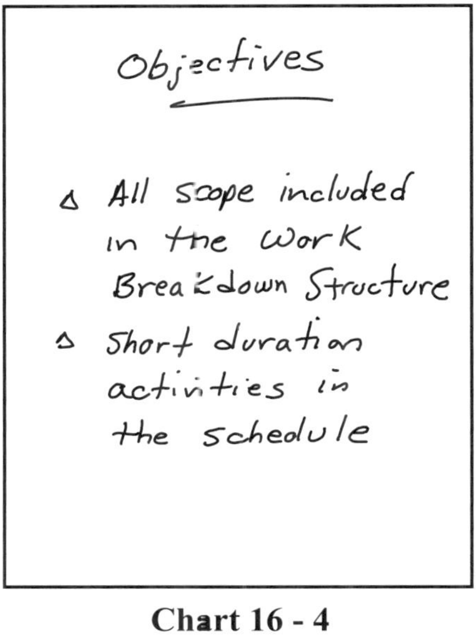

**Objectives**
- All scope included in the Work Breakdown Structure
- Short duration activities in the schedule

**Chart 16 - 4**

the scope management process. List any items that you prepare or create when you're pursuing the scope."

"Do you mean like a WBS?" Alice asked.

"Absolutely!" I responded. "Does everyone know what to do now?"

With three simultaneous yeses, they began the process. After just a few minutes, and a lot of hassling amongst the group as to who thought of some of the items first, they had a good first effort.

Bruce was the first to comment after looking at the three lists. "That was a little too simple if you ask me. In fact, it's actually rather intuitive based on our earlier discussion of scope."

"Absolutely!" I responded. "Preparing an Avoidance Plan doesn't have to be complicated as long as it's clear to anyone looking at the plan as to what your intentions are for managing the particular focus area."

Troy couldn't wait to ask another question. "If the organization developed a good Avoidance Plan format, could it be used for all of the organization's projects?"

"I know the answer to that one," Alice interjected with confidence. "The Avoidance Plan should be like everything else. We can use it for whatever we do. Why in the world would we ever consider managing projects differently down the road?"

The team had made a significant transition towards the acceptance of proper planning from the beginning. It was amazing to see how enthusiastic everyone became when there was a clear idea on how to proceed.

> **OS Phase Avoidance STRATEGY 16**
>
> *If you want authority, you must convince the organization's leadership that you have a plan for how you are going to manage the project. Keep it simple.*

# CHAPTER 17
# You Want It Done...When? The Lighter Side of Managing a Critical Path Schedule

Many envision project management as preparation of sophisticated looking computerized project schedules. Others envision project management as attendance at endless meetings.

If we consider project management in terms of what it should be, then we would be wrong on both accounts! Project management is about managing "all" of the processes necessary to complete the project.

While development and regular maintenance of a project schedule and meetings are important to support the communication process, the world of the project manager should not revolve around either. As we've already discovered, the very first task for the project manager is to develop a plan or strategy for the project, something we refer to as our *Avoidance Plan*. The next step is to define or validate the definition of the project itself, the product description, the *scope*, or the *stuff* requiring immediate attention!

Only after we have a plan for the project and understand the *scope* do we begin the process of developing the detailed schedule or time line for executing the project. Don't get me wrong, scheduling is important, but it is not the first step. A schedule is prepared after we are certain of what we have to accomplish in terms of *scope*.

The sad reality is that teams become desperate from the start, as they are provided with only a rough *scope*, a fixed end date, and a budget ceiling or target. Even if the team begins by validating the scope before agreeing to anything, management will soon raise the bar and encourage a speedier planning process. The error in this action is the obvious lack of realization of what the schedule should be.

> By initially developing a schedule, the team has narrowed their options and will most often forget at least one, if not many, *scope* components. The concept of scheduling has been with us for a long time. Computer systems have allowed us to develop schedules that are more detailed and in some cases, extraordinarily complex. This might seem like a blessing but it is really a curse, as well. Scheduling seems to have lost its credibility.
>
> Think about it. How do we have some of the most sophisticated *processes* and tools in history, but still have many projects that fail or are late?
>
> What's happened?

**B**ruce was the first to return from the break. There was little doubt that he was ready for the next step in the process. It seemed that he'd been waiting all morning to discuss scheduling. After a few of my traditional opening remarks, he began the discussion with his now famous shotgun approach.

Bruce's comments were an exhibition of something that must have been bothering him during our meeting thus far. "The oddest part of our entire discussion today is that we haven't talked any about our critical path schedule. It's hard for me to believe that we've ignored it entirely. The schedule is all we ever talk about around here, especially the last couple of months. Every meeting or hallway discussion starts with some comment about the schedule."

Troy agreed with Bruce, and added his own thoughts. "When we talk about project management around here, we are really referring to the schedule. I'm surprised you haven't asked to even look at it once."

Joining the discussion, Alice asked, "Is our focus on the schedule unusual, or do other companies also emphasize it?"

"You're all correct," I said. "In most companies it's hard to separate the project management scheduling software from the project management processes. What we want to do, though, is not lose the emphasis on scope and remember that scope discovery has to precede scheduling efforts. It's awfully hard to schedule what we don't have details on."

Bruce was listening to my comments directed at Troy, but the explanation didn't faze him at all. He turned around in his chair and looked directly at me, "You've avoided my earlier comments so I'll say them again! Today, the schedule hasn't been mentioned! You haven't asked about the status of the schedule and you haven't even asked to see it. What am I missing?"

"Would it make you feel better if I asked you about the project schedule?" I asked, accompanying the question with a big grin. "The schedule was apparently pretty important before, but it seems the project got in trouble anyhow. I'm not saying that it is wrong to review the schedule, but since you said you reviewed it all the time and the project still hit the OS Phase, what good did it really do?"

"It told me this week that we wouldn't make it!" Bruce said, defensively. "That in itself is pretty darn important."

Alice now joined in to respond to my question. "The schedule represents what we have to do on the project. We were able to determine work to be completed and we were sensitive to the supporting time frame for those work items."

"It was a very effective punch list, you know, a list of what had to be completed," Troy added. "And I agree with Bruce's concern. It would seem that we've spent a lot of time talking philosophy when we should instead be looking at what has to be completed. We will have to have some type of schedule by Monday; even if it's wrong, we need something."

"You can't have a project meeting without a schedule," Bruce added, putting emphasis on the word *without*.

"Alice, what do you think about Troy and Bruce's comments?" I asked with the same bluntness afforded me by Bruce. "Do you agree on the need for a schedule on Monday, no matter if it's right or wrong?"

"That's a loaded question. How could anyone sit here and say it's fine to go to the meeting with a bogus schedule?" she asked. "I think you're getting ready to slam dunk all three of us. I'm beginning to see a mischievous grin."

"Alice's observation is the precise reason I have difficulties playing poker," I replied.

"After just a few minutes of discussion about the schedule, it was apparent how you are driven by the misconception of the importance of the schedule," I spoke in an excited tone, while moving back to the flip chart. "My first experience as a project manager focused completely around a schedule. In various project roles, it became evident that customers always want to look at a schedule.

"For this reason we spent untold hours working to manipulate the computer program to describe what we wanted the customer to see. However, you see, that didn't matter. All you have to do is throw a ten-page schedule out on the table and everyone is happy. If the colors and fonts look nice they might not even look at any specifics. After all, the appearance leads the observer to the conclusion that the details are just as nice."

"You're starting to sound a little cynical," Troy commented.

"A little is an understatement," Alice added. "Experiences with bad schedules have obviously left someone in this room with a bad taste for the process."

Alice's comment evoked laughter from everyone, including myself. Her emphasis on the word bad was classic, and understood by everyone.

To confirm her comment, I provided several horrific examples of schedules manipulated to deceive management. It's almost impossible to read the newspaper without seeing details of a major project that's hit the OS Phase. All of these projects had sophisticated schedules and teams of professionals assigned to them, and they still failed.

Listening intently to the examples, Troy demonstrated his conversion to my position on scheduling. "If you sit back and think about those examples, how was it even remotely possible for a team to manage a schedule, and I emphasize manage, without knowing their project was going to hit a wall or, as we call it, the OS Phase? Either the teams were oblivious to daily events or there was some massaging of the schedule to make it appear to be supporting the target end-date for the project."

Alice seemed disappointed at the bluntness of Troy's comments. Leaning towards Bruce with a sly grin, she asked, "Have you ever embellished the schedule you presented to Troy and me?"

Bruce's silence answered the question. However, before he could respond and incriminate himself, I interrupted the conversation by bringing a broader perspective to the discussion. "Actually, the frequency of this type of behavior is not important. What we have to realize is that it does occur and it's easy to do. The ease at which a team can embellish a schedule and the fact it is even possible would make anyone cynical of the schedule process in general. What's important is the fact that you've hit the OS Phase and you will have to work hard to get credibility back. It would be best if you avoided any representation Monday that the executive committee could question. If I were part of the executive committee and you threw a "new and improved" schedule on the table, you would have to spend a lot of time explaining why we should trust this schedule after we've learned that the previous schedules were bogus."

"I'm thinking about the project schedule…" Bruce said, "…and I agree about leaving it out of Monday's presentation. I'm not sure we can get anything of substance by that time anyhow."

"Does this mean that we won't have a date to provide to the executive committee?" Troy asked, while referring to a subject brought up at least three or four times already this morning.

"It's easy to understand why you want to give them a date," I said, "but you really need their help to establish a realistic schedule. We need to discuss key subtleties of preparing a schedule so you're all prepared in case a question arises, but that's all we can do in the short amount of time we have before the meeting."

Redirecting the conversation away from the schedule for a minute, Alice said, "What we're saying today is that a project should be managed from the scope perspective and not necessarily from the schedule perspective. That's a major change for most project managers. I believe the point is not to avoid using a schedule, but instead look at the project as a whole in terms of the scope, in terms of what we have to do."

Responding with a smile of agreement, I said, "Alice, you're right on point. In fact, if you believe what you just spoke, then you're on your way to understanding what must be done to get back on track. Then we need to move onto the next step and that is to focus on the 'who' as in who will do the work and then, of course, manage the exceptions or, as we call them, the risks."

Troy joined in with an important comment. "All you have to do is remember that scope must be qualified first, then time, and then cost. The Stupid Triangle is a great way to remember that relationship."

Troy then went to the flip chart sheet describing the Avoidance Model and added a triangle above the word *Scope* (Chart 17 - 1). This was very important. Any time one of the three in the room acknowledged the Avoidance Model or Stupid Triangle, it validated their understanding and ultimate commitment to that process perspective.

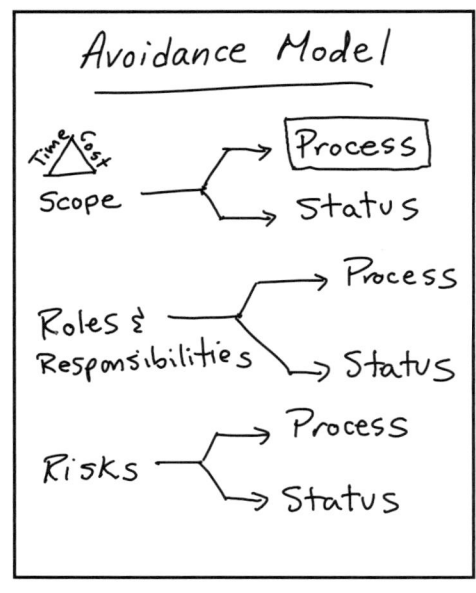

**Chart 17 - 1**

Bruce added his comments, as well. "What we find out when establishing the schedule is that it is much easier to prepare when we know what we're doing…you know, the scope. To support the scope, you have the structure of the project reinforced in the Responsibility Assignment Matrix and you have the responsibilities identified. With that kind of information, putting a schedule together should be a breeze."

As a first step towards establishing a new schedule process, I thought it necessary to make sure everyone understood basic scheduling techniques. Even though all three had adequate experience from a time of use standpoint, it still took some time to reorient them to all of the appropriate scheduling terminology.

It was important to take time to do this because of the nature and impact of failing to have everyone on board. Many errors or deficiencies in schedules could be avoidable if the team using the systems understood the processes inside the computer. Computerized scheduling processes often result in basic omissions and early project misdirection. As I described to the group, we need to make only a few changes in how we look at scheduling. Radical changes are not necessary. The steps necessary to avoid the OS Phase are often a part of existing project management methodologies. We just need to tweak them a little.

Alice was engaged in the discussion and was ready to get into some of the details. "What's the first step to develop a schedule?"

"What we want to do is take the simplest approach possible." I went back to the flip chart to sketch some details. "If we develop a schedule process that only the schedulers can understand, we've created a major injustice."

Continuing the discussion, I drew a simple three-activity precedence diagram on the flip chart (Chart 17 - 2).

"The best technique is to proceed with these processes one at a time and not concurrently."

Continuing, I said, "First we need to develop the definitions for all activities before moving on to sequencing and so on."

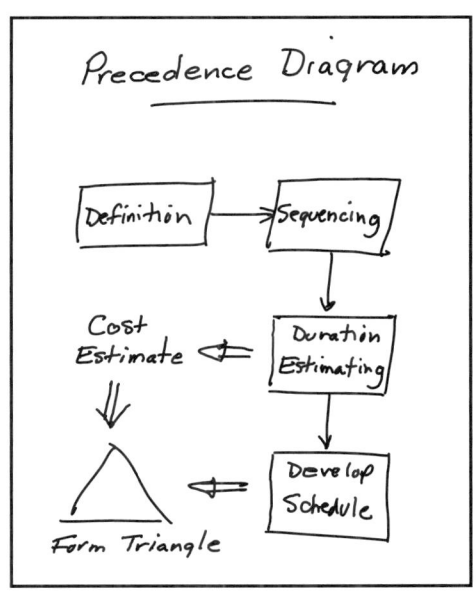

**Chart 17 - 2**

"Isn't that contrary to how many project managers create schedules?" Alice asked. "My experience is that the team would look at the definition, sequencing, and duration estimating simultaneously."

Jumping into the conversation Troy added his comments. "It might be that you haven't defined these processes enough, but on the surface it seems odd to wait on each step to finish before starting the next. How could it make any difference?"

Troy's question was important and is the basis for much of the confusion with those preparing project schedules. I went on to describe a rationale everyone in the room was all too familiar with relating to the scope management process. "The first step, to define activities on the schedule, is a follow-on process, after we first define the scope in the WBS. The activities originate with the WBS. It is important to ensure we have all of the scope before we do anything else. We need to make sure, though, that we've captured the details of each activity and not just used a three word description. The activities represent work, or scope."

It was interesting to see how quickly Alice bought into this process. She continued the discussion by saying, "It would seem that to be effective, the scope process must be separate from the schedule development process. This is a major paradigm shift in how we look at schedules now on this project or in fact anywhere else I've worked."

"Yes, it's a significant shift in focus," I said, while surveying the group to see if Troy and Bruce were also on board. "We always need to look at the schedule in terms of what needs to be completed, not necessarily just for validating dates given to us by management. The schedule would be worthless if it contained only part of the scope. You must be unrelenting in the approach towards gathering scope."

Noticing that I was looking in his direction, Bruce asked a question about the next item listed on the flip chart. "Is the next process—the sequencing of activities—done for all activities before moving on?"

Nodding my head, everyone sensed my next comment. "Again, we must complete this step in its entirety before doing anything else. This is a critical step, but often taken too lightly. I hate rules as much as anyone else, but we have to be diligent in following the proper sequencing and doing each step completely before moving to the next. The underlying basis of the scheduling process is to determine the sequence and timing of work. Logic will be a principle driver and must be incorporated into the schedule without imposing any limitations for resource availability."

"I don't understand what you just said regarding resources," Bruce said. "Why would you even consider developing a schedule without recognizing that it has to be based on available resources? We can't assume that we'll have all of the right people available when we need them. That's an unrealistic risk and won't work in this or any other organization."

"Great call!" I shouted to Bruce, "...converting the assumption into a risk."

Everyone laughed and acknowledged Bruce's quickness on his feet.

"I agree with Bruce," Troy said, while Alice was also agreeing nonverbally. "I think our project recovery planning just hit the OS Phase itself."

The reference to the OS Phase really loosened everyone up again, as it should.

"You guys are way too literal," I responded. "The purpose of developing the initial schedule without consideration for resources is straightforward. If we want to really assess our ability to complete the project on time we need first to know if we could even do the project if there were no resource limitations."

"But we do have resource limitations," Bruce said impatiently. "To ignore that fact is ridiculous."

"Whose job is it to provide resources for your project?" I asked.

"What do you mean by that question?" Bruce responded back. "It's my job to get resources for the project."

"I thought you said earlier that the company itself is configured as a matrix organization, where the different directors 'lend' or 'rent' team members to your project."

"That's right," Bruce countered. "We request the type of resource we need and the managers look to see who's available and then we go from there."

"So the directors are responsible for resources, not you?" I asked with the obvious point slammed home! "It sounds like you don't make resource decisions. Someone else does. Is that right?"

"If you're asking who does the hiring and firing and that type of thing, then you're right," Bruce fired back. "But I'm responsible for managing them once they are on the project."

Alice could see where I was going with the discussion. She didn't waste any time and turned to Bruce with the bottom line question.

"Bruce, have you ever been denied a resource you needed? Was there ever a time you could not get a resource necessary to support the schedule?"

"Sure, in fact it's quite common, but I've been able to manage with what resources I get. I don't see what the problem is with the resource concern."

"I'll tell you what's wrong," Alice said bluntly. "The project hit the OS Phase and now we have to suck up to the executive committee on Monday. That's what the problem is with the resource problem!"

Jumping into the fray, Troy asked, "I think the underlying question Alice is asking is, if you'd had all the resources you needed, could you have met the schedule?"

"Without looking at the details, I'd be afraid to respond with any certainty," Bruce responded. "I will say, though, that I did spend a lot of my waking hours dealing with resource problems."

"What kind of problems?" Troy asked with a puzzled expression on his face.

Bruce was starting to understand where the conversation was heading. With considerably more frustration in his voice, he began to talk about previous problems. "You know, the kind mentioned earlier. Just about the time I would get someone up to speed they would get reassigned or would have other activities thrown at them where they had to multitask much of the time."

"What percentage of time did you spend dealing with resource problems?" Alice asked.

Bruce pondered for a couple of minutes and answered, "It's hard to be accurate, but it wouldn't surprise me if I had to deal with resource hassles at least 30-40 percent of my work day. In fact, the idea of developing a schedule with a target of unlimited resources is making sense now. That way it's possible to see how long it could, and I stress could, take to get the project completed in a perfect world!"

After a slight pause, Bruce continued, "On the project, I loaded resource information into the schedule as I was developing it. For each activity, I included the name or type of resource that was available. I even artificially held several major work areas to dates later than optimum, because I knew I wouldn't have the resources when we really needed them. I never really thought about how this type of scheduling really disguises what is going on. I can't even describe how difficult it was to develop the first schedule. It wasn't the logic or the activities, but instead it was the resource allocations that drove me crazy. By the time I finished with the first schedule I wasn't even sure what I had prepared."

"The more I think about this whole process we did, the more frustrated I'm becoming," Alice said, with a renewed firmness in her voice. "Time spent by a project manager dealing with resource problems is time not spent on doing what should be done. This is a problem we definitely need to present to the executive committee on Monday."

"It would be great if you got this all taken care of before the next project that I'm managing gets underway," Troy said, with a smile and a somewhat constrained level of optimism.

It was fun to observe the intense discussion and to witness the transformation of Bruce. He went from being pleased with the existing resource management process to his concern with the reality that there was a problem. This is so common in organizations where they have beaten it into the project managers that they are responsible for everything.

Realistically, the project manager might be responsible for resources, but they can't be held accountable because they don't have the proper authority. I've watched project managers be criticized publicly by resource managers for problems that were actually resulting from poor resource placement by the resource managers themselves. The sad part about the problem is the reality that project managers learn to accept this type of abuse.

Turning to the group, I summarized this area of concern. "If the project is going to be successful it will be necessary for each of the directors to supply the resources necessary to get the project finished. Any failure on their part will need to be managed as a risk."

Troy moved to the front of the room, stood next to the flip chart stand, and spoke. "We've spent a lot of time dealing with the resources problem. Are there any other details we need to know regarding any other scheduling processes?"

"You're right, we did spend a lot of time with the resource problem," Alice said, responding to Troy on my behalf. "Why don't we take a break for a few minutes and then come back and dig into the remaining processes related to scheduling."

We had spent a lot of time discussing resources and resource processes so everyone took Alice's suggestion without debate. It would be important for everyone to regroup mentally and then come back to the room to dig in and put together a plan for Monday.

---

**OS Phase Avoidance**
**STRATEGY 17**

*A schedule's purpose is to tell you what the dates for the project milestones are…not have you tell it what the dates are…*

*Use the schedule as a tool. Avoid the temptation to use it only for reporting to senior management or customers.*

## CHAPTER 18
# What Story Does Your Schedule Tell?

When reviewing any type of schedule, it is fascinating to look for what story the schedule tells. This is important to understand. A person unfamiliar with a project should be able to sit down with the schedule and visualize the plan for the project during the next week, month, or year. The details in the near term should be clear and should outline systematically what will be occurring.

Despite the mystique associated with scheduling in many organizations, the actual process of creating a time line of events is quite simple and the project manager can apply these same techniques to any size project. In that regard, before anyone embarks on the use of sophisticated computer systems for scheduling, it is important for the user to understand the *processes* of scheduling or time management.

We may not stop long enough to realize it, but most of us use basic scheduling techniques everyday in our personal lives. Wives, husbands, mothers, grandmothers, great grandfathers, and everyone on the planet plans sequencing of activities each day they wake up. No major meal is served without the cook thinking through the sequencing of cooking and reheating and serving. Parents with several children attending sequential or simultaneous school or sports events learn how to cope with the challenges of scheduling. Scheduling is part of our lives and it always will be.

Providing examples of scheduling in our personal lives should not trivialize the tens of thousands of scheduling professionals and consultants in the world. There's no question that we need experts to guide us through schedules of complex projects.

Using experts, though, does not guarantee success. Many large, high profile projects have still fallen behind in their schedules. It's easy to rationalize minor slippages or changes, but months, years, or actual project cancellations are absurd. If you asked ten project management professionals to suggest what the root causes were for schedule failures, you would probably get ten different answers.

We need a *process*, with some thought and communication considerations included. We need a *process* that brings in the relationships of the **Stupid Triangle**. We need a *process* that is simple and credible. We need a schedule *process* that tells us what the schedule needs to be versus our common technique where we force the schedule to fit some arbitrary deadline date pulled out of the air.

The purpose of a project schedule is to tell a story.

What story it tells is up to the project manager!

It's difficult to find a project manager working on medium to large projects who doesn't have some type of formal project schedule in their hands or doesn't have a colorful critical path schedule plastered on the wall of their office or cubicle. Schedules are status symbols for many project managers, the actual accuracy of which is sometimes secondary to their appearance. When it came to the Mountain Adventures project, Bruce and his project schedule hanging on the wall of his office were no exception.

It was easy to round the team up and get them back to the conference room. In his often aggressive tone of voice, Bruce convinced everyone to get back to work so we wouldn't lose any momentum in addressing his remaining schedule development concerns. Preparing schedules was Bruce's area of expertise, and there was no time like the present to get on with the discussion.

Having thought about the resource concern during break, Bruce began the new session with a summary and a strategy for allocating resources after completing the logic-based schedule. "The proper steps for putting our schedule together are to develop logical relationships, estimates for the time required for each activity, and, then and only then, add and evaluate the resource requirements and relationships."

Waiting for a reaction from the others was not necessary. Troy's hand and facial movements demonstrated enthusiastic acceptance of the idea. He responded to Bruce's comments by building on the recommendation. "This idea really makes sense if we first prepare the logical relationship network and save it for use later. It might, in fact, end up being the closest match to the seemingly arbitrary date provided by the customer or sponsor, or, in our case, the executive committee. Taking the logic-based schedule and the resource-based schedule to an executive committee meeting will be beneficial in demonstrating the impact of resource availability concerns within the organization."

Alice was willing to admit that she had never thought of scheduling and resource allocations in this simple way. "When you sit and think this through, the logical schedule prepared first belongs to the project manager. The resource-loaded schedule prepared next actually belongs to the sponsoring organization or senior managers."

Alice's comments in support of the idea drifted off quickly as she interrupted herself with another thought. "I hate to regress, but when we jumped to the resource assignment process and resultant schedules, didn't we skip some important first steps necessary to get the schedule established?"

"I don't think so," responded Bruce, with a new air of confidence. "The first step on the project schedule is to define the activities. The WBS clearly supports the identification step. Next we need to identify the sequence of activities. Our first pass would be to look for those relationships that are mandatory and have no alternative in how we execute them. We then need to establish the discretionary dependencies, the efficient, and nice to have dependencies."

"What happens if we have other activities without any linkages?" Troy asked. "Should we just tie them off some other activity that gives us the date we need? Or should we add an imposed date to hold them in time where we need them."

Troy's question hit a key area of scheduling deficiencies. The schedule for the balance of the project would be facing this concern a lot, since we would be looking at a schedule that was already in progress. Responding directly to Troy, but making sure that Bruce and Alice were listening, I described the best approach. "Although it does happen frequently that activities have no obvious predecessors or successors, there are a couple of strategies to defeat the problem. First and most important is to assign only short durations for activities. Work included in each activity must be very clear to anyone reviewing or executing the work activity. It turns out that if the activities are small enough, the sequencing will be considerably easier, and most activities will turn out to have dependencies. Exceptions would be handled on a case by case basis, hopefully with the person that owns the activity."

"Shouldn't we just ask the person responsible for the activity to determine the dependencies in the first place?" Alice asked.

"That's the correct approach," I responded. "In fact, the best schedule will be a result of the input of those actually doing the work. Unfortunately, this isn't always possible because the eventual resource might not be assigned or even available yet. Whatever we end up with, we need to note the source of the dependency and duration of the assignments. This will help us understand the accuracy of the duration estimate at any point in time and will support the development of a checklist for distribution to team members as the project progresses."

Bruce was thinking through the discussion in his head and came back with a common rebuttal to the strategy of limiting duration lengths for the remaining activities on the project. "If we have short duration activities, won't that result in having to keep track of a ton of schedule activities? I'm not sure we can manage a lot of activities efficiently."

"Remember, think detail, not complexity," I said. "Extra detail will help to ensure nobody gets confused."

"When you suggest short duration activities, is there a rule of thumb to use?" Bruce asked, with a particular interest for his efforts to develop the remaining schedule activities.

"The duration must be manageable," I responded. "A reasonable rule of thumb is to limit the length of any activity to 10 percent of the project's total time duration. If we have a ten-week project, then the maximum duration for any activity should be one week. An exception would be a multiyear project. In that case, it would be appropriate to measure the 10 percent against individual project life cycle phases."

"So 10 percent will work all of the time, for every activity?" Bruce asked, as he was trying to visualize the concept.

"The limit is 10 percent," I responded. "I would actually prefer 5 percent for the norm. What we want is a division of the work that will minimize the amount of multi-tasking we have to plan for each resource."

"I just don't see this working with our team," Bruce answered. "There's going to be a lot of resistance and we'll be accused of micro-managing."

With everyone's facial expressions agreeing with Bruce's comment, I responded with a not so subtle answer. "I agree there will be push back. What we have to consider is why. Why would anybody object to short durations? When you ask the question to these team members, they are cornered. The long durations were giving them latitude to disguise their real performance. That problem alone may be the single most significant contributor to a project landing in the OS Phase."

"Oh, that's right, we haven't mentioned the OS Phase lately. We do have to remember that we're developing a plan to avoid that event," Troy commented, creating a lighter mood in the room.

"I'm starting to like the 10 percent limit," Alice interjected. "When you think of the schedule in those terms, we can limit the amount of the overall project that is at risk at any point in time. If we had some limits this year, we might not be in the fix that we are in now. Actually, the more I think about it, 10 percent of the project duration for what we have left is pretty darn generous."

Looking back at Alice, I responded, "There is nothing preventing you from targeting activity durations that are 5 percent of the project duration or less. This would be a better choice for the bulk of the activities, but whatever you decide, the longest should be 10 percent. You can't waiver from that amount."

"I'd like to slow down a little. I'm still not convinced this is a good idea," Bruce responded. "Remember, it will be me, not you, Alice, that has to go to the team with this new requirement. I might have a mutiny! It will take a lot of effort to break up all of the remaining work into smaller pieces. After we break the schedule down, then we will have the increased effort to maintain each of these small activities, including the regular status that we will have to report against each one. This whole idea is beginning to give me heartburn."

"Let's stop a minute and reflect on what you're saying, Bruce," I said. "The reasoning you're providing is classic. This type of thinking turns the project schedule into a wimpy performance reporting system. We have to remember that the real purpose of the scheduling software is to determine the optimum sequencing of activities. If we end up with large duration activities that have artificial linkages, then we lose the ability to evaluate what is really happening with the schedule."

Alice understood the significance of this concept and cynically delivered her blunt comments to Bruce. "Remember, with our current scheduling process we failed."

"But the people doing the work need long duration activities so they can have a time span in which to do the work. If we tell them the specific sequence, then we are micromanaging, as we talked about before," Bruce said impatiently.

"You're right," I responded with as much empathy as I could muster. "Those are the comments you will get back. But before you get yourself in too deep on this problem, think again about what you would do if the project was a world survival project. Your team must protect the earth from an impending collision with an asteroid. In this case, would you be satisfied that each team member could work on their items 'sometime' within the duration you identified without providing anymore detail than that?"

"Of course not!" Bruce responded quickly, "but this isn't a world survival project."

"Wait a minute," Alice interrupted. "It might not be world survival, but it's a very important project for our company and for all of us in this room. I'm agreeing that team members need to sit down and think through how they plan on getting the project completed. We can't just sit around again and hope all of the team members have the same priorities we have."

While the conversation kept bouncing back and forth, Troy moved to the flip chart and drew some parallel activities on the chart (Chart 18 - 1).

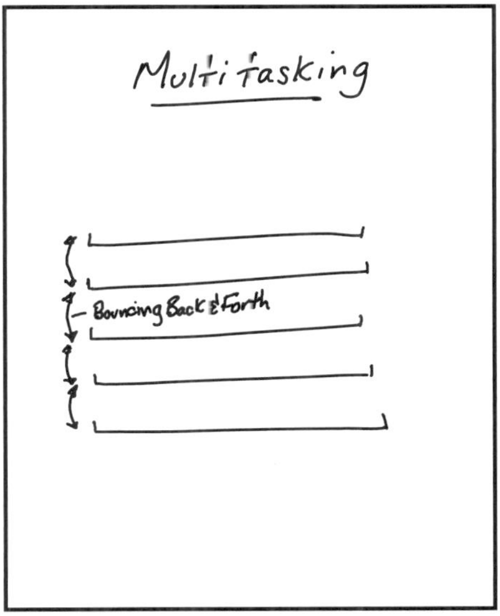

# WHAT STORY DOES YOUR SCHEDULE TELL?  185

Pointing to the chart and moving his eyes back and forth to each of us in the room, Troy commented about the five parallel activities. "If each of these five activities is long in duration and is performed by the same person, we call this multitasking. The person responsible for these activities will bounce back and forth based on what needs to be completed."

Troy added arrows on the flip chart to bring attention to the bouncing process.

Looking to the group, Troy asked a great question. "Does anybody see anything wrong with this picture?"

**Chart 18 - 1**

Alice was on board throughout the whole discussion and was first to respond. "If someone were to give me five tasks and the time period for accomplishing those tasks was similar, my behavior would cause me to not panic until the last minute if I was behind on any of the tasks. However, with the lack of priorities, I could easily procrastinate and find myself in an impossible situation and unable to finish any of the five activities on time."

"That's right!" Troy added, as he was now ready to take over the discussion. "The people working on the project must themselves think through how they are going to manage the activities on their plate. When we allow them to have long durations we are enabling them to get into trouble at the last minute and that definitely looks like the OS Phase."

He then added the OS Phase notation on the flip chart (Chart 18 - 2).

The key word here is "enable."

Bruce was still uneasy with the discussion and threw another wrench in the process. "This is all fine and dandy, but it's impossible to know the details of what a team member will be working on three weeks down the road, let alone two months or even longer. In fact, events happening today might have a major effect on what we do a couple of weeks from now. It seems like everything you do along these lines will have to be done over and over and over."

I waited to see if Alice or Troy would jump to the response, and I wasn't disappointed. Alice reached over the table, took Bruce's arm, and spoke directly to him.

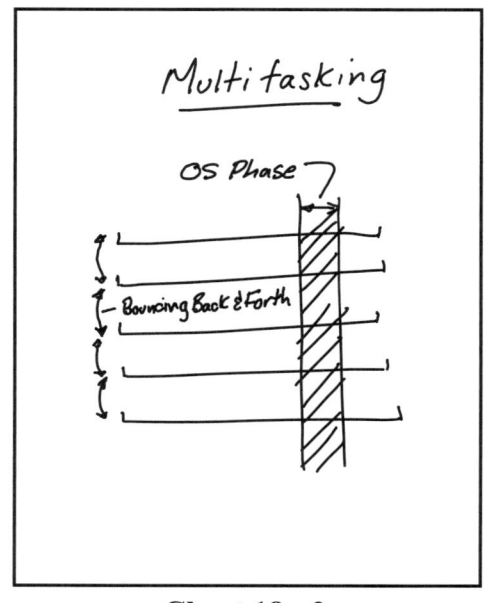

**Chart 18 - 2**

"Let's look back at what we said earlier and, importantly, what we agreed was a good idea earlier. If we're ever going to get better and avoid hitting the OS Phase for the second time, we have to look at the schedule from the perspective of whether or not we can actually complete the work within any allotted time period. To do this with any degree of accuracy we will need to have the work activities broken down to a level where all of the actual work processes are visible. We need to adapt to this new methodology immediately, regardless of how anyone might push back."

Turning to me, Bruce asked, "What about activities quite a bit down the road. Do we need these duration limitations on those?"

Alice answered before I could even muster a response. "Bruce, I hope we don't have many activities that are 'quite a bit down the road' at this stage of the project."

Everyone laughed, including Bruce, as he responded. "I was merely asking a question, you know, for Troy and his upcoming project at the end of the year."

Laughter erupted again and Troy jumped into the discussion. "Thanks for taking care of me, Bruce."

## WHAT STORY DOES YOUR SCHEDULE TELL?    187

There was still a question on the table and I decided to take control of the discussion until we were resolved on this point. "I've said earlier that I detest rules for the sake of a rule; that's dumb and will cause the project manager to lose credibility. We need to manage the targeting of short durations to near-term activities, where we do have the necessary detail. Future activities, at the project manager's discretion, do not have to be broken down until the team gets closer. Depending on the overall duration of the project, a weekly review of future activities should reveal those that are ready for commitment."

"Is that constant review called 'Rolling Wave Scheduling'?" Bruce asked, while showing some clear agreement at the last discussion.

"That's exactly what it's called," I said with a smile and acknowledgment in Bruce's direction. "The concept of Rolling Wave Scheduling is a technique that's been around for a long time."

Alice joined in by saying, "We all are supposed to do 'rolling wave' kind of stuff all of the time. The problem is that we get distracted and forget to do it as a common routine and then we get behind and then we…well we hit the OS Phase!"

Everyone laughed at Alice's description of the process. We knew she was right. The tendency to have good ideas up front and then the ultimate failure to follow through is all too common. We went on to discuss how rolling wave techniques link so closely to the forward-looking characteristics we desire in a project manager. It is important for project managers to spend time with the team looking forward. That rolling wave process is a major preventative action for avoiding the OS Phase.

"I guess it can't hurt if we just try it," Bruce said. "I agree with the phrase that we need to add *detail, not complexity*. If we are ever going to get this schedule completed, we must insist on having simple networks and schedules. It is imperative that we keep our network as simple as possible."

Alice was considering the conversation and obviously thinking of several applications for these concepts. "Rolling wave planning is really just a process of constant knowledge gathering. We want to pay the most attention to activities scheduled in the near future. When the Mountain Adventure Project started, we would have only needed to detail resources for the first three to four months. Then as each month passed, we would add another month's worth of detail. At this time, though, we need to provide details from today until the completion of the project, because we need to know every single aspect of what it will take to finish this project.

"It almost seems odd that we don't use it for everything we do. It's so logical to use what we know today, combined with what we've learned about tomorrow and then apply that knowledge in a real-time method to near-term activities."

Troy was listening politely to the discussion, but at the same time, he was anxious to provide an example of the rolling wave concept. "Last summer, before I accepted my current position, my family and I headed out on a road trip from our home in Las Vegas to Virginia for a little vacation. Our plans were to travel through Dallas where I could meet with Barry and then we would head to Mississippi and on to Virginia. We thought a trip to Hattiesburg, Mississippi, would be great since we were in the area to meet with my sister and aunt. Sounds like a simple road trip, but then a hurricane brewing in the Atlantic struck Florida and was possibly heading for Mississippi and most of our planned travel path. We didn't want to change our route, but now we had to plan our next day's travels daily. Our overall plan for the trip was still sound, but we needed to add the extra knowledge we were gaining each day by listening to the radio and watching the Weather Channel."

Troy's example was personal, and a perfect example of Rolling Wave Scheduling. As he and his family found out more information, they would make mid-course corrections and tweak their original schedule. That's a simple example of what we should be doing on our projects. The little bit of pre-planning made their trip go smoothly and prevented them from heading into a problem, where they would have lost a lot of time.

Alice, excited by how this concept supported her understanding of planning, added her thoughts. "We talk about planning so much, but we actually do very little of it in practice once the project starts. I'm not sure what behavioral trait causes that, but when you think about it, it's a dangerous practice. Throughout my years of experience, it's so easy to recall the times that the project teams didn't follow the project schedule, because most often it was so out of touch with reality. The real truth was that they were themselves out of touch with their responsibility to update it on a regular basis."

"That's right," I added. "A schedule is not magical, it's only a road map, and using Troy's previous example, if we don't keep the road map current with the conditions in front of us, then following it is moot; thus we ignore it; thus we don't even see the OS Phase ahead of us. Then we blame it on others!"

> *OS Phase* **Avoidance**
> **STRATEGY 18**
>
> *If you're talking about it, it had better be on the schedule!*

CHAPTER 19

# An Estimate is Just an Estimate

There is nothing magical about estimating. Just as with scheduling activities on the project, we perform estimates as part of our daily life. We estimate how much we will spend on groceries. We estimate how much we will need in fifteen years for our children's college. Although estimates are important to us, we realize that our personal estimates are not perfect and will need revision when more information is available.

For every element of the project, down to the smallest triangle, we need to capture the *scope* and then develop a related schedule and the effort/cost to complete that work. The purpose of an estimate is to inform others of the expected schedule and cost for each element of a project.

Almost everybody is comfortable with making quick informal estimates in support of daily planning activities. Few, however, enjoy preparing formal estimates. The informal estimates are prepared with little thought as to format or accuracy. They may be requested in a meeting or even as someone walks down the hallway of the office. Formal estimates, on the other hand, have form and content and provide the basis for proposals, official budgets, or authorizations. They are supposed to be accurate.

No matter what your position is about estimating, one thing is true. Most people do not like to have anyone analyze or challenge their estimates. If critiques are expected, it is common for the person doing the estimate to pad it or hide some contingency. Management, suspecting this to be the case, will challenge the performer to do the work in less time or effort, trying to squeeze out the padding. In any case, everyone loses.

After we figure out the level of detail we want for the estimate, the next question is who should prepare the estimate. This answer is not that easy. Initially, the customer or sponsor will

> prepare a high-level estimate, an estimate without benefit of the complete *scope* details and implementation strategies. These high-level estimates are fine if those preparing them are willing to accept a different estimate or forecast value when the details surface. Unfortunately, many times those weak original target estimates remain in place for political reasons.
>
> Welcome to another step on the path to the *OS Phase*!

Bruce's smile faded as he thought about a forgotten task. "So many of the project management processes we need to implement seem possible, but the thought of preparing estimates for each of the remaining work items is a little overwhelming. Estimating is not my strength and there's never enough time to do it right."

"Are you going to teach us how to do better estimates?" Troy asked, displaying a mischievous grin. "We certainly could use some tips to make the process better."

With a grin and a reassuring tone to my voice, I responded to Troy, "No, I'm not going to teach you how to do better estimates. What I'm going to spend time on is making sure you know when and how much estimating is actually required. When we're done talking about estimates, all of you will have infinite wisdom!"

I reluctantly began describing my opinions of the estimating process. "Unfortunately, you've hit a sore spot with me and I'm going to be forced to get on one of my bandwagons and render another opinion."

Everyone laughed at my comments, thinking that I was kidding. They were wrong.

I started the discussion by pacing in front of the conference room. "The project management and cost engineering disciplines have put much emphasis on estimating and types of estimating. I believe they have actually lost sight of what it means to have an estimate and the basics for preparing it. Unlike the way we portray them, an estimate is only a moment in time and may have limited applicability the next day. An estimate is just an estimate."

Alice was the first to speak up after my last comment. "I don't agree with the comment that the estimate isn't applicable the next day. We need estimates so that we can manage performance on the project. If we don't have a baseline, then a yardstick of performance is meaningless."

Troy and Bruce were waiting for Alice to finish before adding their comments, but I cut them all off. "I didn't say that we shouldn't use it to analyze performance, but using your example, Alice, what are you comparing the original estimate to in order to get the performance differential?"

Speaking before Alice could respond, Bruce was quick to add his comments. "We are always looking at actual costs or actual performance and then use that to develop forecasts for the project. Without the estimate, these processes wouldn't mean much."

I was still pacing and decided it was time to present some more thoughts related to estimating strategies.

I started by asking Bruce the first question. "When was the first estimate for the project prepared? And who prepared it?"

"That's easy," Bruce responded. "The first estimate was considered a *rough order of magnitude estimate* prepared before we met with the venture capitalists. Accordingly, the team completed it before starting any work on the project. I wasn't involved at the time, but the executive committee members that were there at the time were very much involved with its development, weren't they, Alice?"

As Bruce turned to Alice, it was obvious that she was a little anxious with the way Bruce just voiced this last question. Turning to me with a slight sign of embarrassment, Alice made a comment that at first caught me off guard. "This morning we've mentioned the executive committee a lot and you've asked questions about how they would react and even speculated about their reactions. Well, I've been less than up front, because as Bruce was insinuating, I'm one of the original members of the executive committee."

"Why didn't you mention that last night when you referenced the committee the first time?" I asked, with a hesitation in my voice from Alice's surprising statement. "That would have been better than holding back some pertinent information. I'm at a big disadvantage here, and that information might have helped me get a better feel of what you guys were up against on Monday."

Alice sat down and addressed me directly. "Actually I thought it might be confusing. The more I thought about it, the more I realized that on Monday our dilemma and recommendation would be quite independent of my role on the committee. In fact, there might even be a coup, depending on what news we have for them and how they react to it. My days on the executive committee might be limited."

I wasn't sure if I accepted Alice's excuse. In my mind her credibility slipped a little, especially after her earlier criticism of anybody that embellished performance. Instead, I decided to proceed with this new information and not let the discussion stall. Turning to Alice, I restated the previous question related to the original estimate. "So I guess that based on these latest comments you were involved and knowledgeable of the first project estimate?"

"If the rest of the truth be known, the estimate was prepared by one other member and me," Alice responded, while walking to the flip chart where she started to draw out a time line of events for the project. "The first estimate was prepared for use as a talking point with investors. No one gave it much credence as having any significant level of accuracy. After we got a go ahead to start preliminary planning, we developed what we referred to as the project estimate. I would categorize the project estimate as mid-grade, kind of what you would use as a budget estimate. It wasn't intended to be a baseline document, but you can probably guess what happened next."

"It became the baseline!" I exclaimed, knowing the answer.

"That's right," she said. "And as I recall, some hotshot project manager saw the number and date and said he could get it done. Do you remember that conversation, Bruce?"

Bruce dodged and hid his head behind Troy.

"You must be talking about me," Bruce said. "I didn't know that you thought of me as a hotshot project manager."

"You definitely weren't shy of any ego," Alice said. "Your self-assurance and project focus gave the executive committee a lot of confidence. In fact, I would say that those attributes have given you a Teflon® type coating throughout the project. No one wanted to challenge you too much for fear that you would put them in their place."

"Let's just hope that he still has some of that Teflon® on Monday," Troy said, directing a smile towards Bruce. "Maybe you have enough to share."

Getting everyone back into the subject at hand, I asked Alice and Bruce if there were any other estimates performed on the project. Alice jotted down a couple of estimating exercises they went through, but nothing of any major significance.

"So the current delay in the project schedule is measured against what was depicted in the original project estimate?" I asked, while looking back and forth to Alice and Bruce.

"Actually, that's not correct," Bruce said, after a few moments of strained silence. "About six months ago we modified our project's baseline and delayed the project a little over three weeks and increased the costs about 10 percent, but I can't recall the actual number. This change was due to suggestions by some investors that we expand the number of locations. It didn't affect the software folks much, but those involved with site logistics were going to have some big concerns. They are the ones that insisted on getting some relief in the schedule."

Turning to Bruce, Troy presented a question that had been bouncing around in my mind for quite awhile. "How accurate have the estimates on the project been so far? What I mean is, do you know where they were soft?"

"Frankly, I haven't paid much attention to the estimates," Bruce responded. "An estimate is just an estimate. I never pay attention to them once we create the baseline, but I'm getting the feeling that you're going to tell me that I've made a big mistake."

Alice and Troy enjoyed Bruce's humor, but knew as well that ignoring estimates was probably not going to be a good approach. In fact, the more Alice thought about the estimating process, the more she was realizing that this was going to be an important area to get resolved.

Speaking directly to me, she asked, "We mentioned earlier about preparing an estimate for Monday's meeting and now I'm wondering what in the world we were talking about. I recognize the importance of having an estimate for getting the project approved initially, but why do we need a new estimate on Monday? That is starting to seem like a lot of work just to appease a process that might not make any sense."

Before I could answer, Troy jumped up and began strutting around the conference room again. "I can't believe what I just heard. How could you possibly think even for a minute that an estimate isn't necessary to reflect our new projection?"

"I'm not arguing that we don't need a forecast for the balance of work," Alice said excitedly. "I'm only questioning a new formal estimate for all of the remaining work."

Troy was visibly agitated with Alice's comments. "How could you think even for a minute that the other members of the executive committee and investors will accept a delay to the project without a detailed accounting of what needs to change? It just won't happen in my lifetime."

"You're right, Troy, but what value will this estimate add?" Bruce asked, while obviously getting frustrated with the discussion. "Preparing a new estimate will take time away from those on the project that need to be getting things done. Instead they'll be bean counting."

In defense, Troy looked at me and asked, "Aren't there different levels of estimates? It would seem that we could prepare a quick and dirty estimate for the balance of this project, but before I start my project down the road, I would work to prepare a detailed estimate."

Alice saw an opportunity to get a message out regarding different types of estimates. Up until now, each time she mentioned the subject, someone changed the discussion. She was concerned that too many times we avoid doing estimates merely because we think there is too much effort involved. Her goal is to get everyone to understand that there are some high level estimating processes, that although not perfect, require much less commitment from the organization to prepare. "If I remember, there are three different levels of estimates: analogous, parametric, and definitive. Did I name these correctly?"

"I hope I can let you down easy," I said, with a modest tone to my voice. "You have described the basic techniques for estimating, not the levels of accuracy, although there is an implied degree of accuracy. But just the fact that you knew those is impressive."

"Suck-up!" Bruce shouted across the room. "Now that you know Alice is on the executive committee, you will want to impress her so she'll bring you back as a consultant."

"Guilty as charged!" I said jokingly, as everyone continued to laugh at Bruce's comment. "I haven't left yet, so I won't worry about coming back until later.

"But now we need to get back to the estimating process. Sadly, for most professionals, the estimating process itself looks complicated. Realistically, though, estimating is something we all know needs to be done. We just need to understand how much time we have for preparing the estimate and how accurate it has to be.

"First, though, we must always remember that the preparation of the estimate is itself scope. We have to be careful not to spend more effort than necessary. As an interesting twist, I'm inclined to strive more for a good scope statement and a rough time and cost estimate for the solid scope, than I would a perfect estimate of the wrong or incomplete scope."

Alice laughed, "Unbelievable. What a concept! The Stupid Triangle really causes a person to pause and reflect about how to proceed. There is no doubt that if we only have so much time or money we should spend our effort to find the most important element of the process…scope."

Troy was internalizing every word. After Alice finished her comments, he responded quickly, "I've never thought about the fact that if we prepared a detailed estimate that the estimate itself is scope. A detailed estimate itself will take a lot more time and money or effort versus preparing a *rough order of magnitude estimate.*

"I know you just mentioned it, Alice, but personally, I keep forgetting to consider that Stupid Triangle thing!"

Troy's comment, although intended to be humorous, was actually quite sobering.

"We just do these things without ever thinking through the whole process," Alice said, echoing Troy's comment. "We must have a good grasp on this part before Monday or we'll …"

"…be hosed!" Bruce and Troy shouted in unison.

"That's right!" Alice said, while laughing at their comment. "Let's get started."

Everyone was now receptive to a little lecture about estimating. I made it clear that while there were different techniques for preparing an estimate, the most important step was to evaluate how certain we are with the result of the estimate.

Starting the discussion, I said, "Maybe the sheer uncertainties for developing estimates for projects leads to the confusion. It's a mess, especially for the novice to try to understand the different types of estimates. It's common to refer to the analogous estimate as a "top down" type estimate. That's wrong.

"When we prepare a detailed estimate, we usually make analogies of similar detailed work. That's where the name *analogous estimate* comes from. We base the parametric estimate on some type of parameter, like dollars per square foot, as a reference point for deriving the costs. The analogous and the parametric processes are actually possible and valid for any type or quality of estimate, from the least accurate Rough Order of Magnitude estimate, to the mid-level quality estimate, called a Budget estimate, or the most accurate Definitive or Control estimate."

While I had their undivided attention, I reviewed the basic steps for putting together an estimating process within the organization. I had to remind them that we were evaluating processes today and not detailing out the project itself. I had to shield them from the human tendency to start producing something immediately, even when things aren't in place.

I returned to the conversation by saying, "There is a lot of attention placed on whether an estimate is top down or bottom up. In addition to the fact that these terms are misleading, the top-down estimate is actually a waste of time. Top-down estimates are inaccurate and often take more time and energy to defend them than it takes to complete a quick bottom-up estimate. The premise of the top-down estimate will get you in trouble every time. The thought is to come up with an estimate at the high level and then figure out the details later. It will usually turn out that later is too late. Often the estimate is inadequate, but still becomes the approved value. Meanwhile when the details are finally obtained, the team is encouraged to *fit* the new estimate into the approved budget."

"And then they're hosed!" Bruce shouted, while everyone else laughed.

"How right you are," I said. "Regardless of the project or the level of detail we have in the planning stage, we need to start at the activity level and prepare the estimate for each line item and then summarize the values upward. "So in effect we estimate what we know," Bruce added.

"Absolutely," I responded. "Whether it's called a bottom-up estimate or sideways estimate, the only thing that matters is that we've prepared an estimate at the level of scope detail that we have at the moment. As the project progresses and the scope is elaborated, the estimate would be enhanced."

Troy was following along with interest, since he was in the process of preparing the first estimate for his new project. To clarify the last point, he asked, "How often do you have to go back and update the completed portion of the estimate? I know that when the scope is elaborated we need to expand the estimate, but I'm trying to get a picture in my mind of what all is being done at each step."

"Actually Troy, the subject that you've surfaced is an area where I differ in my approach from most other professionals. I'm accused of being a little non-standard."

"I think we're all ready for non-standard," Alice said. "We're anxious to hear the process."

Having everyone's attention I began, "For each line item in the Work Breakdown Structure you will have an estimate. As we elaborate the work and define in detail the deliverables depicted in the Work Breakdown Structure, we need to estimate those elements. Depending on the size and duration of the project, you might have to perform this re-estimation process every day. It is important that the project not get ahead of you.

"As far as the maintenance of the Project Management Information System, it would be useful to perform a cost and schedule forecast for each line item weekly, or as often as something changes."

Before I could move on to the next step, Bruce interrupted, "What do you mean by forecast? Moreover, what happened to doing the estimates? We have prepared several forecasts over the course of the project, but they were very cumbersome and time consuming. I can't imagine doing those forecasts weekly."

"I agree with Bruce's point," Alice said. "In addition to the complete project re-forecasts that Bruce referred to, we expected that a forecast was provided to the executive committee at our meeting each month. The team spent a lot of time preparing those, and, as we've discovered, they weren't very accurate."

"I agree with both of your concerns," I responded. "The entire process of re-forecasting becomes increasingly more difficult as time between forecasts increases. The longer you wait, the more difficult the job becomes. The best approach is to do forecasts daily."

"Whoa!" Bruce exclaimed. "If you wanted a reaction with that last comment, you got one. There is no way that I could ever agree to do a forecast every day. That's impossible. In fact, that's all we would be doing."

Recognizing the need to corral Bruce before he got too excited, Troy moved to get control of the discussion. "Maybe we should hear about the details before we judge this recommendation. I don't agree either, but I think there is something I'm missing or haven't thought of, so I'd like to be patient for a few minutes."

With Troy's introduction, I began to describe the details. "Daily forecasting is actually pretty easy. If we think back to the details of the Work Breakdown Structure and the lowest level activity or work package, remember that you assigned a team member to each of these elements. The daily forecast consists of nothing more than directing those responsible for each line item to report back daily as to the individual forecast.

"If the activity hasn't started yet, and nothing is changed, the forecast for that item is nothing more than the previous forecast or original estimate. If an activity is completed, then the forecast is the actual performance, which shouldn't take much time to figure out. The only effort is when an activity is in progress. In this case, the person responsible should be paying attention to what's going on with the work and should be in a good position to validate the original estimate or provide a new forecast."

"That's not so bad when you describe it that way," Troy said. "If everyone does their part, then we will have the effect of a complete project forecast…every day."

"Exactly," I responded, while noticing positive expressions from Bruce and Alice, as well. "Forecasts are easy if you do them every day. Realistically, the effort should only take fifteen - thirty minutes a day…maximum."

Alice, totally caught up in the discussion, now commented, "This is fantastic. In fact, when you look at the way you presented it, we would in fact be doing an estimate every day. That is such a change in the way I've always perceived estimates. At any point in the project, the forecast is actually our latest estimate."

"A forecast is an estimate," Troy repeated. "That is so bizarre. I don't mean to sound so out of touch, but I've never thought of a forecast as an estimate. If we go this way, it means that we would only prepare one estimate or should I say, one formal estimate for any project. We would do the original estimate, and then any changes or elaborations would actually be linked to the forecast."

"That's not all," Alice said, interrupting again. "When you look at estimates as we're describing them now, there would be no such thing as an analogous estimate or parametric estimate for a project in total. The project's estimate would consist of a combination of many levels of detail and accuracy. In fact, even to the very end, some of the elements of the project would still have summary level estimates. The amount of detail and effort we expended on the forecasts would be proportional to the significance of the item itself. And who better to know that than the person doing the work?"

"Taking your comments one step further, if for each forecast or estimate, the person doing the work and estimate assigned a quality or reliability value, let's say from one to ten, or from A to F, then it would be possible to collect the value of each of the estimate categories. It would be simple then to report the percentage of project values based on reliable forecasts and the value of those with rough forecasts.

"Remember, knowledge must be in the hands of the project manager if they are to be successful. This process provides that knowledge."

"The beauty of the process is that the person doing the work is the one that's providing the information," Troy added. "That fact in itself makes the process more credible and, at the same time, drives the responsibility to the proper level of the organization. Too many times Alice and I had to prepare the monthly forecasts because the project team members were too busy. If the forecasts are done daily, it's really impossible to get very far behind in the process."

"That's a clever way to avoid the OS Phase," Bruce said, smiling. "It's amazing that we hadn't thought of this before."

"That's because you're special," Alice responded.

"It's about time you realized that," Bruce quipped back. "But all of this discussion brings up another problem. One of the problems we have is the wide disparity of skill between the different resources supporting the project. Is there a way we can use this same process to deal with this skill disparity? Personally, I think it makes a big difference on our estimates, or maybe I should say forecasts."

Although it was my question to answer, Alice was quick to respond with her suggestion. "Maybe we should have a skills matrix and identify each resource and the information technology or other skills they possess."

"That's not enough," Bruce snapped back. "In fact, that's the problem. We know what everyone can do; it's just that some are better than others. I've felt uncomfortable with grading each team member from one to ten. Although I think about it when a 'four' related performer is assigned to a critical task."

Joining into this conversation, Troy presented an excellent suggestion. "Why not provide each skill area with a distinction consistent with how we often grade others, those being novice, journeyman, or expert. That way, you could apply costs or effort expected by each and you might even encourage those with the lower designations to expand their skills and move upward. I don't think there is any way to lose with this option."

Everyone seemed to feel comfortable with Troy's suggestion but turned to me for my comment.

Responding to their silent request, I said, "Even if you consider the different skill levels, the estimate should reflect what you, or should I say the team members, think the forecast will be. No two humans are identical in their ability to do work, so we need to quit trying to be perfect. We must remember that an estimate is just an estimate.

"A forecast, if it's our estimate, is just a forecast. Some will be right on the mark and others will be considerably higher or lower than expected. If we forecast on a routine basis we will know how we are doing. Moreover, the person doing the work, whether a fast worker or a slow one, will be the one providing the forecast information. You will have to be mature and accept the forecast.

"Remember, everything you are doing is supposed to be another step closer to finishing the project successfully and having the confidence that you are doing something positive to avoid the OS Phase."

---

**OS Phase Avoidance**
**STRATEGY 19**

*Estimate frequently, every day if necessary, and make estimates an integral part of your forecasts.*
*Repeat the following aloud:*
*"An estimate is just an estimate."*
*Say it again. "An estimate is just an estimate."*

---

"Thanks, that's a great way to close out this discussion," Alice said. This area has bothered me more than anything else. I feel very comfortable with where we're going on this now. With this wisdom I think it's time to move on to the next area."

## CHAPTER 20
## Managing Behavior — Someone Has to Do It!

When you ask professionals about project management, responders describe it as a relatively simple, commonsense ***process***, something that we all have done for years. Memories are positively spun. We are encouraged to be optimists—we are "the glass is half full" kind of people.

In other, non-project management related businesses, advertisers direct motivational messages constantly at us in an attempt to form or change our buying or consumer behavior. Advertisers spend millions of dollars to "reach us." However, if they are going to be successful, they first have to "understand us." That's where behavior becomes part of the equation for them as it does for the project manager.

To modify behavior in the work place, managers are trained to be motivators, but this training doesn't always work, especially if the project manager doesn't understand the team members. A message from any manager that doesn't understand the personal dynamics of those they're speaking to may not come across as sincere or credible or both. Poor communication techniques will most often backfire.

Hype and cheerleading are not a sound form of motivation for the long haul.

Maybe I'm alone in my distaste for hearing worn out clichés like:

*"You need to hit the ground running!"*
*"We need a team that will step up to the challenge!"*
*"We are looking for team players that aren't afraid to be aggressive!"*

If you want to inspire a football team at half time, some yelling and hype might work, but you're looking at something that will be with the players for only an hour or so and only if some major breaks go in the team's direction. Projects are much longer and team members often resent off-the-wall motivation techniques and might even laugh behind the backs of those that try them.

Don't misunderstand the message here. Motivation efforts are important. Understanding the complete behavior picture, however, is the real key to a project manager's success.

Remember, project management is all about dealing with people. It's time we stop and recognize that fact and what we should do to leverage this valuable resource if we want to avoid the *OS Phase*!

As we look at the many roles of the project manager, it is important that we keep our messages credible and we have to be careful that we don't become "the glass is half-fool" kind of folk!

With the group's attention, I hit them again with my favorite question. "What percentage of project management involves dealing with people?"

"You've asked that question so many times, that if we answer incorrectly, you'll probably give up on helping us." Bruce responded.

With the expected chuckles from everyone, Bruce continued. "Based on what I've experienced on the Mountain Adventure project, it seemed like close to 140 percent, but I think you told us that it was around 98 percent."

Smiling back at Bruce, I answered affirmatively. "Even though I've referred to the 98 percent value a lot, I don't believe there is an exact answer. Clearly, it would vary from project to project. As far as our discussion today, I've asked the question several times to put everyone in the right frame of mind. Today we need to recognize the importance of the human side of any project. Too many times we get so focused on tools, like software, that we forget that it will take humans to operate the tools and actually implement the processes."

"That's right," Alice added. "When you sit back and think about all of the processes involved with a project, it's easy to forget that each one has humans involved at some point. Even when a process uses machines or computers, don't forget that humans designed these machines and computers. Humans also maintain them. Humans get involved with everything at one time or another."

"A project manager that discounts the significance of humans and their behavior will quickly lose any ability to successfully manage their project," I said, with an apparent agreement from everyone.

"If I had a nickel for each time someone did something that didn't make sense around here, I wouldn't have to play the lottery anymore. I'd be wealthy already," Bruce said, slapping a high-five with Troy.

"I can't believe you have time to buy lottery tickets," Alice interjected.

"Bruce, I agree with your comment about the unpredictability of your team members," Troy added. "But every time I'm surprised by what people do around here, I watch one of those reality shows on television and sit in amazement at some of the stupid things those contestants do each week. Let's face it; the employees of our company are quite normal compared to the fools that show up on television to do those shows."

"I agree," Alice joined in. "How could any of these contestants possibly do what they do? What causes humans to behave the way they do?"

"That's why they call it entertainment," Bruce added. "My favorite show, whenever I have time to watch television is "The Apprentice." On that show, each season or competition ends with a final task for the last two contestants to plan a major charitable event. The editing of the show always focuses on one or more critical decisions made by the winner. The decision most often relates to the team member they chose to help them in the end or with team members they were assigned.

"Now that I think about it, the final test for the apprentices is not as much about completing a task as it is to study the ability to manage difficult situations with team members that sometimes had previously been adversaries. The final task is all about understanding and managing behavior. The apprentice candidate that manages behavior the best usually wins."

"Our own team members are starting to sound more normal every minute," Alice said in a light-hearted tone. "I know we're straying from our problems on the Mountain Adventure project, but I'm intrigued with those daytime talk shows with the live audiences. Some of the themes of the shows are depressing. How can people be so dysfunctional? I actually worry that I'll see someone I know on those shows."

"Please don't tell me you watch those shows," Bruce answered.

Even without dwelling on the details, everyone was able to see the humor in Bruce's comment.

The group's discussion, which had moved from important discussions of the Mountain Adventure Project's problems, was also a sign of behavior. It was easier at this time for them to talk about things they knew than to talk about Monday's agenda, which still had a lot of uncertainty.

As the time was getting closer to Monday's meeting, the group was experiencing a mixture of reality and giddiness. Ironically, this is one of the interesting aspects of behavior, trying to figure out how any team will react in a given situation.

Even though it would be difficult to get everyone's focus again, I wanted to make sure that they really appreciated the difficulties with understanding and managing behavior.

"Let's bring this discussion back to your project," I suggested, while turning to Bruce. "First, let's talk about the performance reporting concerns that we addressed earlier.

"Alice, if I remember correctly, you couldn't understand why Bruce had embellished the monthly reports."

"That's right," she responded.

"Without just picking on Bruce, why does anyone embellish performance when they report about their project or anything they are working on?" I asked. "Why do so many people feel the need to exaggerate status reporting?"

"I would think that there are many reasons why it could happen," Troy commented. "We would all hope that the embellishment wasn't done to cover up anything, but instead was just a poor attempt at optimism. The reality is that behavior is specific to the individuals and the situations."

With a distinct silence in the room, I said, "I think everyone's in agreement with that conclusion. Human behavior and how people react to even the simplest of events will always be puzzling. To demonstrate, let me ask a few simple questions.

"When you actually sit down and think about it, why do we start projects before we even have a clue about the scope?

"Why do we agree to objectives that we know at the start are impossible to meet? Or said another way, why do we agree to start a project with an unbalanced Stupid Triangle?

"Why do we select team members that are wrong for the proposed positions? Is it friendship or stupidity?

"Why do we proceed on projects without even the slightest commitment or understanding of roles and responsibilities?

"Why would anyone start a project without an understanding of the risks?

"Why does anybody do anything they do?"

"Maybe that's the real question," Alice said in response.

"I hear what you're saying, but trying to answer that would be impossible," Troy commented. "That's the behavior piece of the formula. Understanding why people do what they do isn't possible unless you are the person or have a chance to ask them. But until you walk in someone else's shoes, it's hard to really know why anyone does anything."

As he turned to look at all of us in the room, Bruce asked, "So what do we do about behavior?"

Silence took over the group for one of the first times.

"Maybe the most important aspect of behavior we have to understand is that we will never understand it…every time," Alice said, breaking the silence.

Alice's response was accurate, but nonetheless unsettling to the others. Bruce turned to me with a questioning look. He waited for my response without even offering a word.

"Actually, I'm disappointed that our discussion today hasn't helped to answer that question," I replied. "What tools have we discussed that would help to manage behavior?"

Realizing the significance of this question, Alice moved the flip chart and began to write down some tools she thought might work. Simultaneously, Bruce and Troy were calling out additional tools to her faster than she could write with her marker.

Standing back and reflecting after the chart was full (Chart 20 – 1), she said, "We've reviewed each of these tools with respect to how they help to manage the work, but it never occurred to me at the time that these are really being used to support the behavioral aspects of the team members themselves.

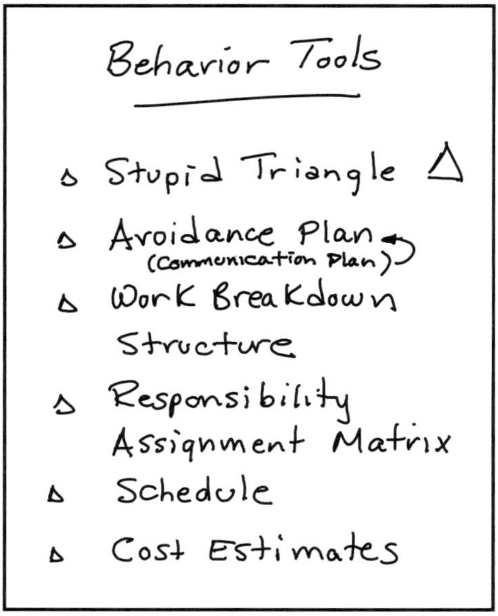

Adding his comments, Troy said, "Absolutely. The Stupid Triangle and Work Breakdown Structure all help to clarify scope. If everyone on the team is confident that scope is being managed, then it will take a lot of pressure off the team as they proceed. Actually, the important part is having some type of process. Without process, humans tend to wander aimlessly and become anxious or agitated."

**Behavior Tools**

- Stupid Triangle △
- Avoidance Plan (Communication Plan)
- Work Breakdown Structure
- Responsibility Assignment Matrix
- Schedule
- Cost Estimates

**Chart 20 - 1**

"I know all about wondering aimlessly," Bruce interjected sarcastically.

Before we went any further I wanted to point out a problem with the list. "I think you left something off the list. In fact, I think it might be the most important tool."

"Risk!" Bruce shouted. "We forgot risk. That's the magical process intended to put everyone at ease. Risk is the ultimate behavioral management tool."

"Perfect," I responded. As we've discussed today, when we don't manage risk our worry level increases every day. Keeping an eye on risks will help everyone sleep at night."

"Well, I don't know if it's that good," Alice said with a smile. "But it should help."

"Excellent," I said excitedly. "We need to always remember the importance of communication, and having clear roles for everyone associated with the project."

"You haven't mentioned motivation. It would seem that it would be an important part of behavior. Where does motivation fit into the picture?" Troy asked.

"I agree," Bruce added. "You've made fun of *raising the bar* and other slogans, but does that mean we shouldn't do any cheerleading at all?"

With everyone looking at me, I addressed his question. "Motivational messages say one of two things about the person screaming the message. Either they really believe that the team can accomplish what they are shouting about, or they're shouting about it because they don't know what else to do. Can anyone think of a time when motivation is proper?"

"I can think of one I do," Troy said. "Everyday we motivate our children to take their first steps or when they get older we motivate them to do better in school because we know they can do it. Part of being a parent is motivating your children to do the right things in life."

"Excellent example," Alice interjected. "That's an example we all can relate to. In fact, I can see where that type of motivation would also be applicable to our employees or team members."

"That's right," Bruce said excitedly. "It's absolutely the right thing to do to motivate our children or teammates, but we would never try to motivate them to do something that would harm them or try to motivate them to attempt something that was not possible. It would be wrong to attempt motivation in either case. In fact, there could be situations where it would be cruel or dangerous."

"That's a great way to look at it," Alice responded. "The irony of the *raise the bar* slogan is that in sports we raise the bar until the athlete eventually fails. I'm still not sure if that's the message we want to use to motivate everyone."

"I'm glad we went over the other avoidance tools before we discussed behavior," Bruce commented. "Even though we've spent time discussing it, I'm not sure if there really is a magic tool to help the project manager deal with behavior issues."

"I agree with Bruce," Troy added. "How do we ever know what to do?"

It was obvious that everyone was still puzzled about behavior. Even with my knowledge of behavioral theories and practices, it's still difficult to know where to start. It was time to give them an example that would help to set a direction.

"Without giving you the perfect answer that you're all expecting, I think it would be appropriate to tell you a very appropriate story where someone actually figured out on their own the secret to this important area."

With everyone's attention, I began. "Several years ago I was working with a client where we had put several groups of project managers through a program to sharpen their overall project management skills. As we were getting ready to start the third session, one of the graduates from the earlier sessions dropped in to help introduce the program. His name was John and as project manager, he was responsible for completion of an internally developed resource management software program. It was an extraordinarily large project involving seven different government agencies and it was still completed successfully.

"When he walked into the session I asked him to describe the most valuable aspect of the program he completed earlier in the year. In retrospect, this was a very risky request on my part because he might have felt uncomfortable or put on the spot. Actually, though, John did not let me down.

"Without any hesitation in his voice, he stood before the group and said that the most important thing he learned was the part about being able to play golf after the scope and roles were in place for the project."

Alice interrupted my story as she abruptly responded to my comment. "You can't be serious. Is that what he said? I think you're playing us as part of the behavioral example."

"I agree," Troy added. "I thought the whole concept of having time to play golf was just a joke."

"Wait a minute. I thought it was a good idea so I've already ordered a new set of clubs," Bruce said, trying purposely to break the seriousness of Alice's comment.

After everyone settled down, I continued, "Yes, he spoke about golf, but you didn't let me finish with the rest of his comments.

"He went on to tell the group that day how important it is to be in a position to play golf. This meant that it was vital to relentlessly get the scope under control and get the roles defined. But he then went on to say that instead of having time to play golf, it gave him the time to deal with all of the employee behavior issues that popped up every day.

"It seemed to him that behavioral issues multiplied exponentially as the team got larger. He said that he could never predict what would happen each day, but he knew that some type of people issue would surface. He was pleased that he had the time to deal with behavior, instead of having to deal with people problems after they already occurred and had influenced the project."

"I'm sorry I interrupted you earlier," Alice said. "This whole idea of playing golf just is so contrary to how I envision a project manager's role, I reacted too fast to the comment."

"That's okay. I expected that you might say that, considering the behavior you've demonstrated since I met you."

Everyone laughed with the analogy to behavior, but even with the light-hearted nature of the comment, it was accurate.

Finishing with my earlier thoughts, I said, "Never criticize a project manager when they have some free time because they're doing everything right. Don't load them down with more projects. The project manager needs that time to deal with the daily behavioral issues that surface on the project they're working on."

"Do these behavioral problems ever get under control?" Bruce asked. "Will I ever be able to play golf?"

Troy jumped in to answer Bruce's question. "I know the question wasn't directed to me, but even if the team members' behavioral issues settled down, I can't imagine a day on a project where they ever really disappear for the customer or our regulators."

"Yeah," Bruce added, "they're always acting weird and you can never figure them out."

"That's except for you Alice," Troy added jokingly. "Bruce forgot to mention that little comment."

Bringing this particular discussion to a closing point, I said, "The important strategy for managing behavior is having the time for managing behavior. If you're always in a rush, you will begin ignoring that very important project component.

"What we have to do is actually think through our options, select a strategy, and then follow through," I said, while moving again to the flip chart. "Members of your project must know their roles and responsibilities for everything you expect them to perform. So what tool will we use to support that process?"

Standing and moving towards the Avoidance Model sheet hanging on the wall (Chart 20 - 2), Troy said, "The Responsibility Assignment Matrix is our tool for understanding roles. And if there is a problem with that process, then we must consider the addition of a risk."

"Excellent," Alice exclaimed. "The Avoidance Model is really a great technique for handling everything, including behavior."

"The model itself isn't a tool," Troy added, "but it gets the process in your mind and once it's there, it will create the thought process we need to implement the right solution. The Avoidance Model is the most important thing I've learned so far."

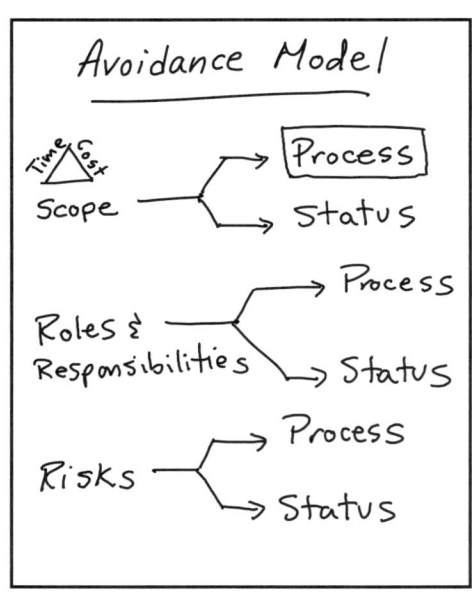

**Chart 20 - 2**

"Behavioral concerns can be overwhelming if we let them," Alice said, while acknowledging Troy's comments with a reassuring nod. "We must have a venting process that allows us to identify a concern and then follow through as we manage the identified risks.

"Behavior is a difficult task for any project manager to have to deal with. Every human is different. Humans associated in any way with the team bring different strengths and weaknesses with them. It is up to the project manager to figure out how they will deal with any behavioral problems as they occur."

"You're right," I responded. "Behavior is a broad area. As far as pinpointing behavior targets on this project, we actually need to cover other concerns first. But do remember that 98 percent of project management is not what we normally think; it's dealing with people. When we lose sight of behavioral trends, we lose control of any project."

> *OS Phase* **Avoidance**
> **STRATEGY 20**
>
> *Failure to recognize and deal with behavioral issues will eventually eat away at the project and provide fuel to get the project to the OS Phase quicker.*
>
> *Project managers must make time for handling behavioral issues with members of the project team and with any support staff.*

# CHAPTER 21
# In Search of the Perfect Project Manager

From birth, setting expectations is part of our life. Our parents had expectations of us as we transcended from childhood to adolescence. When we became young adults, our parents and family had additional expectations. Expectations follow us forever. We now have expectations for our children and, in turn, they have expectations of us. Wow!

As complex as life might be, it is somewhat simplified when we know and, more importantly, understand the extent of these expectations.

Taken as a view from anyone's perspective, there is an abundance of expectations. As employees of a company, our superiors have expectations, our subordinates have expectations of us, our peers have expectations, and, as in the case of our personal lives, we have expectations of all of these folks.

When our role is significant, the size and importance of these expectations is increased. For instance, as the president of any country might expect, meeting the expectations of the citizens is paramount. Unfortunately, as many politicians realize, it is very difficult to keep everyone happy. For a project manager, meeting expectations is the most significant element of their job.

Failure to meet even one person's expectations could result in hitting the *OS Phase*.

We've described the attributes of the *OS Phase*. We've introduced the *stuff* that makes up any project. Now we need to look at the personal attributes of the project manager, the person accountable for getting the job done.

Anyone has the capability to be a great project manager. First, though, they must understand what the expectations are and how to achieve them.

# IN SEARCH OF THE PERFECT PROJECT MANAGER

"After all that we've gone through today, I'm not sure if I understand what we could have done differently," Troy commented.

"Is there such a thing as a perfect project manager?" Bruce asked.

"To find the perfect project manager most people would think they only need a mirror. After all, a characteristic of a good project manager is someone that is confident and self-assured," I quipped.

"You've only known us for a short time. Can you tell from our conversations whether or not any of us would be a good project manager?" Troy asked.

"What do you think, Alice? Do you think Bruce and Troy have what it takes? How about you, Alice, do you have what it takes to be a good project manager?"

"Forget about Troy," Alice exclaimed. "We both know he couldn't manage getting us out of town on time, so why would we even think he has any project manager attributes? So let's forget Troy.

"Do you think I have what it takes to be a project manager?"

With sincerity in my voice, I responded, "If personality and eagerness to learn are any part of it, then all three of you would be the best project managers in the world. Unfortunately, personality and eagerness are only part of what it takes."

With their complete attention again, I thought it would be good to complete an important task before we closed shop. Standing in front of the group and using a strong and challenging tone in my voice, I directed them to complete just one more task. "Now that we're talking about perfect project managers and such, we have thirty minutes before we need to break up this afternoon and head off to Dallas. So each of you need to write down what you think the attributes are for a perfect project manager. When all three of you are done we can compare notes and see what we come up with."

It was fun watching them all ponder the question. I wasn't sure what we would end up with, but with the speed of their hands across their tablets it would seem that the list would be extensive.

After exhausting the ten minutes, I took each of their lists and combined them on some flip chart sheets at the front of the room (Chart 21 – 1 and 2).

| Attributes of PM | Attributes of PM |
|---|---|
| ⚬ Communicator | ⚬ Mentor  ⚬ Flexible |
| ⚬ Ego-less | ⚬ Resourceful  ⚬ Patient |
| ⚬ Driven  ⚬ Leader | ⚬ Customer focused |
| ⚬ Negotiator | ⚬ Takes ownership |
| ⚬ Team oriented | ⚬ Good coach  ⚬ Likeable |
| ⚬ Competent | ⚬ Takes charge  ⚬ Respected |
| ⚬ Competitive/tough | ⚬ Attention to detail |
| ⚬ Organized | ⚬ Non-judgmental |
| ⚬ People person | ⚬ Uses common sense |
| ⚬ Sense of humor |  |
| **Chart 21 - 1** | **Chart 21 - 2** |

Alice was smiling as she looked at the list. "Now that's a lot of attributes. Is it possible that anyone really has all of these characteristics?"

"Hand me a mirror," Bruce demanded and then led a chorus of laughter at this remark.

After the laughter slowed down, Troy asked a well-targeted question about the list. "Bruce aside, the rest of us would benefit from knowing which of these attributes is the most important? If we can't meet every one, we at least need to understand which attributes are important for our current role so we could perform a personal inventory."

"There's no doubt about it. You all hit every possible attribute for a project manager, well, almost every attribute," I spoke in a praising tone.

"What do you mean 'almost every attribute'?" Alice questioned. "I can barely visualize how anyone could even make it through a day on a project if they had to think about managing even half of those attributes."

Responding, I said, "I'd love to answer your question, but as scary as it may sound, the list isn't complete. From my perspective, it's missing some very important traits. Moreover, these missing traits are so important that I wouldn't even consider assigning any project to a person without them.

"For years I've talked about attributes of project managers in the same sentence as looking at the weather. In other words, it didn't bear a lot of relevance. To say that I took it for granted is an understatement. In any training session or seminar, we might discuss attributes, but most often we brainstormed a list, wrote them on a flip chart, and then went on to another *more important* subject. In practice, I don't think I ever thought about a project manager's traits when assigning or working with anyone on a project.

"This all changed several years ago when I was conducting a week-long training engagement at an off-site retreat location. We had a large group of project managers for five days of intensive project management concepts and tools.

"As part of the training and workshops, the manager of the organization, my customer, spoke to me privately and requested that an evaluation be performed at the end of the week. This would include an assessment by me of each of the project managers."

"Whoa…wait a minute!" Alice shouted. "Don't even try to suggest that you have the insight to measure a project manager's worth just from a class or workshop."

"It's great to see you were listening to the story, because you're right. It is impossible, not to mention inappropriate, for someone to make that type of assessment. In fact, the real problem is that someone could believe this was even possible."

"I hope you told your customer that you couldn't do the assessment," Bruce said emphatically.

Smiling, I continued with the story. "Without question, I agree with both of your concerns. We can all agree that working with his team of project managers over the course of five days would not provide adequate insight into personalities and capabilities of the class members. In fact, any evaluation on my part would have been rather shallow and unfounded. The bottom line, there was no way I could agree to do this evaluation."

"So you told him no, right?" Bruce asked again.

Avoiding Bruce's question, I continued. "I should have said no immediately, but an adverse reaction on my part at this time would have disrupted the overall purpose of the class. I felt that the customer asked for the evaluation only because he was uncertain on how best to do it himself. So I thought that I could include some type of evaluation process into the seminar material and it would all work out.

"In retrospect, I think I was floored by the request and really didn't know what to say. The biggest problem for me was that the customer was adding *scope*, and as a principle before I said no, it was important to figure out what the options were.

"Unfortunately, the more I thought about the customer's request, the more I realized that he was looking for a tool or technique that any project management seminar should indeed address. If I was going to give him and his team a quality program, it was essential that I provide this information.

"After evaluating the Stupid Triangle from the perspective of the class, I decided that it would be beneficial to develop some evaluation criteria and I could use my spare time in the evening to do it. It was scope creep, but it was something that I felt I could take away from the seminar, so it made sense to go ahead.

"At the moment as I was dealing with the request, I genuinely felt that satisfying the customer was extremely important and therefore decided that some type of evaluation, maybe of the entire group, would be possible, so I agreed to give it a shot."

"It's hard to imagine what other choice you might have had at that point," Troy added. "I'm not sure where you would start, but it sounds like the customer needed some help and you were conveniently close by."

"That's exactly how I looked at it. In order to evaluate the project managers, I needed a baseline of attributes as a basis to measure against. At first blush, this seemed easy. Develop a list of traits and then use that list to evaluate the project managers. All I needed was the list. I began to reflect from personal experiences and then researched recent literature to develop a list. This task was not that difficult. It seemed that every book I reviewed and every list I found included a similar set of traits. The order of importance was often different, but the items weren't."

"How close was the list to what we came up with on our flip charts?" Alice asked.

# IN SEARCH OF THE PERFECT PROJECT MANAGER 219

"The list was almost identical. But that was a problem. I reflected each evening over the list and then started to consider these traits versus what I had seen from the project managers. Unfortunately, the more I stared at the list, the more the list started to look too basic, almost like standard equipment on a car. I was discouraged.

"Desiring a project manager to be a good communicator is the same as wanting an engine for our car that will run or seats that are comfortable. As consumers, we have grown to expect certain standard components on a car. Likewise, we expect certain basic traits for project managers.

"Something was missing from the list. It seemed that the list was just that, a list. As I started to reflect on what was missing, I organized my thoughts in quite a backwards manner. I thought about the traits of project managers that annoyed me or made me feel uncomfortable, and then I would flip the item around and take the opposite trait as a positive attribute. This reverse thinking is common in decision making methodologies and actually made the process much easier.

"When I began to think about traits that were frustrating, I immediately thought about those project managers or executives that make processes so complicated that no one understands any of them. They could actually be a good communicator, as most often they are.

"They were organized and driven and they incorporated all of the standard project management processes that we wanted, but they were too complicated in their approach.

"They weren't simple!

"Wow! I found the first important special trait. In my experience, I was much more comfortable and had much more confidence in project managers that kept processes simple. How often do we think of the KISS (Keep It

Chart 21 - 3

Simple Stupid) principle when we are listening to a project manager drone on about their project or plans?"

As everyone was anticipating the next trait, I approached the flip chart and began to list the attributes (Chart 21 - 3).

Alice was uncharacteristically speechless. She was making many mental notes about the process, and then commented, "That technique was almost too easy. All you had to do to find good traits was to think about those you didn't want. I can't wait to try that out the next time I'm in the same situation."

"What was the next trait?" Troy questioned.

"The next trait came to me rather easily. I started to think again about traits or personality features that I didn't like and there it was, credible! Too many times I have worked with project managers that were not trustworthy. It was almost impossible to be certain whether or not they were being honest in their assessment of the project or whether they were just saying what they thought we wanted to hear.

"It is difficult to work with a project manager or trust in a project manager that plays games or even appears to be less than honest in their actions. Maybe it is wishful thinking, but I want to believe that there are a lot of credible folks out there and I want those credible people working on my projects (Chart 21 - 4)."

Alice was nodding rapidly in a positive manner and then responded. "Credibility is something we take for granted, but after today it has a new meaning to me and I'm sure Troy feels the same way. It hurt us both to know that we were so gullible to think that the project was in great shape last month. It's embarrassing when you realize that someone played you as a fool."

Bruce brought us all back to reality. "I know that I need to

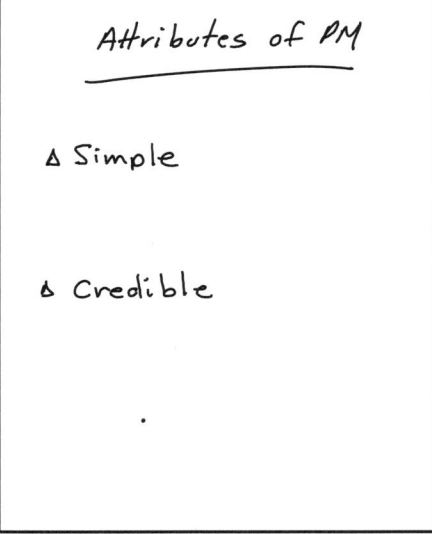

**Chart 21 - 4**

# IN SEARCH OF THE PERFECT PROJECT MANAGER

evaluate my own performance since I began working on this project. It would be great to have faith in everyone all of the time, but history tells us that there are many out there that are not considerate of how their embellishments will impact others."

"That's right!" Alice added. "We have too many things to think about without worrying whether or not our project manager and team are feeding us erroneous project performance information."

Bringing the conversation back to the list, I got everybody's attention again. "Well, it's time to consider the final attribute, which, by the way, is my favorite.

"Again, I thought about those things that annoyed me or made me nervous when I worked with a project manager.

"The last trait, predictive, derives from the knot I often get in my gut when I realize that a project manager has no clue where the project is going and is only looking at what has happened or what the team has accomplished (Chart 21 - 5).

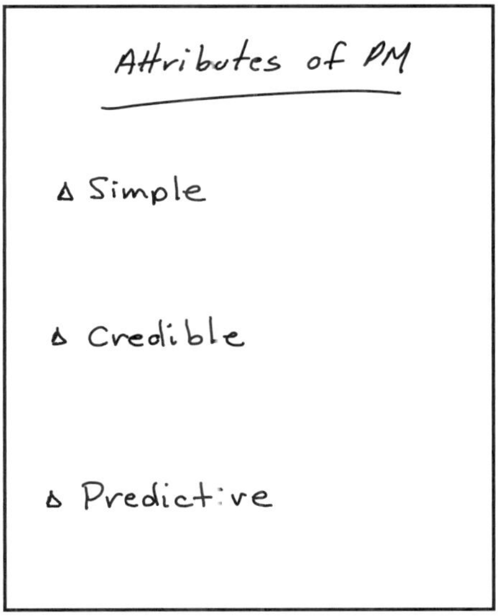

"We use numerous clichés to describe the word predictive. We say that we want someone to be proactive and not reactive. We want forward lookers. We want big picture project managers. Let's make it easy and just say we want someone who is predictive, someone who is looking ahead.

"We know what we've done on the project, we know where we are, but does anybody have a clue where we're headed? Without that information, we are, in effect, traveling blind."

"Not entirely," Alice commented. "It would seem that the project could be headed towards the OS Phase."

"You're absolutely right, Alice," Troy added. "Whenever a project manager understands the concept of the OS Phase, that recognition alone could change how they view their role."

**Attributes of PM**

△ Simple

△ Credible

△ Predictive

**Chart 21 - 5**

Just as everyone was motivated to pursue the traits of a project manager in more detail, Bruce brought us all back to reality. "We've covered a lot of ground this morning, but unless I'm mistaken, we're going to have to leave for the airport soon if we are going to catch our flight to Dallas."

Interrupting, Troy asked, "You almost got away without telling us if you evaluated those project managers at the end of the retreat."

"Good catch," Alice exclaimed. "I would have thought about that story a week from now and realized that we never heard the end. Tell us, what did you do?"

"Well, let me say that it all worked out. I used the same discussion as we just had, but I didn't use the same introduction of how I derived the three attributes of a project manager. When I was finished with the discussion in the group, we took a break shortly afterwards. As I approached my customer, he said something that was very pleasing to my ears. He asked me if I was going to evaluate his team. I told him no. He smiled and said, 'but you've given me the tools I need to do the evaluation.' I smiled affirmatively and the retreat ended up on a good note.

"Speaking of happy endings, we need to get going."

Still excited about the discussion, Troy started to take down the flip charts hanging on the wall. As he was rolling them up together, he made a suggestion. "Maybe we could sit together and work some of this out during our flight."

I took at least one second to respond to the suggestion. "Great in principle, Troy, but poor for those sitting around us that would prefer having some quiet time during the flight. When we get to Dallas, you three can wrap up the discussion at your office, or off site if you are worried about who else might be in the office over the weekend. At a minimum, you need to have a draft of your Avoidance Plan with the supporting Avoidance Model Processes outlined. I would suggest that you prepare and present a simple PowerPoint presentation as a springboard into any detailed discussions. Be careful not to put too much detail on the slides."

"I don't expect that we will have many details by Monday!" Bruce added, as everyone laughed nervously. "But we will consolidate everything we've talked about today."

"Sounds like a plan," I said, while gathering up my notes and arranging them in my briefcase. "My hotel arrangements are already in place at the Meridian in downtown Dallas, so after you work out the details for the presentation, you can call me at the hotel if you want me to review anything before Monday morning. When you call, let me know if you want me to attend or participate in the meeting. Monday and Tuesday are open on my calendar so I would be willing to formalize our consulting relationship and help you follow through with the next critical steps. But to follow Troy's advice, we need to get a move on to the airport. Traffic to O'Hare on Saturday is sometimes worse than during the week!"

"Sounds like a plan," said Alice, as Troy and Bruce nodded affirmatively.

---

***OS Phase* Avoidance**
**STRATEGY 21**

*Take the time to be predictive every day. It is important to evaluate your routine activities and determine how many are predictive in nature.*

*Remember, if you're not looking ahead to where the project is headed, who is?*

# A World Without the OS Phase

# Chapter 22
# Understanding the Processes
# of Project Management

It is now the perfect time to reiterate a point made earlier about *processes*. Projects don't fail, *processes* fail!

The blame game commonly narrows in on a specific project and its participants after it hits the **OS Phase**. The correct response would be to examine the processes that failed. Projects are unique and we may never repeat a project even close to the one we're working on today, but the processes used to support the project will be used over and over again.

The group of processes that make up a company's or organization's way of doing business is referred to as the Management Control System. This system can be informal manual systems for small developing companies or extraordinarily complex computerized models for large corporations. Subsets of the Management Control System include groups of processes or modules for handling specific interest areas such as those that support project management, referred to as the Project Management Information System or PMIS.

The strong interest in project management is heartwarming, but in many companies, the big investments in their sophisticated computerized PMIS hit the wrong target. What's needed is a straightforward PMIS that supports a likewise simple Management Control System set of processes.

We need to have processes in place that provide accurate and timely information about each project to the executive leaders. Project managers in turn, need data management tools in order to spend more time focusing on the project and less time on finding and exercising the data.

Before you become awe struck with the fancy artwork and professional looking management reports, make sure your PMIS has a sound process for managing *scope* and for linking the "complete" project *scope* with the related time and cost. Remember, *scope* management processes will drive the entire project.

The corporate organizations that figure this out and make it work will take major leaps over their competitors in their respective business sectors.

Monday morning arrived with the normal fanfare of an unscheduled executive committee meeting. The air in the room was not moving. The lack of smiling faces from the meeting initiators created suspicion and tenseness. After the usual pleasantries and greetings, everyone took a place around a large oval conference table. Along with the air of uncertainty in the room, the reason for my presence wasn't clear to those on the committee. I was pleasant but to avoid attention, I positioned myself in an inconspicuous location. I could offer support and encouragement, but Alice, Troy, and Bruce were the ones that had to believe in their proposal.

Alice had asked me to attend the meeting to add moral support. I agreed to the request, but I made it clear that their journey after the meeting had to be on their own. My engagement starting on Wednesday was not subject to change.

Alice took a position near the large, white, ceiling-mounted projection screen and began the presentation.

As the project management office director for the Mountain Adventure Corporation and a member of the executive committee, she will be the person responsible for providing details of the bad news to the others at the table.

The executive committee consisted of the seven senior managers of the company. All but Raj, the chief financial officer, were part of the original brain trust that came up with the mountain adventures concept. Raj joined the team when it became apparent that they needed someone with Wall Street experience in financing to coordinate that vital element for the company. Considered by many on the Street as the best at getting investors to join in on new ventures, Raj had gained his experience working in various Wall Street start-up organizations.

He joined the Mountain Adventure Corporation so he could take a break from the unending rigor he experienced on Manhattan Island.

At this time, these seven individuals owned equal shares of the company. Raj earned his share by obtaining generous venture capital financing without forcing them to enter the market as a traded company.

Edward is the information systems director. His team is responsible for the web-based applications and any other infrastructure computer systems. These web-based applications start with the customers and then tie to the supply chain processes. Edward's background relates closely with the integrated application under development.

Barbara is the supply chain director. Her role is to establish new supply chain processes that ensure each customer will receive the equipment and accommodations they order. Accuracy of the ordering system is important for her team's success. To date, she is pleased with the deliverables completed by Edward's organization.

As the director of the project management office, Alice is responsible for staffing and oversight of all project management processes. Troy reports to Alice and is project manager for internal improvement processes. In that role, he is responsible for integrating lessons learned and feedback from existing activities and then incorporating them into standard practices as the corporation grows.

Troy is preparing himself for the project manager role in an upcoming web-based project still early in the planning stages. Bruce also works for Alice and is the project manager responsible for the first rollout of the new product concept. He is responsible for managing the integration of all aspects related to the completed adventure delivery model. Bruce came to the group with a proven record of accomplishment in managing these types of projects; however, none of his prior experience included a project of this overall magnitude.

Gene is the operations manager. His role will be to take the completed project and then manage the teams responsible for taking and fulfilling orders. This role wasn't well defined yet, but Gene was attempting to clarify roles whenever conflicts or gaps surfaced. At this time, he is trying to finalize the participants involved with the travel agent-related activities, such as car rentals, air travel, and hotel accommodations. Currently Barry, the administrative director, is coordinating those efforts.

In the corporation's early days, Barry was responsible for financing and human resources processes including hiring, and firing, and basic office management. When it became apparent that he was uncomfortable with major financing strategies, Raj joined the team. After that point, Barry didn't have a strong role in any specific area so he became the managing director by default, responsible for managing day-to-day activities. In a law firm, his title would be managing partner. In this organization, most thought his role was more like a pain in the butt. He would be the toughest person to deal with on the executive committee!

As director of marketing, Rich claims to have had the original idea. It's been reported that there is a Starbucks napkin with the project concept drawn out, but that's no longer important. Rich is always challenging everyone to stretch performance levels. He tends to think of the project in very high-level terms and has a lot of difficulty whenever someone wants to formalize processes. He was instrumental in convincing the financial community about the strengths of the project. He was also the first project manager for overall integration. This only worked for a short time, due to his lack of focus on important management processes. His entrepreneurial behavior is in direct conflict with Barry.

After exchanging pleasantries around the table, Alice introduced me as an observer and consultant to her on the project. Barry immediately swung into form and asked her why she thought she needed a consultant and bluntly asked where she found the money for such a frivolous expense.

She was careful not to tell her associates that she and Troy picked me up at O'Hare Airport and then I followed them home to Dallas. It would sound too much like a lost puppy story. Instead, she ignored Barry's comment and announced that the project was in trouble and that this was the purpose of the meeting. She provided her assessment that the adventures project would be unable to meet its target completion date and budget target. As soon as she said that to the group, there was an anticipated level of unrest at the table.

As it turns out, other than the changes requested by the investors that Bruce had mentioned back in Chicago, the project had not had any major upset since the initial funding fiascoes by Barry. Even to this point in time, everyone was proceeding without knowing that anything could be wrong with the project.

As we had discovered after reviewing the problems in detail in Chicago, very few around the table could escape some element of involvement in the problems contributing to the OS Phase. Getting everyone to admit involvement and then to accept the situation and help to develop a new plan would be difficult, at best. Alice had her work cut out for her this morning.

Not wasting any time in the introduction, she began the presentation by introducing a PowerPoint slide with three basic areas of failure on the project identified (Exhibit 22 - A).

*Project Issues*

- **Poor data management support processes and systems**
- **Poor project definition and unrealistic baselines**
- **Poor project management implementation techniques**

The Mountain Adventure Corporation

**Exhibit 22 - A**

As she started discussing the slide, I couldn't help thinking about how easy it would have been to predict the behavior of those at the table.

As soon as a presenter, in this case Alice, introduces the project's various problems, everyone around the table always seems shocked.

It's only natural for the various directors to take the criticisms personally and even connect a particular bulleted item on the slide with themselves. I've always thought that it would be much easier to insert pictures of each member of the team, in this case the executive committee, into the presentation software and have the faces appear next to the item that they own. Imagine everyone's smiling or actually frowning faces by each item. This sounds bizarre, but in this conference room at that very moment, everyone at the table was doing the same thing in their mind. Each member was looking at these items and seeing them as bullets pointing directly at them or even to the member of the executive committee sitting beside them.

The challenge will be for Alice to keep any finger pointing at a minimum and to seek a future path for the project (and as it will turn out, the company).

"We lost control of the project after a culmination of many failures. Our Management Control System failed completely." Alice spoke with a degree of certainty in her voice that made it difficult for anybody to say anything, except for Edward.

It would have been an understatement to say that Edward became unglued. Before he could mount a good defense, however, I interrupted his initial utterances and took a few minutes to explain the terminology. I pointed out that Alice was referring to Management Control System as the various processes that a project manager has to rely on to get a project finished. The computer systems supporting the project manager are often called the Project Management Information System.

There are many analogies drawn from the data management failures on the project. As expected, Edward was sensitive to any criticism. He was correct to the point that the failure or apparent failure of the Project Management Information System was not the only reason they hit the OS Phase.

Shaking his head and with a mild case of frustration in his voice, Edward backed out of the conversation by adding, "Sounds like a bunch of fancy multi-syllable consultant buzz words to me."

This comment by Edward brought a few cynical laughs and jeers from everyone at the table.

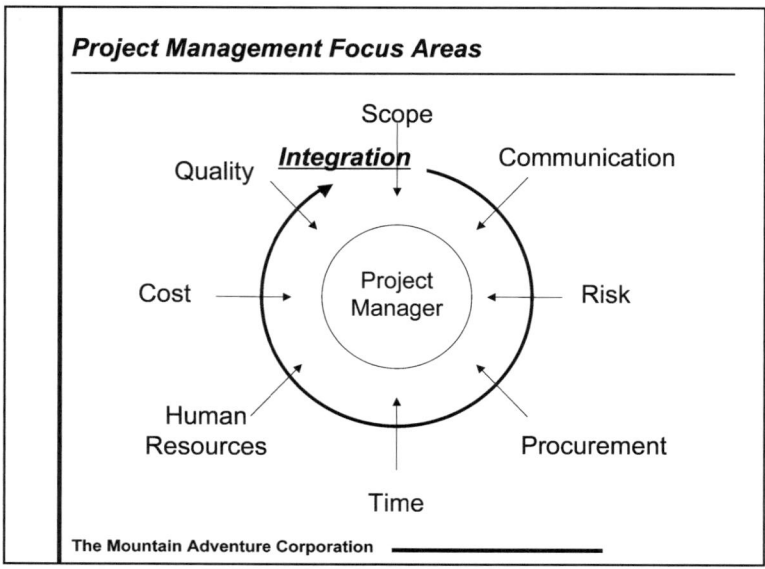

**Exhibit 22 - B**

After things calmed down, Alice flipped to the next slide in the presentation and described the Project Management Focus Areas (Exhibit 22 - B). She took several minutes to review them, making sure the committee was following her presentation with no difficulty.

Then Troy took the floor and described the importance of managing Scope, Roles, and Risks on the project. The discussion intensified, but Troy did a great job keeping everyone on track. At one point, Bruce stood up and joined him. At this time, Bruce presented the Stupid Triangle and provided examples of how pertinent it was to the project. Watching his passion and thorough coverage of the Stupid Triangle was like watching your child take their first step or go out on their first date…a very, very, proud moment!

An actualizing moment for any consultant is to see the student take the role as teacher. In this case, we had three new teachers and they were turning the meeting attendees on their collective ears. It was a crowning moment as Edward, a cynic up until now, turned to the others of the executive committee and announced that they should plan to review the complete recommendation before drawing any conclusions.

Score one for good project management processes!

> ***OS Phase* Avoidance**
> **STRATEGY 22**
>
> *The project manager must understand all elements of the Management Control System, including details of where the project related data resides, and how to get it.*

# CHAPTER 23
# Welcome to the P.O.T.P. Convention

The *OS Phase* doesn't just happen.

Criticism for any project's failure is to be expected and is most often appropriate.

Actually accepting blame, though, is different. All too often, after the *OS Phase* occurs, there is a lot of finger pointing aimed directly towards the project manager.

Whether it's deserved or not, the blame game is a giant waste of time and effort. Everyone involved must focus on fixing the project, not on pointing fingers. Blame at this point creates a negative diversion that uses up valuable time. If we see everyone involved stepping up to admit their element of blame, somehow we can live with everything much better. If no one steps up and we feel alone, then anger and frustration set in quickly!

In practice, we find that many are to blame. If we can get everyone to accept their piece of the blame, then it is easier to move on.

In 1988, Gary Larson created a Far Side® cartoon that depicted a large contingent of his funny-looking characters all gathered at a *25th Annual Part of the Problem (P.O.T.P.) Convention*. This cartoon is perfect as an introductory slide for a management review meeting for a project that hit the *OS Phase*. If everyone at the presentation, including executive management, laughs at the cartoon, then the meeting will usually go well. If no one laughs, then it could be a predictive sign that the team is hosed!

Accepting blame for failures on a project is an essential part of the successful restart and eventual conclusion of a project. Team members and management must clean the "blame slate" before they can build a strong relationship.

After the blame buffet is completed, it's time to move on and deal with the problems as a team!

It was surprising that all members of the committee were so attentive. After the initial criticisms and related denials, everyone confirmed that delaying or canceling the project was not an option. The project had to be finished as soon and as efficiently as possible. Arguing at this point was not constructive.

Barry turned to Alice and made his thoughts very clear. "Alice, we all are depending on getting the first phase of the mountain adventure concept in place. We are confident that the demand is there and we want this first rollout to the public to work and work well. It's true that our enthusiasm may have clouded our judgment of the project's performance. I feel strongly, though, that we can't let this happen again."

"Fortunately, we are only advertising the mountain adventure concept and haven't started taking orders yet," Rich added. "Listening to the discussion this morning is causing some concern in my mind about risks associated with day-to-day operations after initial rollout. We also need to focus on future operations activities and make sure they are in place. For this reason, I am willing to accept the delay, contingent on members of the executive committee providing increased oversight."

Continuing, Rich added, "I can't speak for everyone on the committee, but I believe we understand the processes well, but we didn't pay as much attention to the project as we should have, considering the importance. We are all part of the problem by being too willing to think that everything was fine. I'm embarrassed at how easily I ignored the real performance of the project."

"I agree with your comments related to reviewing our processes," Gene added, directing his comments to Rich. "We need to assess operational risks and we need to get the ordering software in place so that we can begin to take orders. As you recall, that is one of the features currently behind schedule."

Barry acknowledged Gene's comment and added a surprising recommendation. "After we complete the review of the proposed recovery plan, I would like to suggest that Troy take the lead in reviewing all of the company processes as they relate to what we've talked about this morning."

"These project management processes are applicable to almost everything we're doing on a day-to-day basis," Raj added. "We have to be successful during the operational phase. In fact, we can't forget that some of our first customers will be some of our key venture capitalists. I expect they will be critiquing every step of the process."

Barbara started the search for a new, more meaningful way to measure performance by getting everyone focused on vision and process, which turns out to be a profound combination of project attributes. "First, we must understand the vision of where we want to be at the end of the project and then we need to understand the processes that get us there. When we draw out the processes, we will be able to visually see where some new performance measures might be hiding."

Turning to me for a reaction to Barbara's comments, Alice asked, "How are we doing? Will our efforts of looking at the processes illustrate the performance measures we are looking for to ensure we meet our objectives?"

"Absolutely," I responded confidently. "Projects are composed of processes, and each process contributes to the ultimate vision. Many of them are repeated hundreds or thousands of times. It is the consistency and efficiency of these processes that will determine your ability to complete the project successfully. We need to identify where those processes produce vital project data, and then we need to capture that data."

Troy had kept quiet for quite awhile but now entered the discussion, maybe because of his future role on the next major project. After all, any corrections on this project will be golden nuggets for him down the road. "It was hard for me to appreciate that a project manager was actually managing processes, that is, the processes of project management. That's bizarre when you think about it. We're so conditioned to understand the difference between projects and processes that it's odd to change to this thought process."

"I agree!" Gene exclaimed. "In my role as operations director, I dabble in the quality and process improvement areas of the organization. Even though my thoughts are always towards process, I guess I've never really thought that a project consists of processes as well. From this perspective, it becomes obvious that knowledge of the processes is vital for any company or organization. This is a major change in the way I look at everything."

Raj, who had been listening intently, spoke with similar enthusiasm. "I agree with everyone's comments so far. If you look at projects as a grouping of processes, we need to understand each of them and seek out performance measures that drive behavior within the project team. After we finish up with projects, then we need to make sure the rest of the organization is aligned and working properly."

At this point, I drew out a couple of flow charts of key project management processes and depicted examples graphically of where the team could be creating data (Chart 23 - 1).

Speaking again, Raj added, "The fascinating aspect of processes and data is that only a process can create data. As important as data is to an organization, understanding the process where it originates is definitely the first step. As obvious as the relationship of data is to process, I have never thought about it before today."

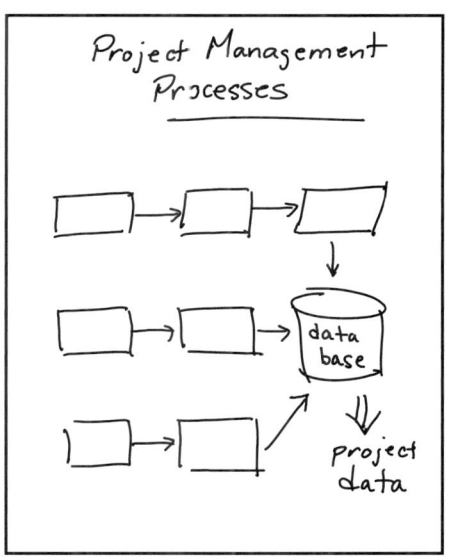

**Chart 23 - 1**

Alice was pleased at the discussion and purposely said very little. The process review recommendation was on the table and that's all she needed to worry about at this time. Turning to me, she asked a question that was on everyone's mind. "Where are we going next?"

"First things first," I said. "It's important for us to take an hour break so that everyone can get their house in order for the next couple of days. When we return, we are going to work together on some steps that will help everyone understand and validate our processes and then develop an Avoidance Plan."

"What are we avoiding?" Raj asked, with a somewhat puzzled expression.

> **OS Phase Avoidance STRATEGY 23**
>
> *When you're reviewing processes, don't just look at the high visibility processes. Look at everything, even supporting processes. Follow the complete dataflow throughout the company or organization.*
>
> *The importance of supporting processes is significant. If processes break down, it may go unnoticed for a while and the project will be quietly off and running to the OS Phase.*

Laughing politely at the comment and not at Raj, Alice responded, "We'll talk about what we're avoiding when we return. We've only begun to describe what we've learned over the weekend."

## CHAPTER 24
# It's All About Data! Pass It On!

It is becoming common for organizations to implement large corporate-wide computerized software systems to manage all of the organization's data. Often though, these systems are entirely too complex and are not flexible enough to meet a project manager's needs. They simply don't get the job done!

From the vantage point of the senior management team running a company, the actual design of the computerized data management system is supposed to support all of the organizations within the company, but, importantly, these systems are there to capture key data for corporate accounting and reporting purposes. Although not intentional, there is often little attention placed on what project managers might need. Executive management's heavy investment in these corporate-wide computerized systems is so significant that it's considered career limiting for the project manager to criticize them as being inadequate.

As project management rises in visibility in corporations today and the needs of project management receive more attention, this gap in information will close. It is important that this happen, because from the project manager's perspective, it's all about data! The lack of good data and poor data management will lead directly to the *OS Phase*.

Data management is the top issue influencing the successful implementation of project management methodologies in most companies. The chances of having a successful project in terms of controlling *scope*, time, and cost baselines is difficult enough when *scope*, time, and cost are linked and in the same database. When managed separately or not at all, success decreases exponentially. In the first case, you can see the *OS Phase* coming and can do something about it before it's too late. In the second scenario, you don't even know what happened until it's over!

> The Work Breakdown Structure becomes a project manager's key tool for managing project data. Early on in the project, it is important for the project manager to understand how project data is *processed* and how the relevant data eventually ends up in the Work Breakdown Structure elements and related reports.
>
> *Processes* that depict organizational workflow and the related data capture *process* steps require immediate and thorough attention.
>
> Remember, the first steps on a project reinforce the notion that it's all about data!

Not surprisingly, everyone returned to the meeting and were seated before the one-hour break was over. It was important to pick up where we left off.

Alice began, "Without losing the point related to the data concerns, I still believe the project must have better data management if we are ever going to have the level of success that everyone expects. We are going to present our plan to avoid any return trips to the OS Phase, and in that plan we have identified better data management as a requirement."

Listening with an obvious interest in this part of the meeting, Edward turned to Bruce to get a clarification of his earlier statement. "Bruce, you said the Management Control System completely failed, but didn't you say there were other processes that were a problem?"

"That's right; we had process concerns overall," Bruce said. "But, and I mean *but*, an important supporting process for any project manager is one that provides important data from which they make decisions. I remember a discussion from a seminar where the speaker described data management and data warehousing in terms of something we could all understand.

"The speaker said that Information Technology groups had one primary mission in support of the company infrastructure systems. This mission is to develop systems to collect data, store the data, and then make it available for retrieval when needed.

"What the speaker used as a comparison was a full-service grocery store. As crazy as it sounded at first, in the analogy the grocery store is a data warehouse that has all of the various kinds of data. It's easy to imagine the benefit of this giant store having a good directory for where the products are stored. Most of the items are clearly marked as to freshness, or in the business world, as being 'current' data. The data we grab and put in our cart becomes information specific to our needs. We might feel like Italian while someone else wants Chinese. Depending on what we need to buy, we have several choices of data retrieval systems, or carts, that we can choose.

"Sometimes our choice of grocery stores is not like the store I described. Maybe the store doesn't have the specific foods we want or the aisles are marked poorly and we spend a lot of time looking for what we want. It's frustrating when the only choice we have is a store without these features. If we want a specific brand or style of food, forget it! The freshness of the data, oops…I mean food, will be something that will require our attention.

"Even the deluxe store might not be easy for us to navigate twenty-four hours a day. I have a mental picture of project personnel digging through pallets dropped in the aisles late at night for restocking empty shelves. It will be necessary to rout through each pallet piled with groceries still in their boxes and held together with cellophane wrapping.

"When we don't have the deluxe store or we don't have it available when we need it, we literally have to take it or leave it. From the data management perspective, until we place the data in the proper location, the process of finding it is futile and non-productive."

Bruce told the story almost without taking a breath. It was hard for him to keep going with all the laughter around the table. It was clear that Bruce had created a vision in everyone's mind. His story telling ability might be his greatest strength!

With everyone still joking about the analogy, Alice joined in and added more fuel to the fire. "Users, not the Information Technology group, should define data and data needs. The argument that we should give information to certain levels of management is unfair to those sitting in those positions. Analytical project managers will want a great amount of detail. Others will not. The data warehouse or *grocery store* should let them choose for themselves. Some Information Technology folks want us to buy what they want to sell, not what we need. The correlation to a convenience food store hits all too close to our situation, high prices, and minimal choices. Oh yes, but everything is convenient."

Alice's extra description sobered the group a little. Edward turned to the back of the room where I was sitting and asked pointedly, "Surely you can't say that the problems are due only to bad data? Isn't that particular excuse a little old fashioned and actually nothing more than a cop-out to divert us from the real reasons the project failed?"

"No, it's not a cop-out. The time that a project manager has to spend to find needed project related data, that should have been available, is wasted. Absolutely wasted," I said in a firm, direct response while taking the floor. "Every time we make fun of a project manager that complains about not having timely cost data, imagine yourself in a car. You are driving down the road being told that you have to finish an 800-mile trip as fast as possible, but you can't run out of gas or get a speeding ticket. It's possible, but the task would still be a challenge. Oops, I forgot to mention that the car doesn't have a speedometer, odometer, or gas gauge. In fact, the car doesn't have any gauges at all."

"Sounds like my old '49 Chevy," Barry added, bringing the smiles back to everyone's expression.

Continuing with the analogy, I described even more details related to the data diet that project managers face everyday. "With these limitations in the car, if you are to be successful and not run out of gas or get a ticket, you will be forced to stop and fill up the car many more times than if you had a gauge. If you had the time, you might research and find out the actual capacity of the tank in the car. But you could only do that by asking people along the way, because the driver's manual or any type of instructions are also missing from the glove compartment. You might take a chance and guess that the tank is fourteen gallons, and then calculate gas consumption by checking mileage from road signs. Oh, I forgot to mention that you will actually receive the mileage and gas consumption data, but it will be 60-90 days after the trip is completed."

The room was silent as I continued. "This is what your project manager, Bruce, and others on his team deal with everyday. He has few choices. One choice is to be distracted from driving the car, which we will parallel as the real scope of the project, to spend time calculating gas consumption. The inevitable situation is one where he just throws up his hands, drives the car, and doesn't worry about running out of gas. If he ends up on the side of the road, or hits the OS Phase, then so what! He did the best job he could with what he had to work with."

Barbara turned to Bruce and asked, "Is that what happened here? Were the data systems inadequate? Is that why the project hit the OS Phase?"

"Yes to both questions, there is no doubt that the data concerns made me crazy. They made everyone crazy. We spent a lot of time

---

*OS Phase* **Avoidance**
**STRATEGY 24**

*Before imposing a major straightjacket on your organization with a complex computerized data management system, study the data. Draw out all processes associated with collecting and managing the data. Understand what data is important, identify what data is mandatory, and specify what data is nice to have but not essential.*

*When shopping for a formal computerized Project Management Information System to support project management and to manage the data, don't be taken by the fancy bells and whistles. Price and complexity are increasing each year along with the problems associated with unnecessary features.*

*Get involved with data management. Don't be just a bystander. Understand the processes. Understand the data. Remember, it's all about data!*

finding the correct data and then we ended up with a lot of redundant systems just to manage basic information," Bruce said in a frustrated tone.

"But I want to be careful and not blame data management problems for everything that happened. The three of us have realized in the last couple of days that there was not just one area where the project failed."

Interrupting, Alice got everyone's attention while introducing the next area for the group to address. "This discussion is a great introduction to the next one. We need to look at the organization as a whole and find the attributes that will make us all winners down the road."

# CHAPTER 25
# The Attributes of a Great Project Management Organization

A study of Management Control Systems teaches us that whatever we develop must be *simple* and repeatable. In that same way, project management processes are a subset of the organization's overall Management Control System and themselves need to be *simple* and straightforward.

As the team proceeds, events might happen that threaten successful completion of the project and the project manager needs a little more time to fix the problem. Maybe just a little embellishment will be okay until everything gets back on track, and while you're on that track, it's not a train you hear coming...it's the *OS Phase*!

Depending on the severity, inaccurate performance reporting in the form of inflated percentages completed could evolve into a major *credibility* concern.

The implication that a process or project management team is not *credible* isn't meant to be an indictment against either. However, in 2002, corporate executive *credibility* lapses resulted in stock market losses measured in the trillions. Few people were untouched in one way or another by these corporate collapses. Just how important is *credibility*? Although it's hard to measure precisely, it's BIG!

Striving for *simple* and *credible* are easy compared to being *predictive*. Forward *predictions* are difficult and don't have the same level of certainty that previously completed events have. The fear of being wrong on a *prediction* can be overwhelming to many project managers. It is important to lead by example and correct the behavioral tendency to only focus on what's known and to avoid what isn't known. It is mandatory that we encourage project managers to look into the future and to dwell on the past only when it leads us to where we're going.

> Any project manager that is *predictive* in their approach is demonstrating a strong sign that they understand their project.

After everyone was comfortable around the table, Alice proceeded with the next area of discussion. Based on my earlier suggestion, she asked me to lead an exercise to get everyone up to speed on the proposed new processes.

The first step was to break into three teams (Chart 25 - 1). I explained the concept of the Avoidance Attributes for a Project Manager: simple, credible, and predictive. Now I wanted each team to take one of these words, study it, and then present back to the others the relationship of that term to what they needed to do in the future on the project.

Alice had presented these attributes to the executive committee in the earlier morning session. Everyone appreciated the significance of the attributes.

```
Team 1       Bruce
"Simple"  ⇒  Edward
             Barry

Team 2       Troy
"Credible" ⇒ Gene
             Barbara

Team 3       Alice
"Predictive" ⇒ Raj
             Rich
```

**Chart 25 - 1**

The exercise now would be a test to see if they really connected with the concept. It was certain that everyone was engaged in the day's activities, but it was important to know that they would leave the session with the points internalized.

It was great to see the teams working together to brainstorm characteristics and considerations for each of the three Avoidance Attributes. After just short of half an hour all three teams were ready to present their findings. We then began what would be a major transition in thought processes for this outstanding team.

Edward and Barry took the lead in presenting their findings on the term *Simple*. Barry started out by going to the flip chart at the front of the room. First, he summarized his team's key points. "We've learned today that a fundamental principle of project management implementation is to keep processes simple. Unfortunately, the concept of simple flies in the face of many concepts we have used so far."

Joining in, Edward picked up the discussion. "Simple just isn't as much fun as complex and our nature has driven us towards complex, technically complicated solutions. In our information technology world, frills and fancy gadgets rule the day. As a result, we have encouraged Bruce to deliver techniques that are glitzy and, in many cases, specific only to the problem at hand."

"We all agreed that it would be unfair to state in a categorical sense that these strategies are flawed," Bruce added. "History reveals that the processes we were putting in place can work and we had a reasonable basis to consider using them. Unfortunately, their complexity often confused the team and executive management, because they did not have time to dig through the details. Too much faith was necessary for techniques and strategies that required too much time to understand their implications."

Edward now took the lead and said, "What we want is something that is easy to explain and, most importantly, easy to measure success from. To reiterate the earlier discussion, we need data that is easily available for anyone that needs to use it. *Simple* must represent techniques that can be implemented today!"

The focus of the first team was excellent. Bruce turned, looking for comments, and I complimented their effort. "That was an excellent synopsis of *simple*. When we apply the term to project management processes, it's odd, but we want our project management techniques to jump out at us as being obvious. Almost too simple, but that's okay."

Edward added, "Do you mean that promises of exciting things in the future instead of simple things result in major disappointments?"

Everyone at the table smiled.

Barry jumped back in and summarized the team's conclusions by reading from the flip chart, adding some more detail to each of the bulleted items. (Chart 25 - 2) "Simple project management strategies won't require extensive training to be used.

"Simple stands for results easily understood by all levels of the management team.

"Simple is anti-complicated.

"Simple stands for a concept discussed and rolled out throughout the organization without having to meet delays associated with major corporate initiatives.

"Simple is the ability to look at one or two performance charts and know immediately whether a project is moving forward successfully or not.

"Simple is actually understanding what is going on and being able to communicate it to others that need the information (Chart 25 - 3).

"Simple is looking for some type of performance metrics or critical measures that actually represent important elements of the project and are easy to capture.

"Simple is using and understanding the Stupid Triangle and being able to explain it to others."

After answering a few questions, Bruce, Edward, and Barry finished their synopsis of *simple*.

---

Simple is...

- Project Management process requires only "minor" training
- Anti-complicated
- Everybody (management) understands results
- Straight forward and quick roll-out
- Easy to read performance reports

**Chart 25 - 2**

---

Simple is also...

- Understanding what's going on ⇒ can explain it to others
- Using performance metrics that are easy to capture and easy to understand
- Simple = (OS Phase)

**Chart 25 - 3**

---

Based on the discussion, it was obvious that the concept of *simple* wasn't present at anytime before today. This is true especially before the project hit the OS Phase. However, it was certain that this was going to change and change quickly. *Simple* was about to become part of everyday life.

The second team was eager to discuss the significance of *Credibility* in the organization. The best part of this assignment was their initial feeling that everyone in the organization was already credible and they would have an easy time with the subject. Initially, Troy, Gene, and Barbara had a difficult time deriving any concerns with credibility because of the perceived project team's conformance to that standard. After discussions with others in the group, the team was able to get a better perspective of some deficiencies and then developed some great recommendations.

Gene went to the front of the room and started the next discussion. His approach was different from the first team's. Instead of presenting findings, he asked the other members of the executive committee for input on what they thought were suggestions to instill credibility into the daily processes of team members.

Since it was important to hear from each team before engaging the entire committee, Gene was stepping out of the prescribed game plan. I politely interrupted his request and asked that he and his teammates first present the specific findings of their group, and then we could hear what others thought.

Gene smiled and said, "I was just trying to cheat a little."

They laughed at Gene's comment, as everyone except me knew him for his practical jokes. He enjoyed getting that type of reaction and it was good to see some humor in the room. I just would have rather not had it sent in my direction.

Still smiling, Barbara joined Gene at the front of the room and began the planned presentation by examining the concept of *credibility*. "When we started brainstorming, we all just sat and stared at each other. The concept of *credibility* seemed almost too happy, too easy. We all agreed that *credibility* should be a standard operating mode for a project manager. Actually, it should be a standard operating mode for everyone in the organization. Everyone must be *credible*, that's a given!"

Gene then added, "At this point we realized that *credibility* is closely linked to *simple*. This would imply that anyone trying to complicate a process might, in fact, be trying to hide something. This was one of our most important revelations."

Barbara continued the discussion by describing one of the team's strategies. "To get some type of validation of this presumption, we secretly sent Troy over to the other team to pull Bruce aside and ask him if he had, in fact, been credible on how he reported details of the project. While Troy was talking with Bruce, Gene and I collected our thoughts on how we felt about the project's performance information. Was it too complicated, or was it simple and on target? Gene's comments were a real eye-opener for me.

"Go ahead, Gene, and tell them what you told me," Barbara said.

"Thanks for putting me on the spot," he responded. "When I look back at the monthly review meetings, we were presented a lot of charts and tables of numbers, supposedly representing performance on the project. There were many times that I literally didn't have a clue about what was being presented. Anytime I personally didn't understand something, I always assumed someone else did. In fact, I would look at Raj's reaction whenever Bruce or Alice presented the different financial reports. He is our numbers person and there was no doubt in my mind that he would react to any information that represented a problem."

"Sounds like that makes you point person for interpreting project performance," I said, while turning and addressing Raj. "Hopefully you understood Bruce's reports."

Raj's facial expression said everything as he responded to Gene's comments. "Wow! I had no idea that you respected me so much. I'm speechless and definitely flattered."

Raj's response elicited laughter. It was amazing to see how this forum was letting everyone speak freely about how processes occurred in the past. It's sad that a problem must happen for organizations to finally talk candidly with each other.

We talked more about roles and responsibilities. We emphasized how important it was to make sure someone is responsible for each element of the review.

Raj stood and addressed the group, reinforcing the discussion of roles and responsibilities. "I'm not sure if others counted on me like

Gene did and, for the record, I'm agreeable with that. It would work better, however, if you told a person about this added responsibility. I might have taken a different approach to how I reviewed the information if I had understood my role better."

"I wasn't speaking for the group," Gene added. "Maybe I was the only one of the group that did it."

"Well, I did it a little," Barry said. "And looking now at everyone else's facial expressions, I don't think Gene and I were alone."

Rich broke his silence and made a significant point to the group. "Sometimes information about projects and project management in general is handled like there's a cloak of secrecy surrounding it, or at least that's how it seems. The numbers and other verbal performance information provided were convincing enough and because the performance reports were always positive, there was no reason to challenge anything. It was easy to let the team enthusiasm become blinders. I don't think the deception was criminal, just hurtful."

Not wanting to stay quiet any longer, Bruce moved to the front of the room with Barbara and began to present his part of the story. "I never looked at anything that was reported as being deceitful. It's hard to draw a line between embellishment and deceit. At this time, it doesn't really matter because everything from this point will be reported candidly the way it is, period! It wasn't until Troy asked me the question about how I had reported performance on the project that I even imagined the reporting process to be a contributor itself to the project's demise. That was a real eye-opener."

I took the opportunity to leverage off Bruce's comment and began a discussion of how poor reporting can actually affect the project and make it worse. "The connection of performance reporting to performance isn't obvious at first. The problem derives from the delay in responding to the concerns. The project was getting in deeper trouble each week. The collective wisdom around the table might have intervened and corrected the problem if they only knew. Unfortunately, the performance problems weren't discussed and Bruce probably breathed a sigh of relief after each executive committee meeting only to have the problems get worse during the next period. The OS Phase was emerging and no one knew it was coming."

"Is it common for project managers to manage the news?" Raj asked.

Responding directly to Raj's comment, I said, "Actually, it is considered by some as a strong attribute or personal strength for a project manager to be able to manage the news or as it's sometimes called, spin the news. Most of the time we don't think of performance reporting on a project as part of the project itself, but, instead, just as a cost of doing business. We only do it for that reason. We refer to this as 'compliant behavior.' If we had a choice to present performance or not, the answer would most often be 'not' —that's the reality." We often consider performance reporting as unavoidable and not something intended to add value or solve problems. The goal for many project managers is to present project performance without anybody asking any questions. Think about how many times we present some type of information and we hope, or should I say pray, that there aren't any questions. In fact, it's common for senior managers to evaluate presentation performance based on the number and type of questions asked in any given presentation. This whole process is a big deal. What Bruce did was unfortunate but it isn't uncommon. He has repented and probably shouldn't be hassled anymore about it."

Bruce responded by gently slipping a twenty dollar bill under the folder lying on the table in front of where I was sitting.

"Here I thought he'd seen the error of his way and there he goes… bribing the consultant," Barbara said, while reaching over and grabbing the twenty dollar bill.

The reaction by everyone was positive.

"Thanks for giving me a second chance," Bruce said with a reassured smile. "When Troy asked the question earlier I told him that I had exaggerated earlier on the project when I reported progress. I honestly never thought there was anything wrong with what I had done."

With a sly grin towards Alice, Bruce continued by saying, "Before we leave this subject you might want to ask Alice if she ever added an even better spin to my status before presenting it formally to you as the executive committee."

Alice's smile provided her answer and before she could say anything in her own defense, Barbara turned to Bruce and asked, "Have you thought about how this happened? What causes someone to embellish project performance?"

In a convincing tone, Bruce responded to Barbara's question. "The embellishments weren't meant to be deceitful. We just weren't making enough progress and I thought we could make it up before anybody really noticed. I really wanted the project to be successful, and somehow the lack of progress was personal. At least I took it personally, and I always had the interests of the company as a priority. When I finally woke up and realized that I couldn't change the outcome and we couldn't make the project's end date, I reported it immediately to Troy and Alice."

"We've been through that, Bruce," Alice interjected. "You did tell us, but the timing was terrible. In fact you only told us on Friday because you hit the OS Phase and couldn't hide it anymore."

Gene now saw this as an opportunity to take control of the discussion again. "Bruce was not being credible, but he is a team player and he was trying to do what he thought was right. Our team determined that the silence of the executive committee contributed as well to what happened. We never made our position clear on how important credibility and accurate reporting are to the project. They just can't be taken for granted. This may be the most important lesson learned today. It is essential to present expectations at the beginning of a project. As an executive committee for the project, I don't recall when we ever invited Bruce to our gatherings. We communicated everything through Alice…."

"That's it; let's blame Alice for everything!" Rich chided. "We will fail as a committee if we don't end up blaming someone today. I think the responsibility to cast the blame on someone is part of our job description."

Everyone laughed at his comment; even Alice smirked!

"Who would have thought that discussing the aspects of credibility would have brought out so many goof ball comments?" Barry added, while poking Bruce gently in the ribs.

Gene continued with a convincing tone to his voice, "In fact, this discussion is really now getting everyone on board. It's a shame that we didn't set better expectations at the beginning of the project."

"But it's never too late," Raj added, after listening intently to the discussion. "I'm really encouraged by where we can go with this in the future."

Gene went on to describe his team's analysis of *credible*. "Unfortunately, many projects are founded on a lot of arm waving and promises that are discovered as being hype after it's too late. Project management techniques themselves must be credible. Failure to implement credible processes, and, most importantly, the lack of credible performance data as the project proceeds, is a major contributor to projects reaching the OS Phase undetected."

Troy joined in and turned the flip chart to a new page (Chart 25 - 4). "Credibility concerns manifest themselves in numerous ways. Building fat and hidden contingency in a schedule or budget does not support the concept of being credible. This is especially true if the team intentionally hides the contingency from others."

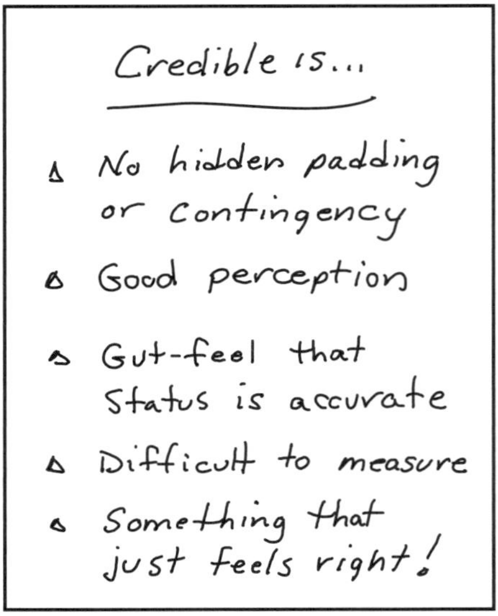

Troy turned the discussion over to Barbara, who then pointed to the balance of items on the flip chart and began describing each item.

"Credible is often more of a perception than an object we can actually measure.

"Credibility is that gut feeling that something just isn't right at the project performance review meeting."

Credible is...
- No hidden padding or contingency
- Good perception
- Gut-feel that status is accurate
- Difficult to measure
- Something that just feels right!

**Chart 25 - 4**

Congratulating the team on a great and thorough effort with their synopsis, I went on to close out this session by adding, "The problem of credibility can be devastating to the project manager. When credibility concerns surface, confidence in the project manager and team becomes suspect. Outside consultants appear for more reviews. Whether or not the project manager created the credibility concern purposely or not, the effect is the same, and additional delays are to be expected. The OS Phase terminology will become part of their new vocabulary."

The last team, consisting of Alice, Raj, and Rich, almost forgot they had to present their findings related to the goal of being predictive. The concept of predictive project management focuses on the real heart of a project—when will it be completed? The project manager must be equipped with the tools that make the prediction process better than looking at a crystal ball and remain credible at the same time.

Raj started the discussion. "The insinuation that the executive committee may be guilty for the apparent lack of a critical critique leads us to one of our first observations when it comes to the need to be predictive. On any given project, there may be many people involved with the day-to-day activities. There might be various sponsors, each with their own vested interest. When we brainstormed a list of the various project stakeholders, we realized that the project sponsor or customer are most often busy managing many other activities besides the specific aspects of a given project.

"Project team members, whether totally committed to the project or not, focus only on their portion of the project and are, for the most part, only contemplating near-term events, not the completion activity details related to the project. These realities leave only one person to watch the project as a whole. That person is the project manager. If the project manager is caught up in minor details or technology concerns, then no one is looking at the end of the project."

With growing enthusiasm, Raj continued with his comments. "When I look at the financial management of this company, there is no doubt that I have to manage the day to day cash flow and financial concerns. Likewise, it would be fool hardy if I didn't pay strong attention to where money markets are moving. In order for me to take advantage of better financing possibilities, I have to look at many market variables and then project them forward based on my experience and instincts."

"In other words," Rich said, "you have to be predictive or our financial well-being will be jeopardized!"

"Exactly!" Raj added enthusiastically, while looking around the room for other confirmations. "This discussion has validated standard processes that I use but had never really thought about their significance."

"Speaking from a marketing perspective," Rich said, "predictive behavior is essential, but it's not easy. When you look at how we report to the executive committee, it's much easier to dwell on what has happened because we know that for sure. Predictors, however, are quite a bit more difficult."

"Our team realized that the Stupid Triangle sets the basis for our initial project understanding," Alice said. "The Stupid Triangle will help us to set a course for avoiding the OS Phase. Our relentless pursuit of scope will then ensure the accuracy of our project predictions."

Rich added the classic consideration when it comes to being predictive. "What started to interest us is the question of how a forecast is derived? Is the evaluation based on a crystal ball approach or is it based on relevant performance metrics?"

"We all know the correct answer, but like everything else we discussed this morning, the challenge of most project strategies is the dependence on people to make them work," Alice said.

"It is possible to know to the penny how much a project has spent to date, but what purpose does that level of detail serve? We labor over minuscule values, when the numbers we derive are only moments in time. They will have no credible purpose after the project is completed.

"If the project or program manager can't be predictive, then the system itself must provide predictive information or else everything is lost."

Jumping in the discussion, Gene added his thoughts. "Sponsors and executive managers often seem to rebuke managers that want time to discuss projects that are in fact on schedule, but might have some problems with the future, predictive concerns. The tendency to spend the majority of time dealing with one crisis after another has become a corporate culture."

"That's a good point, Gene," Barbara added, "let's change the culture before it's too late. I'm starting to see some of the same tendencies here and it is troubling to me. I don't like seeing the wrong people getting rewarded."

Gene responded, "I haven't noticed it as much here, but on my previous job, it was common to promote those that were always knee deep in crisis events. Let's make the change here and reward those project managers and project personnel that are looking ahead on their projects and let's reward them by giving them time on our calendar to meet with them."

Barry was soaking in all of the discussion. He joined in by making an interesting suggestion. "We could make this happen if we initiated a process to schedule meetings between eight and ten in the morning with project managers *who have their act together*, then everyone else after 10 A.M. You can almost hear the hall chatter. 'Gee Harold,

---

### *OS Phase* Avoidance
### STRATEGY 25

*Simple is the basis of this book. Simple techniques are presented that will not require more details to implement than are provided to the reader. The simple techniques will not require extensive procedures to implement. The simple techniques will not require the user to seek permission to use. The simple techniques will not violate existing requirements and, most importantly, will not detract from the actual execution of the project.*

*Surround yourself and your organization with only credible personnel. Do not do business with vendors or customers that are not credible. Life is too short to waste on those who will abuse others so that they themselves look good or are successful. Tolerance of this type of behavior reflects poorly on how others perceive you.*

*Predictive project managers should not play a secondary role to other project managers whose projects are suddenly in trouble at the last minute and as a result are monopolizing all of the executive manager's time.*

when's your meeting with the boss? Noon? What's wrong with your project?' It would be amazing to try."

"There is no doubt in my mind that if we'd done any of these processes we wouldn't have hit the OS Phase and we would be busy selling what will be a very hot product," Alice said, while pacing on the long side of the conference room. "As senior managers we must make available at least two hours per day for predictive activities. Eventually, we will have eight hours for predictive and two hours for crisis, that being the entrance into the perfect world."

Everyone was pleased with the discussion. The hope is that they all will walk the talk and take these Avoidance Attributes seriously for the balance of this project and future projects or processes down the road.

# CHAPTER 26
# Tracked, Discussed, But Never Managed ... the Real Life Cycle of Risk Management

There are many ways to implement *risk* management within a project. The single most important step is to ensure that the discussion of *risk* is on the agenda at every project meeting. *Risk* management will never become part of our culture if it doesn't become part of our day to day work *processes*.

It is common to have a lot of hype and excitement about *risk* management, but after the dust clears, and the excitement wanes, *risk* management often becomes just another unfunded mandate. *Risk* is something that managers have to consider, but they aren't given additional financial resources or time to do it. In these cases, aspiring project managers will comply with the minimum *risk* management requirements, but it won't be anything more than that.

When we consider the *Stupid Triangle*, we understand that *scope* must correspond with the time and cost on a project. In the same way, *risk* must correspond with any reserves we've allocated for both time and cost. Managing *risk* has some important advantages, not the least of which is that *risks* occur only in the future and are there whether we want to recognize them or not.

The *predictive* nature of *risks* allows us to consider or act upon mitigation strategies before we get in trouble. *Risk* helps to keep our day-to-day focus on the *predictive* elements of the project.

Successful companies manage *risk*. Sometimes they manage *risk* using complex statistical analysis. Sometimes they manage *risk* in their heads and don't put words or numbers to paper. Regardless, the *process* of *risk* management is present.

If you are not discussing project *risk* items at staff or project review meetings, then what are you discussing?

Think about it!

The reaction to the Avoidance Attributes was great. Everyone understood the significance of the three Avoidance Attributes, both for the project manager and for project management in general. Before we went too far into the details, Troy described the Avoidance Model we had presented in the morning meeting. Alice had directed her earlier presentation to getting the important processes in place and not so much to what each process represented.

When asked to present, Troy was still a little uncertain about his knowledge of the subject and he suggested that I do the presentation instead.

I let him down as easy as I could. "Sorry, Troy, this is a test. Since you will be responsible for the next project, it's appropriate to put you on the spot to make sure you truly understand what you have to do. In fact, it wouldn't be surprising if you do a better job than I would have done."

Barbara was eager to get started so she grabbed Troy's arm and pulled him to the front of the room.

Gene laughed and said, "It looks like Troy was a victim of the supply chain process. We just witnessed another just-in-time delivery."

Everyone laughed at the horseplay of Barbara and Troy. As it turned out, the distraction caused Troy to relax a little and he calmly presented the relationship and importance of scope, roles, and risk as it related to the current project and he even tied in the discussion with the upcoming effort associated with the next release.

After completing the presentation, he took the flip chart sheet and hung it on the wall next to the chart depicting the attributes we had discussed earlier.

It didn't take long for the members of the committee to notice the relationship of the two charts. Barry spoke first, "It's amazing when you put those two flip charts (Charts 26 – 1 and 2) next to each other that there is such an incredible linkage between them. Scope and Simple line up, Credible and Roles line up, but the most remarkable coincidence is that Predictive and Risk also line up."

"Absolutely," Gene said, as he interrupted Barry in mid-sentence. "We all agreed earlier that being predictive was vital. Now we know how important risk management is in accomplishing this objective."

# THE REAL LIFE CYCLE OF RISK MANAGEMENT

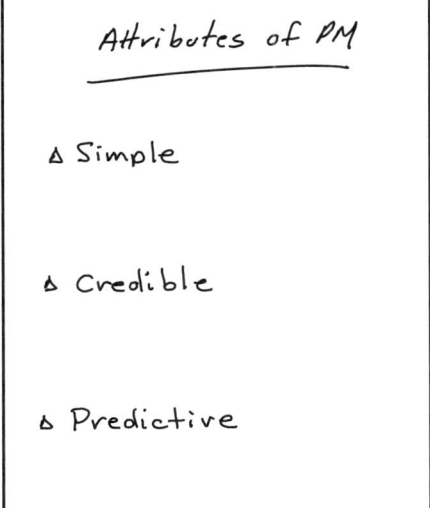

**Chart 26 - 1**    **Chart 26 - 2**

Bruce smiled and replied, "What I've learned in the past couple of days is that without managing risks, it is impossible to be predictive. We can think we're taking care of business all we want, but we're in a happy world that will eventually come crashing in on top of us, reminiscent of the OS Phase effect. My only concern is explaining this concept to someone else. It's difficult for me to distinguish between gloom and doom, being predictive, and just covering our collective butts!"

Everyone nodded in agreement to the importance of risk management in the OS Phase avoidance strategies. It was apparent that Alice and Troy were delivering a compelling demonstration.

Raj then turned to Bruce and asked, "It seems that I recall some listings of risks when we started the project. Am I just imagining things or did we attempt risk management early in the project?"

"Raj, that's why we all love ya so much; you never let us forget anything," Alice said with a smile. "Risk management is not new to the project. We have tracked risks and have discussed risks, but we didn't manage them. Bruce would bring up risks and we pooh-poohed him every time. I'm speaking for Bruce, but I think that the executive committee's lack of interest in risks probably caused him to start ignoring them as well."

Turning to me, Edward asked, "Is our behavior common? Or do other companies follow the risk management processes with more discipline?"

"I wish I could say that you're the only organization that ignores the process, but that would be a gross misstatement," I responded, while noticing the group's keen interest in my response. "In companies where they've implemented even the most comprehensive program, it's very common for everyone to talk a good game, but that's all."

"Sounds like that compliant behavior thing again," Alice said.

"That's right," I agreed with an affirmative response. "If the project manager has to present project risks at the monthly portfolio or project manager status meetings, they will print them out just before they're needed, take five minutes to update them and that's all. Unfortunately, it's more of a show than anything else. To compound the problem, the reviewers see the compliant risk forms filled out, ask a few questions and that's it! They often dismiss the process even more so than the project manager."

At this time, everyone turned to Bruce to see his reaction.

He was learning well. He definitely took the high road.

"I'm not going to let the committee take all of the blame," he replied. "Everyone throughout the organization dismissed any concept of risk management. We were all convinced that we could do anything. Looking back now, it's so obvious that the invincible attitude is great for keeping morale peaked, but it can go too far. In our case, it caused us to be too optimistic. I was glad that the risks weren't considered because that made one less thing I had to worry about. Ignorance is bliss! I thought ignoring the risks would make my life easier. When I look at it now, paying attention to them would have made my life much easier. I never made the correlation of how important they were to the project."

Continuing, now with a totally engaged group, Bruce finished his thoughts about risk. "I can't speak for everyone in the room, but based on what I've learned the past couple of days, I realize now that risk management is pertinent to what each of us does each day. Risk management will be a major part of our project management processes from this point forward if I have anything to do with it."

Adding to Bruce's comments, Alice said, "Failure to understand future risks will blindside us to the point we might lose everything. We almost lost it all, but now we have a second chance. I'm not going to throw that second chance away. We're changing how we do business. Our team is going to manage risk daily."

Listening to the discussion, Edward directed a related question that was probably on everyone's mind. "We've talked about managing risks so we can avoid them, but what should we do if a bad risk actually happens? Supposing the risk was even on the list and its impact was managed, but it was unavoidable and it happened."

Without hesitation, I responded, "Give the project manager a pat on the back and offer support to clean up any debris that happened as a result of the risk's occurrence.

"The key is to avoid being negative with Bruce or anyone on the project team. It was their job to identify risks, quantify them, and then manage them. Sometimes it is just impossible to avoid a risk."

"Sounds like the cliché, 'timing is everything' might be relevant here," Gene added.

Moving up again to the front of the room, I addressed the group. "Timing will be the difference between success and failure; it's that simple. It's the way it's always been in the past and it's the way it will always be in the future. If we can identify a risk before it happens, we at least have a chance to consider some mitigation strategies. If we didn't have the risk on our radar, then we might not have a chance to manage its impact."

I went on to describe one of my favorite examples of risk management — a real life example that would fit the concept of mountain adventures, with a built-in twist of how the severity of risk fits into the picture.

"I learned to appreciate risk and levels of risk while living in Idaho. During the winter, the temperature can turn very cold. Acquiring and maintaining survival supplies and equipment is essential. Freezing to death is a risk that everyone should take seriously. When driving around town in a 4-wheel-drive vehicle, the threatening nature of the weather doesn't seem ominous, shelter is all around wherever you drive. It is important to have good tires and a worthy vehicle, but it's not life threatening if you break down. In this case, the risk of having a vehicle problem is low and the impact is actually quite low as well. However, when traveling to the Grand Tetons or other nearby mountain ranges, it's essential to carry extra warm clothing, sub-zero sleeping bags, or other survival gear. Why? Because risk or, as we're referring to it, project risk, increases significantly when leaving town. There is no law requiring all vehicles to contain survival gear, just like there's no procedure or regulation that we have to take project risks seriously. But we recognize the folly of those that don't. The probability of the risk increased slightly, but the impact increased substantially."

"Wow!" Alice exclaimed, "now there's an example that's easy to relate to."

"That's right," I said, and I wanted to capture the essence of the example. "Risk has two components, probability of occurrence and impact. To really understand a risk, we need to evaluate both elements for each risk."

Continuing, I provided another very recent example. "After moving to Virginia, my wife and I began to restore an historic two-story farmhouse. Recently, I pointed out to her an area of the roof where I wanted to install gutters. The location was two-and-a-half stories above the ground. I explained that I wanted to purchase a heavy-duty ladder so that I could do the work myself. For what I paid for the ladder, I could more than offset the cost of hiring a contractor to do the installation and I would be left with a nice shiny ladder, or new toy, as my wife described it, to play with when the work was completed."

Everyone laughed at the description of the ladder and then Alice said she thought she knew where I was going with the example. "Did you even consider that there is a chance you might fall from the ladder?"

"That's exactly what my wife said. I told her that I've climbed structural steel during my career and although my legs were getting a little less stable, I wasn't really concerned with the task at hand. If the ladder was a good one, everything would be fine. Her next comment, however, made a point that was hard to argue. She agreed that my chances of falling were remote, but if I did, the impact could be fatal."

"So what did you do?" Barry asked.

"Good question," I responded quickly. "Actually, if the weather is good in Virginia today, the contractor should be working on the gutter as we speak."

"That is a great analogy," Troy commented. "Too many times we take *risks* without really thinking about the consequences. In that case, I believe the correct term is that your risk response was to transfer the risk."

"Excellent!" I said, while trying to get back to the project.

"What happens in the case where a risk occurs and it wasn't on the list of risks that we manage?" Edward asked.

"Then you're hosed!" Bruce said in his now traditional vocal burst. "You're hosed big time!"

"Bruce is right, and it's at that point where we take you behind the barn and beat you senseless!" I said, while trying unsuccessfully to keep a serious look on my face.

After the laughter stopped, I went on to provide the more professional response. "I think you know the right answer. This is where you have to take the occurrence as a failure of the risk management process. It will be important for you to identify the areas of failure, what processes failed and then fix them. The project manager definitely has some answering to do before they can continue on in their role.

"Remember, the project manager's key role is to be predictive. If something unexpected happens, it will be necessary to evaluate the potential of a repeat situation down the road," I said in a serious tone. "The project manager's role is to avoid the OS Phase. Risks will knock a project to pieces quicker than anything out there."

Alice joined in with a great correlation to the seriousness of risk management. "We always talk about how awful it is to have to deal with scope creep. The creeping scope will take precious time and money to accomplish. The risk that happens without any warning is like scope creep except that it is so much more significant."

"Anytime we omit a risk from our planning, we put the project and organization in jeopardy. The question of why a risk wasn't on the list must be determined quickly," Edward said in a convincing tone. "We won't be allowed to drag you behind the barn, but we must take the

> **OS Phase Avoidance**
> **STRATEGY 26**
>
> *Risk management is the project manager's secret weapon. It is imperative that project managers identify and manage risk. Risk management is the best tool available to support the predictive facets of the project.*

breach seriously. We just can't afford to play this out too many times."

# CHAPTER 27
# Avoidance Metrics

A long-time favorite cliché in quality management circles is "you can't improve what you don't measure." Although few will argue with the validity of this statement, few actually practice what they preach!

This is where we introduce a new tool entitled *Avoidance Metrics*. The idea is to put related performance metrics or measures in place to track project performance towards meeting project *objectives*. As we look at *Avoidance Metrics*, it will become clear that it's not enough to just have project *objectives*. But to make them work, we must also have strategies for achieving each *objective* and a way to measure our chances of meeting them.

A classic example of our tendency to lose sight of *objectives* centers on the dieting process. "My *objective* might be to lose twenty pounds in the next four months based on my doctor making me promise that I would lose the weight. Even with this commitment, my return visit to the doctor is a long time away. There shouldn't be a problem with me eating a candy bar today if I want one." Hmmm!

To be successful, we have to link the candy bar today with the *objective* to lose twenty pounds in four months. Unless we link each action along the way to a cause and effect relationship, a candy bar each day could easily become routine. That is, of course, until we have to return to the doctor's office and weigh in. At that point, we have in effect hit the dietary *OS Phase*.

Experience reminds us that actual identification of *objectives* can be easy, whereas accomplishing the little rascals is more difficult. The *Avoidance Metrics* will help us to keep our focus and to *meet* them, every time! We use metrics for almost every other aspect of business. We look at consumer price indices; we watch and try to predict interest rates and stock market performance.

> However, when it comes to projects, we jump into the process without so much as a clue as to what is important to know about the project. *Avoidance Metrics*, or sometimes called Critical Success Factors, measure performance areas vital to the project. If chosen correctly and with appropriate thought to the *processes*, the *Avoidance Metrics* will be *simple* but effective *predictors*.
>
> Just like a light or temperature gauge on a car that provides a warning when the engine is getting too warm, *Avoidance Metrics* will tell us when our project is overheating!

Engaged in the discussions up to this point, Raj was evidencing discomfort with the absence of any discussion related to performance monitoring techniques for the project. In an excited voice, he zeroed in on his concern. "It is one thing to say we need to be predictive and it is another to actually do it! There is little argument that managing risks is important, but I need some type of indicator or group of indicators that will keep us from hitting the OS Phase again without prior notice. The events of today are a major surprise to us sitting around the table. This can't happen again! We must have some formalized process to provide accurate performance of the project."

Barry jumped in and added, "Raj must have sound data before he or any of us can approach the venture capitalists and request additional funding. Corporate financial decisions rely on massive amounts of financial information, either gathered by the company or acquired from outside monitoring services. Project specific data can only originate in one location, and that my friend, Bruce, is with you. You must provide us with the details outlining where the project is going."

Gene was processing and agreeing with every word uttered by Raj and Barry. "It's going to be difficult not to feel the need to micromanage Bruce from this point forward. My experience tells me that doing so is wrong. What we need instead are measures that will micromanage Bruce on a regular basis but without the hassle for him or us! We need a measure that reassures us that the project is proceeding well, without having to stop Bruce all the time so he can prepare status."

Everyone laughed at Gene's last comment, but his grasp of managing performance-related information definitely hit the mark. What a concept — monitoring without hassling!

Alice turned to me, looking for any comments I might have. Responding, I said, "In a perfect world, we want to remove the perception that we're micromanaging our team, but at the same time we want some assurances that the project is progressing according to what we deem is important. The unfortunate result many times, though, is a request from management to measure and report on everything! When this happens, the over-reporting is a distraction for the project. It is all too common to create an overload of measures after a project hits the OS Phase. It is a natural reaction to have a perception that a lack of measurements before the OS Phase caused the problem. This is a fallacy!

"What we don't need is a long list of measures, but, instead, only a handful of relevant ones. How these measures are developed is not set in stone, but each metric should link to the project's high-level objectives."

Bruce went back to the Stupid Triangle and spent more time describing the deliverables and objectives. After his discussion, everyone agreed that we needed an updated list of objectives.

Raj was in strong agreement about objectives, but Rich brought everyone back to earth. "What good are objectives if we don't know we missed them until we missed them? Looking at the original objectives, we were convinced at the time that they were wonderful, but look what happened. It's as if they didn't have any affect at all on the outcome."

Before Rich could think to ask Bruce if he managed the project to the original objectives, I jumped to my feet and charged up to the front of the conference room. I had to do something to get everyone on track with objectives. Thinking through my options, I ended up with my favorite analogy and began the sensitive discussion about losing weight.

Turning to the group and trying to make eye contact with as many in the room as I could, I began the discussion. "Even if your weight is at the proper level, it is impossible to escape the constant daily discussion in the news and magazines of the overweight dilemma that has reached almost epidemic proportions.

"Let's tie Avoidance Metrics to losing weight. When we initiate a personal weight loss program, we immediately start getting on the scales each day. We're going to compare what we see on the scales to what our doctor or weight loss author says we should weigh."

While moving my focus to everyone in the room, I asked, "Now based on this scenario, what is our objective?"

Barry spoke first. "You could actually have two objectives depending on how you want to measure. One objective would be to weigh a certain value; in my case, I want to weigh 185 pounds and that value would be my objective. Another way to look at the same effort would be to say that since I now weigh 205 pounds, the objective is to lose twenty pounds. Either way, you get to the same result."

"The only result I see now, Barry, is that men lie more than women about their weight," Alice said, while bringing everyone in the room to a roar of laughter. "If you weigh 205 pounds, I want to borrow your scales."

Blushing, Barry looked at Alice and said, "I was only saying that as a hypothetical example."

As expected, more laughter erupted throughout the conference room.

It took a few minutes to get everybody calmed down and back on track. Barry was good-natured and he disregarded the jabs about his weight. The discussion did point out the problem with weight loss. We get so fixated on the scale's value we lose sight of the process of weight gain or weight loss.

Continuing with the example, I wanted to relate the example to their project. "We have grown to believe that to lose weight, we have to get on the scales everyday. That's insane. The scales tell us how much we weigh, but they don't tell us if our weight loss program is on track or off track. When we climb on the scales and they shout that we weigh more than the previous day, what does it mean? Our objective might be to lose twenty pounds. We're measuring our objective, but nothing is happening! Bruce had project objectives set in place by everyone in this room, but the project still failed. What happened?"

Rich was the first to see the relevance of the example. He started by focusing back to the weight loss example and challenging the benefit of getting on the scales. "The measurement on your bathroom scales is only a result of other factors. It is a direct result of the number of calories or specialty food types consumed each day. It is a result of the number of minutes of exercise logged each day. It might even be a result of the amount of water consumed or not consumed each day. The weight value on the scale itself doesn't change anything; it is only a result of these other items."

"That's right," said Alice. "To lose weight, we must measure the factors that contribute to our weight. Understanding and targeting these metrics will result in change, not getting on the scales."

Quiet since his earlier ribbing, Barry joined in the conversation. "It is possible then to calculate daily calorie intake and exercise parameters over a designated number of days, stick to those values and lose weight, without ever getting on any scales."

"That's a fantastic observation," I said, while looking for agreement from everyone else.

"This is so contrary to anything I've ever done in the past when I was on a diet, but it makes sense," Barry said.

Tying the discussion back to the project, I addressed the group, with each person in the room clearly focused. "Unfortunately, just as Bruce was conditioned to look at actual costs to date figures and current schedule performance, we are conditioned to get on the scales. All that any of these things tell us is some value that we can graph, and that's the extent of it!"

Bruce, although silent so far in this discussion, now made a rather astute comment. "Think about it. The scales don't predict we will gain weight, they tell us we HAVE gained or lost weight. If our calorie count consistently exceeds a reasonable target each day, we have a good predictor that we will ultimately gain weight. It's just a matter of time, but it will happen."

I walked over to the flip chart and wrote down the attributes of the Avoidance Metrics that we'd been discussing (Chart 27 - 1).

Rich laughed and asked, "Is there anything that shouldn't be simple, credible, or predictive?"

Smiling, I looked at Rich and gave him and everyone else the answer they were expecting, "No!"

Barbara was pleased with the correlation of these attributes to project metrics. "It's about time we all started doing everything in accordance with these three attributes. I believe we should not limit their application to projects. They fit everything we do at work…"

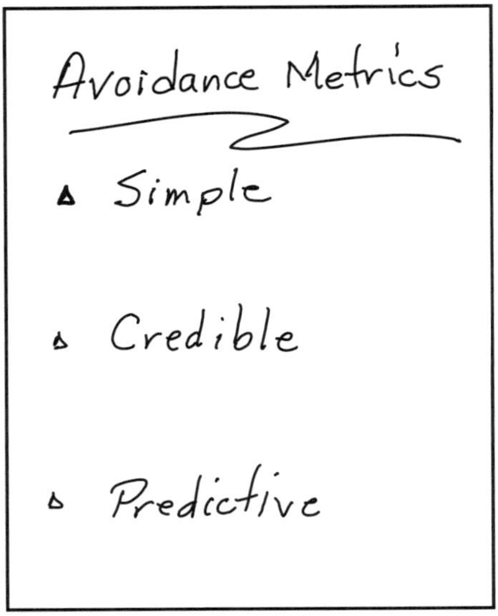

"…and at home," Gene said, finishing Barbara's sentence. "Making a correlation of these concepts to my personal activities helps me to appreciate their value. We need to simplify our lives, not complicate them even more."

Avoidance Metrics
- Simple
- Credible
- Predictive

**Chart 27 - 1**

We don't want to develop metrics that are there just for the sake of having measures. Each metric should have a sanity check to make sure it is simple to capture, the data is credible and can't be manipulated in any way, and it supports our need to be predictive.

Bruce was thinking of several possibilities for metrics, but became stuck on a common dilemma. "The idea of Avoidance Metrics is great, but how do we get those that have to support the collection and processing steps to do what they are supposed to do? The Responsibility Assignment Matrix we discussed earlier could be a great tool, but it's not uncommon for some team members to ignore their own specific assignments."

"Bruce," Alice responded, "as we said earlier, you need to treat that situation as a risk. If you can't get the responsiveness needed, then the executive committee will be presented with the associated risk."

"Would Bruce have any other choices?" Troy asked. "You can't spend all of your time identifying and floating up new risks. There just wouldn't be time in the day to do anything else."

"I'm glad you thought about this before you actually jumped into the processes we've described here this morning," I said, while noticing some confused looks around the table. "Risk management is an important process on any project, but it is difficult to do properly. Any time we can resolve a problem before going through the risk management steps is time well spent. In fact, when you bring risks to management it is important to have as many supporting documents as possible to support the concern. Display of Avoidance Metrics is totally appropriate."

Based on his facial expressions, Raj had a lot going on in his mind related to Avoidance Metrics. After the linkage of Avoidance Metrics to risk management, he joined in on the discussion. "This conversation is relevant to my area of responsibility, almost 1 to 1. In order to successfully manage the financial health of this company, it is necessary to pay attention to numerous indices provided in the marketplace. Although interest rate levels today are important, the best information is what will help me predict the future levels of interest rates. I can't wait until I miss our financial target, or our financial objective, before I adjust our financial position in the markets."

"So then your objective is to meet certain financial targets and the market indices you use are the same as Avoidance Metrics?" Alice asked.

"Absolutely," Raj responded enthusiastically. "I've been doing everything perfectly and didn't even know it."

Rich smiled and spoke what was on everybody's mind. "No, Raj, you're not perfect, just slightly ahead of the rest of us!"

"Can you imagine how well Avoidance Metrics would work with monitoring the various team members on follow-through and action item assignments?" Troy asked, while moving around the conference room.

In response, Barry added, "This is where Avoidance Metrics falls into play. Instead of wasting time nagging people to do their jobs, measure what you need them to do. Remember, the secret is to get the team to tell you what they will do and then expect them to do it! They all need to look at their processes and explore possible points to capture the relevant data."

Barbara interrupted the discussion by expressing her displeasure with the current situation. "Accepting the delay is difficult for me. Even though we don't have to report to stockholders or a board of directors, we still should be ashamed of what happened. We've talked about the problems, and there are some great suggestions on the table, but let's not forget that as a group we will all suffer financially and could even lose our market position before we start. Any other potential competitors will be pleased to see our delay and will mock our stumble out of the gate."

On a roll, Barbara kept the floor, moved closer to Bruce without formally confronting him, and said, "And I'm personally disappointed that the executive committee wasn't advised of the problem earlier. It wouldn't surprise me if everyone else in the industry knew about this problem before we did!

"With that said," she continued, "it is obvious that the executive committee might be partially responsible because we failed to use the right metrics to measure the project's performance. Announcements like this today should not be a surprise."

Turning back to the others on the executive committee she asked, "Does anyone even know what metrics we see each month? I ask this question because, in all honesty, if you asked today what metrics we use, I'm not sure that I could recall even one."

The silence was very telling.

Barry was the first to speak. "The monthly reports always seemed to make sense, but now we realize that our metrics were inadequate. As a committee we have several key decisions to make this afternoon, and I believe the most important is to decide on some realistic metrics that will be a valid reflection of the project's performance."

Barbara's intensity actually had a calming effect on Barry and everyone else in the room, for that matter. Her skills as a manager are part of the normal folk lore. Her passion to get the project back on track was a welcome sign and might be the most significant contribution. Barbara's experience in supply chain management taught her to measure key processes if she was going to keep a step ahead of the company's Operations organization. She was pushing the group towards development of metrics for the project, believing that with the right measures, the executive committee could use these metrics to keep abreast of project performance from this point forward.

She didn't know how right she was!

Looking around the room it was easy to see that there were many eyebrows raised in agreement with Barbara's challenge. It was neither the time nor the place for Alice to debate Barbara's earlier comments. It was time for her, instead, to sit back and listen to what her peers offered as suggestions. With the poise of a seasoned professional and the humility of a fallen executive, she turned to Barbara and thanked her for the support and then turned to the balance of the executive committee and thanked them for their support.

Looking back again to Barbara, Alice smiled and turned the discussion over to her by asking a question. "What's the best process towards developing some metrics? How is it possible to have measures that offer better information than those we used before? Remember, Troy and I were also oblivious to problems on the project."

The earlier discussion energized Barbara and she was now excited to take charge of the discussion. Her first approach was right on target. "We've talked a lot today about predictive measures and I don't recall any of our reports including much in this area. If we are to avoid the OS Phase in the future, we need to have measures that warn us when we're heading that way. But before I spout too many of my own opinions, I'd like to see what everybody else thinks."

"I agree wholeheartedly with the need for metrics," Barry added, while shuffling through his notebook jammed with previous project performance reports. "We need measures that stand alone and give us warning before we hit the OS Phase. I also like the concept of *simple* that we discussed earlier. I used to like a lot of detail, but there just isn't time to sit down and analyze detailed spreadsheets of numbers. We need some metrics that are easy to graph and tell the appropriate story."

Raj was deeply engaged in the conversation. He waited for Barry to finish shuffling his paperwork and then added his own comments. "The idea of *simple* is great, and the concept of striving towards *predictive* behavior is even better. From a financial perspective, we must always be looking forward. It's odd that so many project management metrics focus on history. From my vantage point, accountants keep track of the past, and that's important, but investors want to know what the future holds and in today's world, we have to be pretty close with our predictions."

Barbara was glad to see the support to develop metrics. She went to the front of the room, turned to a clean sheet on the flip chart, and directed her attention to the group. "Let's first think about what's important for us to know from this point forward."

"Good strategy. First we figure out what we need to know and then develop measures that will ensure we get there," Rich said enthusiastically. "We need to get rid of any metrics that are currently required but have no purpose."

"Who came up with some of the measures we have now?" Gene asked. "All I hear is complaints from my team whenever I ask them for performance data each month."

"Let's not debate what we're doing now, but, instead, take advantage of this problem with the project to reexamine all of our metrics," Barbara added. "As we discussed earlier, we need metrics that are simple to develop and understood by all. They must be credible both to us as a committee and to the staff themselves, and, most importantly, we need metrics that are *predictive*."

Barbara's reference to the attributes of a strong project management program was a boost to everyone. She was now directing her earlier criticism towards solutions that everyone supported.

Barbara's mind filled with more thoughts relevant to the new process. "From a supply chain perspective, I should be measuring the number of intended deliverables that are overdue. Up until now, I just focused on having the final deliverables completed by a certain date, an important objective, but if that's all we focus on, then it's too late if we miss it. Measuring how many deliverables are overdue at any point in time doesn't leave much to the imagination."

Troy was still pacing around the room. His mind was traveling at warp speed as he was trying to internalize this important concept. "Avoidance Metrics will be fantastic on the project. If I understand the concept, I'll have some of the same Avoidance Metrics on my follow-on project, but I'll also have some that are unique based on that project's specific objectives. That's kind of frustrating."

Responding to Troy's comment, I concluded the thought by adding, "Defining Avoidance Metrics is not easy because this will vary with almost every project or company and can vary even within similar projects within the same organization. You will have Avoidance Metrics for the initial phases of your project, whereas Bruce is past that point and those Avoidance Metrics won't benefit the project. It may seem strange, though, but the most beneficial part of Avoidance Metrics is the actual process of deriving them. Sitting with the team and then the executive committee to look for those items that most clearly define the success of the project is an important part of the Avoidance Metrics definition and buy-in process. The project team must work together to seek out performance criteria that have meaning and that everyone understands."

Turning to Edward, who was not yet totally convinced, Alice provided an example related to software development. "One of the objectives we came up with over the weekend was to have "zero" critical and high defects on the release of the new booking and delivery system. The Avoidance Metric might measure how many unresolved critical and high defects are on the list. When an Avoidance Metric is forecasting steady increases in unresolved defects, instead of a decrease over time, then we need to add that item to the project's risk list. It is important to keep the Avoidance Metrics and the supporting processes simple. In fact, the more I think about the discussion, it would be a great strategy to consider Avoidance Metrics that provide a signal that any individual risk we are tracking is actually getting worse or, in fact, might be about to occur. I believe we call this a 'trigger.'"

Edward commented to the group without hesitation. "Alice's example makes sense. I've never really thought about having these types of metrics in place, but it's clear how they might help us out from this point forward. When should we do them?"

"Now!" Alice exclaimed. "For our project the time is now! We don't have any time to waste if we are to feel good as a committee on where we are going."

"I agree," Raj commented, while starting to sketch out some ideas on his note pad. "If we have the right metrics, I can see our financiers buying into our plan much quicker and with less hassle."

Quiet during the last discussion, and usually a cynic when it comes to performance metrics, Barry asked a common question for anybody embarking on development of metrics. "Is there a list anywhere of Avoidance Metrics that we can use so we can start immediately?"

After sending a less than affirmative non-verbal response to answer Barry's question, I suggested that as a team we develop some metrics that relate specifically to the project. I spent some time listing 'typical' metrics, but fell short of saying that the list was even close to being complete (Chart 27 - 2).

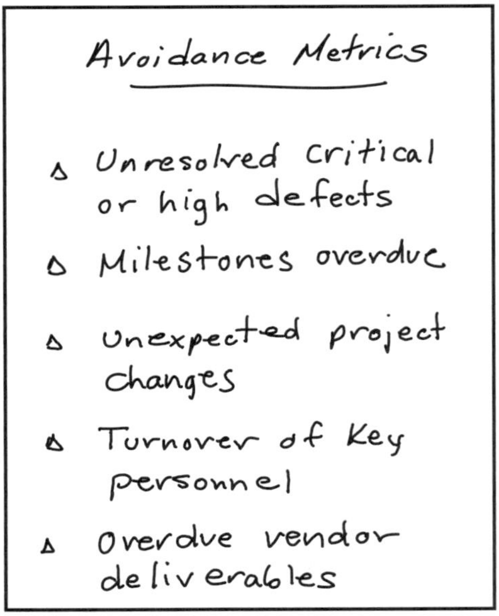

After I finished presenting the examples, I turned to Barry and said, "Maybe if we do a good job developing Avoidance Metrics, you and I could co-author a book with suggestions for developing metrics. We could even include a list of the top 100 project performance metrics."

This suggestion kept the mood in the room light, but, at the same time, Barry seemed to have taken the suggestion seriously based on his energies at taking copious notes about the discussion.

*Avoidance Metrics*

- Unresolved critical or high defects
- Milestones overdue
- Unexpected project changes
- Turnover of key personnel
- Overdue vendor deliverables

**Chart 27 - 2**

As we were finalizing the first pass of a list of Avoidance Metrics, Barry stood and got everyone's attention. He began his comments in a tone that captured their complete attention. "I've sat here this morning and had to curb my anger and frustration at the delay, with confidence that the team can actually finish this project. When I first suspected that the project had serious problems after my discussions with Bruce over the weekend, I was ready to boot some of our team out the door this morning. After our discussions, and Bruce's obvious acceptance of his role in the delay and willingness to change his processes, I'm convinced that the project will get back on track, and I'm further convinced that the next project down the road will be even better. Troy's enthusiasm and the lessons he is learning from today will be invaluable for our future projects."

After getting non-verbal agreements from the other members of the executive committee, Barry continued his comments. "If I've learned anything this morning, it's that the biggest problem we've had is admitting there was a problem. Even though I was disappointed with the news this morning, I can't say that I was really surprised. We were zooming along at a fast pace, but we didn't really have any metrics substantiating that we were going to be successful. It is imperative that as executives we have metrics in place to predict problems before the project or work task gets in trouble. They can also substantiate that you're proceeding or planning properly. I, for one, believe that the Avoidance Metrics we've looked at will make a big difference."

Gene was the first to acknowledge Barry's comments. "I agree with everything you said and I hope that this was more than lip service this morning. I expect great things from the team. Also, Barry, I was wondering if your new book on Avoidance Metrics would be available on the company's new web site?"

Gene's comment about the book caught everyone off guard, in a good way! It was great to see everyone on the same page and ready to move on to the next area of discussion.

---

*OS Phase* Avoidance
**STRATEGY 27**

*Avoidance Metrics should be simple, credible, and predictive.*

*Identification of Avoidance Metrics will guide us by defining the effort it will take to meet all project objectives.*

*Having a truly representative Avoidance Metric is like winning the lottery...almost.*

CHAPTER 28

# Understanding Earned Value Management

The use of *Avoidance Metrics* is an invaluable tool for the project manager and team. If derived properly, they will drive specific performance needs or provide early warning systems for deficiencies.

The beneficial features of *Avoidance Metrics* can also be their curse. When used properly, metrics drive behavior on specific project processes or problems. Only those needed or adding value are used. Even with the significant value of these metrics, it's a disadvantage if we couldn't use some of the metrics on every project, in every phase, in every business sector. It would be beneficial to have key *Avoidance Metrics* that were the same for every type of project, from information technology related initiatives to traditional construction projects.

Metrics deriving from the use of **Earned Value Management** techniques will provide the common measures that we need.

**Earned Value Management** provides metrics that evaluate how well the schedule as a whole is performing to the target schedule and how close actual costs are coming in based on the budget for work performed. Since time and cost are elements of all projects, regardless of type of project, using **Earned Value Management** provides the standard methodology we were looking for as a tool.

An incredible benefit of **Earned Value Management** is how well it links with critical path analysis for the schedule and appropriate cost performance analysis, to become one of the best *predictive* tools available. **Earned Value Management** takes project performance to date and provides an unbiased forecast for the schedule and cost outcome.

If basic guidelines for using **Earned Value Management** calculations are used and agreeable to all parties, it is a great way to calculate progress payments to subcontractors, another area where consistent application of methodologies is mandatory.

Despite the fact that some professionals depict **Earned Value Management** as a very complex series of formulas and terminologies, it is not. When implemented properly, it definitely meets our framework of *Avoidance Metrics* to be *simple*, *credible*, and *predictive*.

Used properly, it will help us avoid the *OS Phase*.

Bruce's mood and enthusiasm were improving, especially after Barry's vote of confidence. He knew that support from the entire executive committee was essential if the project was to succeed. He was still interested in understanding all of the potential Avoidance Metrics. He started the new discussion by summarizing all of the project management tools discussed earlier onto the flip chart (Chart 28 - 1). "We're working to get the processes of project management in place. We will be using a WBS to keep track of scope and a Responsibility Assignment Matrix for managing roles and responsibilities. We will identify and manage risks on a routine basis using both the WBS and Responsibility Assignment Matrix. After these are in place, we will implement Avoidance Metrics to keep track of performance and to be predictive."

"Am I on track?" he asked.

"Yes, these are definitely the right steps to take to move forward with the project," I responded enthusiastically. "If you put these tools in place as we've described them, you will have an Avoidance Plan that will work. It is important,

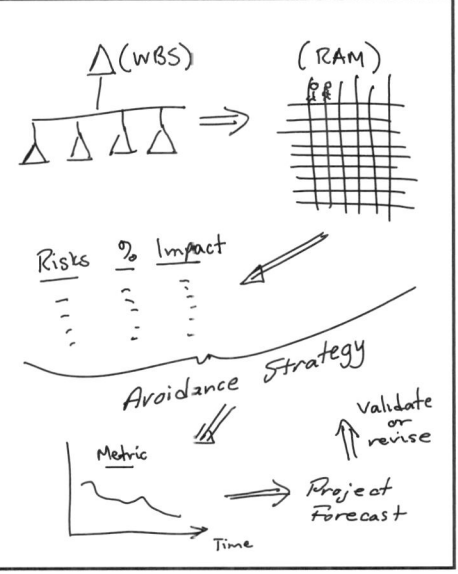

**Chart 28 - 1**

though, to focus at all times on the predictive elements we discussed when we presented the Avoidance Metrics. In general, tools are just things unless they're used to our advantage. As you develop more Avoidance Metrics, you will begin to feel the predictive nature of things. In fact, you will soon realize that Avoidance Metrics represents the most important tool for any project manager."

"Whoa!" Bruce exclaimed, smiling and shaking his index finger at me as if to scold me. "There you go again, presenting another project management tool that you define as the most important tool for the project manager."

"I agree," Rich added, smiling as well. "Pretty soon, you're going to tell us that everything is important."

I laughed and then compared Bruce's comment to one I had received some time ago from a young project manager that I was mentoring on a rather difficult automation installation project. "Each month when I visited the plant and mentored the on-site project management team I apparently presented a new tool, similar to the list Bruce articulated perfectly a few minutes ago. Without realizing it, each month I had commented that the new tool was the most important thing that a project manager could use for managing any project. The young project manager stopped me in mid-sentence on my third or fourth visit, I can't remember now which one, and challenged me.

"He said that I presented a new tool every month and each time I said that it was the most important tool for the project manager. I think he was excited to think that he had caught me in a slight embellishment!"

Bruce was glued to every word and could hardly wait to comment, "I can't wait to hear how you got out of that one. In fact, I'm surprised that you are so willing to admit that you are an embellisher yourself."

Everyone enjoyed Bruce's horseplay and listened to hear the response.

Laughing aloud at Bruce's comment, I closed with the perfect response. "Bruce, I told him what I will tell you today. A project manager must choose from numerous tools available for use on the project. As it turns out, each step of the project has a new tool that emerges as important. This doesn't diminish the significance of the others, but it does put in perspective the constantly maturing nature of a project. In the beginning, having a solid Avoidance Plan is important, but once it's in place, the project manager must focus on the next step. Once the project is defined with a WBS and Responsibility Assignment Matrix and there is a schedule and cost baseline in place, then the project manager must develop metrics to ensure that the agreed upon targets are met. Without those other steps completed, the metrics themselves would have little value."

Bruce smiled and acknowledged my response to his challenge. "Even though life might become boring when we all become good at project management, it sounds like there is still a lot of work involved to get there."

"Oh yes, the project manager's job might become boring when everything falls into place, but the steps to get it there will always be fun and exciting."

Raj enjoyed the bantering back and forth, and as he was listening to the discussion, he began to wonder how Bruce would incorporate some of the project's previous tools in the days and weeks ahead. "What about the Critical Path Schedule and our monthly budget expenditure reports? Will they work for Bruce as tools after they're updated based on the new events happening with the project? I need something that validates our cost forecast and something that confirms our ability to meet the revised delivery schedule."

Before I could respond, Bruce turned to Raj and answered from his perspective. "With the focus on the critical path, using our schedule will definitely help us stay in tune with what's important for us to work on to finish the project. The schedule will be a vital tool for the team and me. Targeting our cost objectives will help us keep the project profitable, which I know is a big concern for everyone."

"That's right," Alice said, joining in the conversation. "These are both important, but as we learned with the Avoidance Metrics, we must finalize some key measures that will help to make sure we are predictive and stay on track to meet our new targets. I believe that the Avoidance Metrics should be linked with an unbreakable chain to the critical path schedule and the monthly budget spending plan."

"I don't think we can wait on Barry's book of Avoidance Metrics," Raj said, invoking a few smirks from around the table. "So I am curious whether or not there exists some standard schedule and cost metrics that we're not aware of that could be used on the project?"

"…or on my project even though it's a ways down the road?" Troy questioned. "We are really interested in the importance of being predictive but I keep going back in my mind how difficult it is to actually accomplish this feat on most projects."

"When you think about it, if *percentage complete measurements* are flawed, what other choices do we have for our project?" Alice asked.

Based on the discussion, I thought it was the right time to introduce some special metrics to satisfy everyone's interest. I began by addressing Raj's comment. "My sense is that being predictive is a way to take historical performance data and use it to demonstrate relevant trends. We've talked about the key tools, but now you need to have some type of measure to make sure you are doing things correctly. That's where a concept called Earned Value Management comes into the picture."

In an abrupt change in attitude, Barbara began shaking her head in frustration. "You're talking about Earned Value Management as if it's the easiest thing in the world to do, and I have real problems with that. The applications I've seen of Earned Value Management were neither easy nor were they worth the paper they were printed on."

"I agree with Barbara," Gene added. "When you start to look at all of the acronyms and fancy formulas associated with Earned Value Management, it looks like some type of shell game. I've seen more people cheat on progress reporting using that process than I've seen cars on our Dallas expressways each day. I think anyone with even marginal intelligence could figure out a way to cheat, or maybe I should say embellish Earned Value Management processes. If we're criticizing Bruce for how progress was being reported, I'm not sure Earned Value Management is giving him a replacement methodology that is any better."

Defensive over the last comment, Bruce commented back to Gene in a blunt but clear way. "I'm sorry you think I 'cheated' the system when I reported back to the committee. I never deliberately lied, I just didn't drill down or show data that cast a negative perception of the project!"

Alice immediately jumped to Bruce's rescue. "Bruce was being optimistic, just like we wanted him to be, and we discouraged him from looking at risks. We are just as guilty as he was when it comes down to the actual reporting processes. I do have to agree, however, with everyone's negative comments about Earned Value Management. I've seen it used, and don't remember much of the details other than it didn't leave a good taste in my mouth."

"At least you have some kind of taste in your mouth," Rich said. "I've listened to this conversation for the last five minutes and don't have any idea what any of you are talking about. You keep referring to the term Earned Value Management, but what do you mean by the word 'earned' and how does that apply when you add the word 'value' with it? It's as if you all are speaking in a different language."

Turning to Rich, I thanked him for his comment and then offered some explanation. "The concept of Earned Value Management is predicated on the word 'earned,' where the project manager identifies what needs to be completed in the future and assigns a value to each work item. The value is most often the cost or hour budget for each activity. As work is completed, the project manager 'earns' the 'value' of the item, thus the term 'earned value.' We add the word 'management' with 'earned value' to make it sound official."

"Adding words for the sake of adding words does not make a concept simple!" Rich commented in a joking manner. "I'm okay now with the other two words, but why not just call the concept Earned Value?"

Before I could answer Rich's question, Alice provided the correct response. "The term 'earned value' often refers to the value that was earned. I know that sounds like double talk, but think about it for a minute. If you call the process Earned Value and the measure itself Earned Value, then possible confusion exists, and that, Rich, is not simple. Adding the word 'management' clarifies that reference to the process, not the measure."

"Let me repeat my earlier comment about Earned Value Management being a shell game," Gene interjected. "This last discussion demonstrates how crazy the concept really is, especially for those of us that don't have the same attention span as some of the younger team members."

While still pacing back and forth I turned to the audience with a serious look and said, "If I told you that I agreed with everything you've just discussed, you would think I'd lost my mind. But truth be known, I have witnessed some of the least effective applications ever attempted of Earned Value Management. There probably isn't a single project management process with more of a potential to demand a lot of work with a minimal benefit to a project."

"After that endorsement I can't wait to see what your proposal is for Earned Value Management on the project," Raj said, displaying his usual cynical grin.

Without addressing his concerns directly, I decided that further explanation was necessary. "There are many ways to implement Earned Value Management. Some of the processes will yield nothing and other processes will yield some impressive results. So now I'd like to make a note for the record. If I can convince everyone here to use the techniques that are proven successful, and after Bruce's team begins using Earned Value Management, the executive committee needs to return to this discussion sometime in the future to see if you still are skeptical."

Continuing, I asked for their support. "I just ask that you not dismiss it until we've had a chance to discuss it and make sure we all understand how it works. Everyone in the room has exhibited patience and professionalism today, and it's time to continue that mode of operation."

"This is getting way too serious for me," Bruce said, while bringing some levity to my serious comment.

After letting the laughter and snide remarks calm down, I began presenting the details of Earned Value Management to get everyone on the same playing field.

The most important steps were to describe how each measure of earned value links to the vast number of *Stupid Triangles* that makes up the project. At the flip chart, I wrote out the three key definitions (Chart 28 - 2). Each term provided key information for our performance measurements.

It's impossible to present these terms to a group of professionals without getting questions fired back immediately from someone trying to understand the concepts.

Bruce was the first to raise a question. "What do you mean by work scheduled? I understand that the value we're talking about is a budgeted value, but what is the time period for the work scheduled? Is it the entire project?"

Barry smiled as he responded to Bruce, "I'm glad you asked the question, Bruce. I was lost ten minutes ago but didn't want to admit to it. These terms are almost like a secret code. I remember now why I never took up spying or other covert operations; it was way too complicated!"

> Key Terms
>
> BCWS – Budgeted Cost of Work Scheduled to "time now"
>
> BCWP – Budgeted Cost of Work Performed up to "time now"
>
> ACWP – Actual Cost of Work Performed up to "time now"

**Chart 28 - 2**

Barry's comment lightened up the mood, but he made a point that is so common in the area of Earned Value Management.

I spoke quickly to agree with his concern, "I think half of the people that either use it or have it reported to them don't really understand the terminology and, therefore, don't trust it or just plain ignore it. Anybody that's listened to me speak about earned value has heard the term 'alphabet soup' because that's my nickname for it. I'm not sure there is any other methodology with so many 2, 3, and 4 letter abbreviations."

The best way to describe Budgeted Cost of Work Scheduled is to depict it on a project schedule, so I drew out a very simplistic schedule example on the whiteboard (Example 28 - A).

Pointing to Budgeted Cost of Work Scheduled as the budget value of the scheduled items shown to the left of the data date or time now line, it becomes clear as to what it represents. "Budgeted Cost of Work Scheduled is the summation of the budgeted values of the work that was to be completed to date."

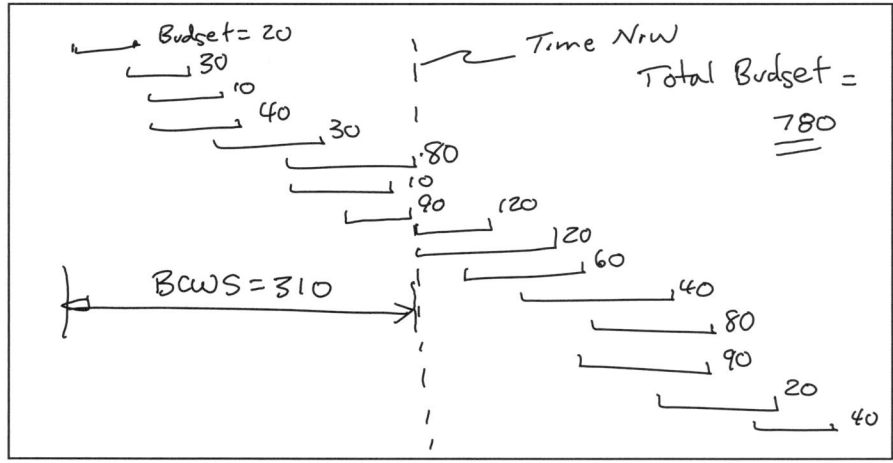

**Example 28 - A**

Troy looked up after scribbling on his note pad and asked, "On the first day of the project the Budgeted Cost of Work Scheduled would be 'zero' and on the last day it would represent the entire budget, right?"

"Exactly," I said with a strong level of encouragement in my voice. "In simple terms, Budgeted Cost of Work Scheduled represents the value of the work that should be completed through the current reporting date or in simple terms, the date at which current data for the project has been reported. Earlier I referred to this date as the data date and on the whiteboard schedule, I called it Time Now. These terms are synonymous for our example. In order for us to evaluate the value of what we have earned, it is important to understand how recent the data was reported."

"The reporting date definition is clear to me now, but could you explain what you mean by the term *value*," Troy said.

"This is where the benefit of Earned Value Management starts," I said. "First we need an estimate or weighted value for each work item."

"What unit should we use for estimating?" Alice asked.

The interest was increasing and it was obvious that most in the group were desperate for some type of analytical measure that would help them understand the performance of the project. My excitement apparently was contagious. Turning to Alice, I wanted to give her an answer that fit her paradigm. "Actually, it doesn't make any difference

# UNDERSTANDING EARNED VALUE MANAGEMENT

as long as they are the same on every item. The estimate must represent some type of equivalent effort. It could be hours, dollars, Euros, anything." The value for Budgeted Cost of Work Scheduled will be identical to the Budgeted Cost of Work Performed when the task is complete. Remember, Budgeted Cost of Work Performed represents the value of the work that actually was completed so far and Actual Cost of Work Performed is what we've spent on the work performed to date."

"Perfect," Alice said, while scanning the conference room for any puzzled looks. "As the project proceeds from the first day forward, the Budgeted Cost of Work Scheduled increases based on the new work that is supposed to be completed."

"That makes sense!" Barbara blurted out. "So then the Budgeted Cost of Work Performed would represent the value of the work actually completed and then you can compare that with what you should have done. Right?"

"Perfect," Alice responded, as she marked up the whiteboard to reflect activities that had progressed and then addressed the team (Example 28 - B). "The heavy lines indicate the amount or percentage of work completed."

As I watched the dynamics in the room, it was interesting to see everyone's reaction when Alice highlighted an item past the data date or time now, indicating that it had Budgeted Cost of Work Performed because it was complete.

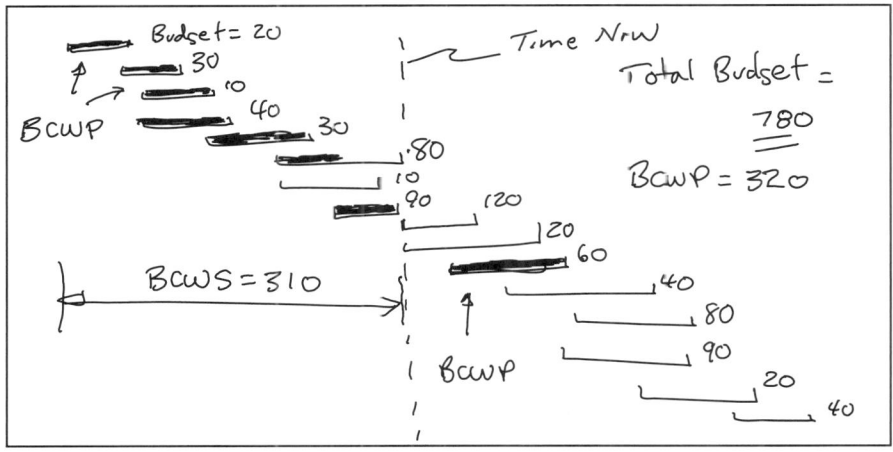

**Example 28 - B**

Sensing the questioning looks, Alice clarified what was happening. "We scheduled the activity to be completed in the future, but we completed it early and must include it in the work performed value. This is one of the most difficult aspects of Earned Value Management to understand, or maybe I should say, accept."

"Perfect again," I said, while working to maintain the momentum that Alice had displayed. "Now the only thing left is to compare the actual costs against the value of the work we have completed. The term Actual Cost of Work Performed would represent the actual costs linked to the same time period as the values for the work scheduled and earned."

"Oops," said Barbara. "I think we just found the Achilles heel in the process."

"You can say that again," Bruce said, joining in.

Everyone in the room, except me, knew what the problem was on the project. Actual costs for the project are not available from the accounting system for several weeks. Measuring actual costs against the Budgeted Cost of Work Performed will not be as easy as just suggesting that we do it.

"Well, it looks like we're back to a data management concern again," Barry said. "I'm not sure if we can get that resolved soon enough for this project."

"If you can live with late performance metrics for cost, the late reporting of actual costs will not prevent us from using Earned Value Management for a schedule performance metric," I suggested, trying to salvage the discussion. "Schedule performance analyses will compare what was scheduled with what was earned, and as long as we have a schedule and pay attention to what we're earning, you will have some good trending to work with as a project metric."

"What's the best way to display earned value?" Barbara asked. "Should we use a table of numbers or should we create trend curves for some of the data, similar to the Avoidance Metrics we discussed earlier?"

Alice answered before I could even muster the first breath. "The table of numbers is not an option. We've all realized the disadvantage of that type of reporting. As far as graphing the numbers, isn't there a

# UNDERSTANDING EARNED VALUE MANAGEMENT

common term called Schedule Variance (SV) that we would use? If I remember correctly, Schedule Variance is the difference between what we earned and what we should have earned."

Turning to the flip chart, she wrote the formula as she remembered it from her previous project some time ago (Chart 28 - 3).

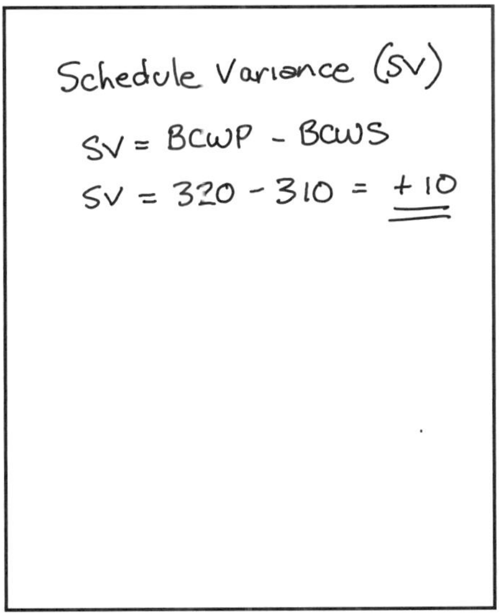

"Excellent!" I exclaimed. "Someone is a closet Earned Value Management fanatic! But it's a shame that you remembered the one term that is absolutely worthless as a measurement of performance."

"Whoa!" Raj exclaimed. "I remember seeing that term a lot. I think it is very common on government projects and I know the Project Management Information Systems have that formula pre-programmed into their programs. Somebody thinks it's the right type of measurement, even if you don't!"

Raj's comment silenced the room. They all had a great deal of respect for Raj and were aware of his ability to focus and analyze proposals. So far, the acceptance of using Earned Value Management was tenuous at best.

Addressing Raj directly, I went to the formula that Alice had written on the flip chart and added an additional formula for Cost Variance (Chart 28 - 4).

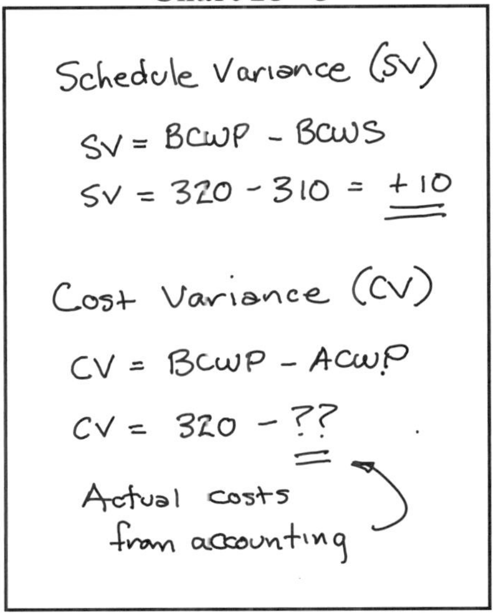

Schedule Variance (SV)

SV = BCWP - BCWS

SV = 320 - 310 = +10

**Chart 28 - 3**

Schedule Variance (SV)

SV = BCWP - BCWS

SV = 320 - 310 = +10

Cost Variance (CV)

CV = BCWP - ACWP

CV = 320 - ??  ← Actual costs from accounting

**Chart 28 - 4**

I then went on to explain the formula. "Before we look at alternatives, I wanted to show the corresponding relationship for measuring cost performance. The Cost Variance is a measure of how much we are over or under budget at the moment. The calculated value represents a point in time and does have significance for a financial manager. Cost Variance evaluates the difference between what we've spent versus what we've earned."

"How is this better than comparing actual costs to budget?" Barry asked.

"Thanks for asking," I responded. "This is where Earned Value Management separates itself from most cost measures. With the Cost Variance formula we are comparing what we've spent versus what work we've completed. It could turn out that our actual costs are below what was budgeted in the cost baseline through that point in time, which looks good on the surface, but if we haven't accomplished much work, it's easy to draw the wrong conclusion."

Taking this comment and summarizing it, Barry concluded, "The schedule and cost variances are beneficial to the point that they report performance to date, but they provide little vision into the future, and that's a problem."

"Isn't that where the schedule comes into play?" Troy asked. "The critical path would tell us if we are going to meet the scheduled milestones."

Bruce jumped into the conversation with a perfect response. "If the work that comprised the negative SV wasn't on the critical path, you wouldn't know you had a problem with that work falling behind unless you also used Earned Value Management."

"That would be easy to fix if we had a metric that measured those activities," Gene responded.

"STOP!" Barbara shouted, while nervously beating on the table with her hand. "I'm getting confused."

I let the group banter back and forth for a few minutes before I jumped back into the conversation. It was clear that in addition to Barbara, others were also getting a little anxious.

Getting everyone's attention, I went back to the board and addressed the group. "By what you all are saying, you're now realiz-

# UNDERSTANDING EARNED VALUE MANAGEMENT

ing the rationale behind Earned Value Management. Current budget evaluations and schedule measures are flimsy at best and don't really provide the simple detail necessary to be predictive. Earned Value Management provides a basis for measuring schedule performance against what should have been completed and cost performance against what we've actually spent."

Alice responded to my comment almost instantly. "But didn't you say that Schedule Variance and Cost Variance weren't any good either?"

"That's right," I answered. "What I would like to present are two alternate measures called Schedule Performance Index and Cost Performance Index. These measures help us to step back from the confusion of pure schedule and cost measures."

On the flip chart, I wrote the two indices I was referring to and then explained them (Chart 28 - 5). "When we mathematically divide the same values we saw before, we create an index of performance, similar to an Avoidance Metric. By themselves, these metrics don't tell us much, except that if either the cost or schedule value is less than "1" then we are not doing well for that particular area."

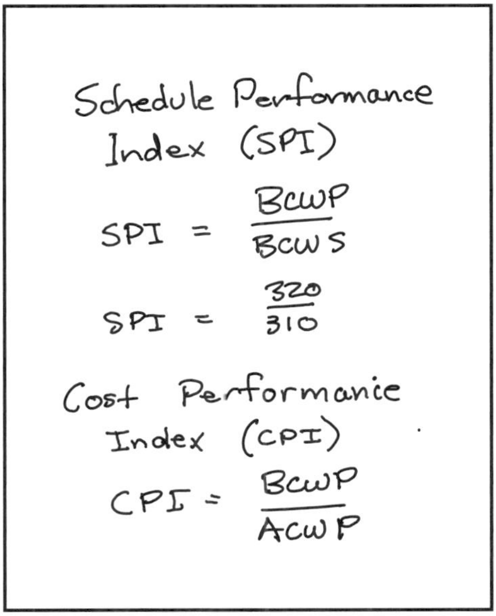

Raj was obviously getting impatient or confused by the discussion. Recognizing a good talking point, he jumped back into the discussion. "I don't see the advantage to the Cost Performance Index. With Cost Variance, I had a value that I could work with to assess the project's costs. With Cost Performance Index, all I have is an index. I can see why most people use Cost Variance, but I'm lost as to why Cost Performance Index is better."

Schedule Performance Index (SPI)

$$SPI = \frac{BCWP}{BCWS}$$

$$SPI = \frac{320}{310}$$

Cost Performance Index (CPI)

$$CPI = \frac{BCWP}{ACWP}$$

**Chart 28 - 5**

"I agree with Raj," Alice said, serving as a spokesperson for the group. "Why would anybody use an index when evaluating project performance?"

As I looked over at Raj, it was clear that Alice's comment struck a chord in his mind.

I asked him a question that he was already contemplating. "Raj, you mentioned earlier that you used the Consumer Price Index and other similar metrics to help you predict the market. Why in the world would you use an index instead of real numbers?"

To say that everyone in the room realized the answer to that question at the same time would be an understatement.

"Indices show trends without having to get bogged down with incomprehensible numbers. Indices provide a quick assessment of what is happening in the financial world," Raj responded.

"And they're simple!" Alice exclaimed.

Gene was obviously engaged in the concept. He walked to the flip chart and added some more details on the Schedule Performance Index chart I had drawn earlier, then spoke to the group (Chart 28 - 6). "If we show the end date of the project with the 'X' then we realize that Schedule Performance Index must equal '1' at that point. There is no choice, because the Budgeted Cost of Work Performed has to equal the Budgeted Cost of Work Scheduled or we wouldn't be at the end. With that in mind, at any point in the project, if we are trending downward away from '1' then the project is hosed!"

Everyone laughed at Gene's comment, but he was right.

Bruce was silent for much of this discussion, since he was

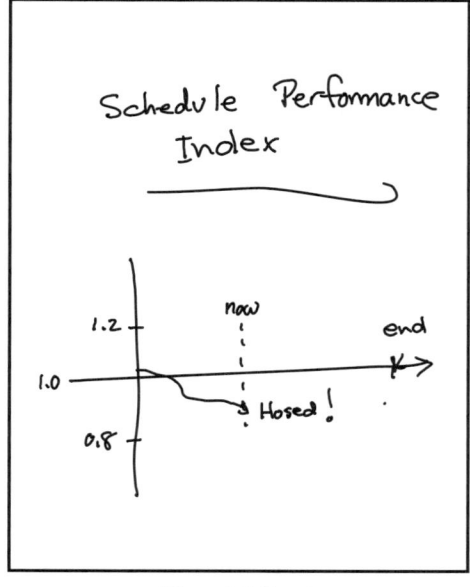

**Chart 28 - 6**

learning a concept with which he was totally unfamiliar. He laughed while adding, "That downward curve not only says we're hosed, but it's a solid predictive warning that we are headed to the OS Phase."

"That's right, Bruce," Troy joined in. "The Schedule Performance Index and Cost Performance Index are both linked to the schedule. The schedule links to the scope by way of the Work Breakdown Structure. These measures then provide a clear indication if the project team is doing what they said they were going to do for all of the key parameters."

"I'm sold," Raj said, while mimicking 'The Wave' by raising both hands high in the air. "As the executive committee, we need to get a proposal as to what the team plans to do and then we compare that curve, each week if necessary, to see if they are getting it done. Schedule Performance Index and Cost Performance Index are clearly the capstone of all Avoidance Metrics."

With the total group now engaged and supporting the concept of Earned Value Management, I presented some more details related to other benefits of these indices and captured them on the flip chart (Chart 28 - 7). Then I suggested we take a short break before moving on to another important area.

It was becoming apparent that the executive committee was gaining confidence, but it would be just as important to make sure they gave Bruce the time to prepare a thorough plan. Actually, I was beginning to think that several on the executive committee might even want to help him since they were demonstrating such a genuine interest. With all of the new experts on the team, Bruce was going to have his work cut out for him.

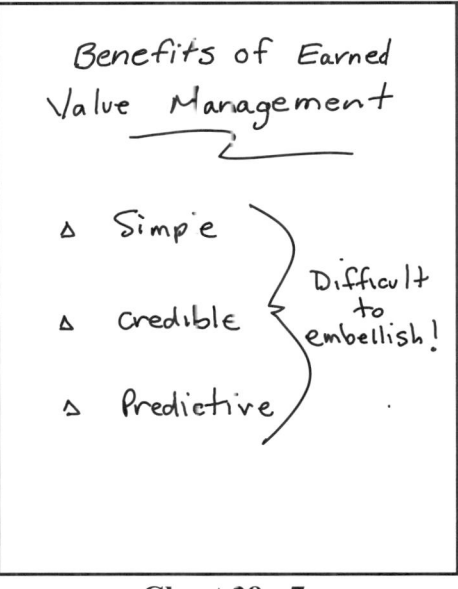

**Chart 28 - 7**

> ***OS Phase* Avoidance**
> **STRATEGY 28**
>
> ***Earned Value Management is an excellent predictive tool for predicting the cost and schedule outcome of any type of project.***
>
> ***Schedule Performance Index and Cost Performance Index might be the best metrics ever developed to quickly and accurately assess the performance and forecast of a project.***

# CHAPTER 29
# Avoiding That Déjà vu Feeling

A great tragedy associated with project management is the often common repeating of the same mistakes. When an organization repeats problems, we shake our heads and ask, "Why did they do that again?" or "How could this have happened knowing what we knew?"

Unfortunately, no matter how many times we are shocked at how projects repeat the terrible mistakes of the past, we would be remiss if we thought that particular occurrence would be the last time it happened or would happen. History will more than likely repeat itself...over and over!

As bad as it is to repeat mistakes, it is unforgivable to squander good lessons that we've learned by failing to make them part of our best practices. Failure to share lessons, both good and bad, has an irreversible negative effect on future projects.

Few will argue with the relevancy of capturing important lessons learned on a project, but at the same time, few actually take the process seriously. Just as with *risk* management, where everyone speaks of the importance of managing *risks*, few actually implement meaningful systems to manage lessons learned. If anything, the perception of the "final lessons learned report" is less than glamorous. With the wrong attitude, lessons learned gathering is a far cry from real project management. In addition, if a report is required at the completion of a project, then it's only completed as a compliant step. When the report is completed, it will collect dust on the shelf.

To wait until a project ends to complete the report is ignoring the dynamics of the project environment. An analogy would be to write down the checks from your checking account only once every six months or so. The personal memory has too many things happening to allow completion of the project successfully.

> Ignoring the busy lives of project team members or anybody, for that matter, is a mistake. If something isn't written down or captured in some way, the chance that it will be lost is increased significantly.
>
> The human race grows and prospers based on the sharing of lessons learned from one generation to the next. Project management teams need to prosper as well. Any tendency to avoid sharing experiences will stunt the growth of the organization and will cripple the ability to learn from mistakes. Success in lessons learned is necessary to drive the organization towards maturity.
>
> Support for lessons learned must start at the top of the organization.
>
> That is a lesson learned many times in other organizations.

It was encouraging to see how focused the group was with the discussion of project management concepts and processes. Everyone in the conference room was making a significant professional transition as they began to understand the relevance of these key, yet simple concepts.

"If we had only thought about these things before starting then we might not have hit the OS Phase," Bruce said, with genuine frustration in his voice.

Rich, not one of Bruce's strong supporters, was conciliatory as he responded to Bruce's comment. "The important thing is that it is never too late. The project deadline and budget are history, but the new project assessment will provide the target for where the project is heading."

"Everything we've talked about up to this point seems to make so much sense. It is embarrassing that we don't practice these concepts all of the time," Gene said.

"It's that simple part of the process that we most often forget," Barbara shot back. "Human nature around here is to seek out the complex solution because we have a special project. We always have a special project."

"That's right, even with tens of thousands or hundreds of thousands of projects that started on the same day as ours, our project is special," Barry added between snickers from everyone.

"I don't feel special," Bruce blurted out, while everyone laughed at his candor.

"Yes, Bruce, you are special," Alice said almost sarcastically, while bringing everybody back to reality. "The challenge will be to have the entire management team support the simple solution. This is a much greater challenge than one might expect. You can't believe how often *simple* is criticized for the very reason that it is too simple."

With a questioning look, Alice replied, "Thinking about these concepts we have discussed so far, it is amazing that we repeat the same mistakes so many times. It's like a bad dream…over and over…."

Troy commented as well. "The project started repeating problems that I know our organization has experienced many times before. It's as if we never learn. Even little kids learn not to touch a hot stove the second time. But we, as adult professionals, just start down the same path that led to failure the last time; each time we think it will be different."

"Repeating problems is a common process in companies," I said. "When we try to understand why this happens, we need to look at the basic elements that drive us to where we are today. First we need to determine whether the problem is a behavioral or process concern."

Troy was puzzled, "What do you mean, behavioral or process?"

Before I could answer, Alice was there with the perfect response. "When we look at a problem or deficiency as a process concern it makes the fix seem rather easy. All we need to do is review the process with the right people and then make the change to the process. We might need some retraining, but again the adjustment is rather straightforward.

"Behavioral concerns are more complex. They deal specifically with humans," she continued, as everyone laughed aloud. When the group calmed down, she continued, "If a step is missing in a procedure, it's easy to see what needs to be done to fix it. When humans mess up, it can get very complicated when we try to understand why in the world they did what they did!"

"Amen on those humans," Gene interjected with a sly smile.

Troy threw out a slight word of caution. "I agree with the concern about making processes too complicated, but it's imperative that we have processes defined and we definitely need to incorporate them into written procedures to make sure everyone understands and adheres to every step that needs to be performed. Without defined processes, formalized in a procedure, we would have chaos. Wouldn't we?"

"The answer to the question is a big yes," I responded. "Without that type of definition, the organization would not be able to repeat any successes or avoid any failures. We just need to remember to keep the processes and their supporting procedures simple."

Gene's operations experience gave him a great perspective on the discussion. He listened intently to the conversation and then spoke candidly to the group. "Having processes and supporting procedures is not the problem. But having too many of them is! When we add or modify a process step we might have fixed the concern from the process perspective, but we have in turn created another compliant requirement for the humans to adhere to. That is bad!"

"That's right, Gene," Barbara said, while addressing his concern. "Fixing a procedure is the easiest thing to do. Dealing with behavioral problems, the 'why' the person did what they did, is much more difficult. Even though the new requirement or procedure will fix the problem, if the new step doesn't appear to add value, then it might be ignored. Based on many attempts to make this work at previous companies, I realized that the technique of capturing lessons learned and then incorporating them into the organization can be quite difficult."

Troy, puzzled by Barbara's last comment, asked, "Where does the concept of adding value tie into lessons learned? I don't see the correlation."

At the flip chart in the front of the conference room, I presented a simple prioritization tool that I often use on projects (Chart 29 - 1). "One way to analyze requirements or procedural steps on a project is to look at each of them based on how they fall into one of four different categories. Let me show you what I mean."

Continuing with the discussion of the matrix, I provided a relevant example of how the Avoidance Matrix could apply to the project. "A table like this is great when looking at scope or more specifically, requirements, for a project. It also works with any other process or procedure to evaluate the things we do on a continuous basis. It helps to categorize or group items so that those we should avoid are pinpointed."

Troy and Alice both agreed that this technique would work great when initially setting expectations with the project stakeholders.

Alice commented, "Even though the table's categories seem simple enough, I can image that there are some heated discussions regarding where a particular item falls."

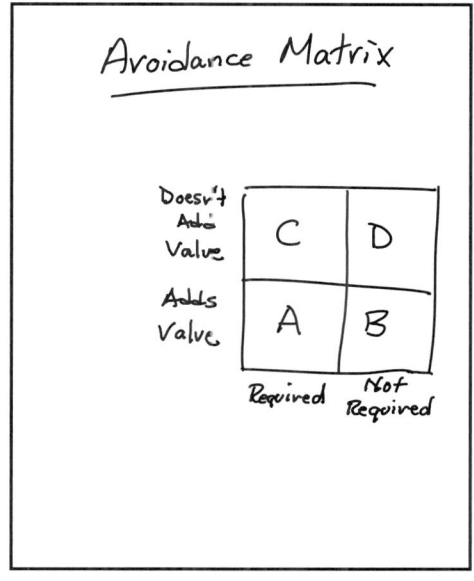

**Chart 29 - 1**

"Oh yes. That's what makes the project management role so exciting," I responded. "Project managers get to work with the people aspects of the project."

Rich came to the flip chart to join me, as he seemed to be thinking about how this might work in his Information Technology group. "Actually, when you think about it, the *Required / Not Required* designation is not too difficult to determine. Either there is a requirement to do something or there isn't. Although interpretation of requirements is added to the equation, it's still possible without much argument. The *Adds Value / Doesn't Add Value* on the other hand often depends on the unique perspective of the person you ask. As we've been discussing, as soon as you include humans with the equation, behavioral concerns enter into the picture."

The group seemed impressed with Rich's perception of the problem. With everyone now listening for my response, I asked a question instead. "Where do you think lessons learned fit on the matrix?"

Rich was puzzled at first with the question, but quickly understood the problem. "It's easy to see what can happen with lessons learned. They may add value for future projects but it's hard to see how we get excited now about fixing things for future projects."

Alice commented, "It's pretty easy to understand that if any process is not perceived to add value then it probably won't get done."

Rich took the marker, modified the flip chart, and commented, "Now let's look at where lessons learned fit into the picture."

After modifying the Avoidance Matrix on the flip chart, it is easy to see why lessons learned processes fall through the cracks (Chart 29 - 2).

Adding to Rich's comment, I said, "This Avoidance Matrix really spells out the difference between process and behavior. Initially all of the requirements of the organization fit in as Type A, B, C, or D. Behavioral attributes drive us to adhere to those requirements or rules that are most important. As a result, anything that is a Type C or D has minimal chances of getting accomplished."

**Chart 29 - 2**

"But if the process step is a Type C, it is required and will be done. Right?" Barry asked.

Answering the question, I turned to Barry and said, "Unless we have blatant disregard for procedures, you are correct, Barry. Problems will still occur if only the minimum intent of the process step is accomplished. This minimum accomplishment is very evident with lessons learned. For instance, procedures may require that a lessons learned report be prepared at the completion of each project, but if it's perceived as only a compliant requirement and not something that adds value, then only a minimum amount of effort will be forthcoming. Just enough effort will be made for compliancy and to satisfy the intent of the rule."

Edward added another question. "Why wouldn't a project manager understand the importance of lessons learned?"

Turning abruptly to Bruce and Troy, I addressed Edward's comment. "I'll answer that question with a question for these two project managers. How do you, Bruce, and you, Troy, feel about completing lessons learned at the end of projects?"

"Okay, you got us!" they answered simultaneously.

"Right!" I responded. "You're busy doing what you think is important and you just don't see any relevance to doing something like lessons learned. Remember, lessons learned is something that is prepared for managing future activities. If you don't complete the lessons learned report until the end of the project, it's easy to see how you would be complacent about doing it."

Going back to the earlier discussion about behavior versus process origins, Alice joined back in and concluded, "This now makes it a behavior concern, which means that we have to change behavior in order to accomplish what we want with this process."

Bruce was listening, but he gave the response that we've learned to expect on a regular basis. "We need to remember that the reason we don't want to do lessons learned is because we don't see the immediate benefit for our project. We need to see how we can get it to add value or else nothing will change. Forget the fact that we will lose important history for future projects. That's not in our view at all."

Continuing, I said, "In fact, we've entered into a common rat hole."

Troy was quick to recognize where we were going. "Bruce, you must be talking about the…*what's in it for me?* syndrome."

"Perfect," I said. "It's easy to see how this behavior element will drive our success and failures."

Bruce reversed directions and countered with the all too common excuse for ignoring lessons learned. "When you think about lessons learned, why are we even wasting time now talking about them? We have our project that is in trouble and you are introducing us to something that makes sense, but won't get us out of our current jam. We've hit the OS Phase and that's the bottom line. What we need to understand is what we need to do next, on *our project*, not one down the road."

"Way to go!" I said excitedly, catching Bruce a little off guard. "I couldn't have scripted it better. Bruce, your comments are consistent with what we encounter on a day-in and day-out basis. The complication is the fact that you are accurate in your question, but only to a point."

Continuing, I said, "First, let's look at how lessons learned can help out your project. The measure of value added on the left hand side of the matrix is actually multidimensional. It is easy to see how differently someone might react when we consider whether something adds value to our current project or whether the value added actually benefits someone else. It's nice to draw these 2x2 matrices and then proclaim that they represent all possible scenarios. But, that conclusion is often incorrect."

Alice agreed, and added, "But at least they get you to think about the various choices."

"Perfect," I said, with a proud tone to my voice. "Internalizing these concepts is vital to finding the best solutions. It's obvious that you both are well on your way. Now to some very complex concerns related to behavior.

"What about the executive committee?" I asked. "Does anyone here think they might be driven by the same behavioral tendencies?"

"To them, or I guess I should say, to us, it's all about priorities we have to deal with everyday. We don't seem to have much choice on where we spend our time anymore," Alice answered, while slightly laughing at her own comment.

Troy's smile represented clear agreement to this concern. "In our organization, the executive committee often supported our lack of emphasis on lessons learned because they are only focused on the project. We really need to pay attention to what's happened each day, even though bad lessons learned are clearly something we do not want to do again."

Raising her hands and passing them back and forth in the direction of her fellow executive committee members, Barbara added her comments about the discussion. "I think I speak for everyone on the executive committee when I say that lessons learned are important. It is important that we don't get distracted from the main project at hand, though. Someone needs to capture the lessons learned and then present back to us those that are relevant."

Barry, quiet up until this point when it came to lessons learned, joined in with his comments. "It's been a long time since I managed a project the magnitude of this project, but it's easy for anyone to overlook the future benefit of something when they are dealing with significant crisis day in and day out."

"It's just very difficult to get everyone focused," Bruce added. "If we don't have enough time to do a good job with lessons learned, then we will usually do just the minimum."

"Let's develop a database where we can store lessons learned for others," Edward suggested.

"That's okay," Barbara said. "But you really need to be somewhat more active than just storing them. The important benefit is to process each of the lessons learned. Add them to a procedure or create a list of best practices or make them a risk but be careful about just storing them. That only creates another database that we have to deal with."

"When we think of lessons learned, it helps to consider the good experiences and the bad experiences," Raj commented, while drawing another Avoidance Model on the flip chart, only this time, focused on lessons learned and incorporating Alice's comments (Chart 29 - 3).

"The importance of using lessons learned certainly becomes evident when looking at Raj's graphic," Gene added.

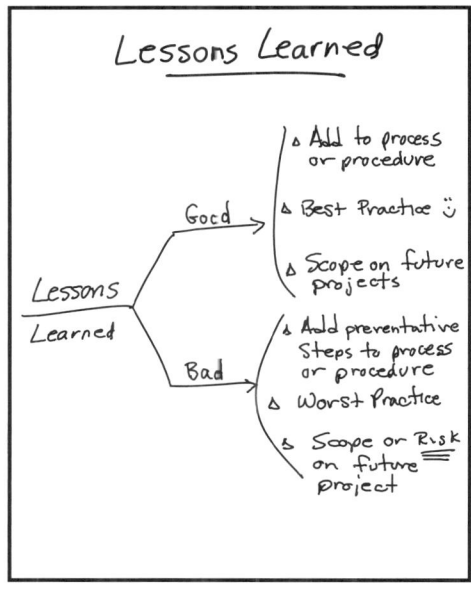

**Chart 29 - 3**

After a few seconds of silence while the importance of lessons learned sunk into everyone's mind, Alice introduced a totally off-the-wall analogy. "The best football team coaches and any team sport coaches study films of opponents and of themselves. They do this before a game and, now with current technology, do it throughout the game itself. Unfortunately, project managers don't have a chance to review films related to their project. They must rely on memories of others. Again, imagine the football coach depending on the memory of some people that watched a previous game. A lot of the key information will be forgotten."

Everyone was now seeing the significance of lessons learned. Summarizing his process depiction on the flip chart, Raj concluded his thoughts. "We totally bought into the importance of managing scope, roles & responsibilities, and risks and now it's easy to see the connection between the Avoidance Model and the lessons learned process. For any area of importance we need a process for managing it."

Bruce added an important context of the lessons learned process. "In order to be certain that we've captured the proper scope, we must understand the risks, and to understand both the scope and risk we need to review lessons learned from our project and review lessons learned from other similar projects in our company."

"What are you going to include as a major project deliverable when you finish the project?" Alice asked, looking at Troy and Bruce.

With just a little thought, Bruce answered, "A comprehensive lessons learned report for the project."

"Great answer," she said. "When you think about it, lessons learned from a project represent perhaps the most important deliverable for the project. We want to think of our project as our legacy, but this is a great fallacy. We're back to that joke about our project being special. In reality, by the time any project manager finishes a project there may be another project that is already in the works to replace it."

Adding to her comment, I contributed my own thoughts on the subject. "Very rarely does the legacy of a project manager live on with an individual project. The naming of most projects to build a big building or structure is consistent only with a big contributor or sponsor; nothing refers to the project manager. The only real legacy that any of us ever leaves on *every* project is the lessons learned."

Alice smiled, "Actually when you look at it that way, even a failed project can produce a valuable product at the end."

"Sounds like we're talking about 'the glass is half-full' philosophy," Barbara added.

"There is nothing wrong with thinking that way," Edward interjected, while still running these concepts through his mind. "The wisdom of what went well, mixed with the caution to watch out for those steps that didn't fare so well, is important. This is especially true if you are working in the Information Technology world."

"There you go," Alice said jokingly, "announcing again that you are special."

Edward agreed and added, "Then in order to get the benefit from lessons learned it is imperative that the organization benefit and learn. Otherwise the experience is wasted."

"Exactly. When we finally adopt the truth that scope takes time and costs money then we have to recognize that the lessons learned were scope and did cost time and/or money."

Alice was smiling, "Just think, if I touched a hot stove for the first time and I could talk, I would get on the Internet to tell everyone how bad it was. I would want to make sure that no one else had to endure my painful experience. It is amazing that we actually deal with lessons learned everyday at work and in our personal lives."

I couldn't help smiling as I responded to her brilliant example. "Alice, when you think about it, the whole concept of learning from our mistakes is incorporated in our daily lives as humans, but somehow when we go to work we often go out of our way to cover up the problem. This is totally nuts when you think about it! Managing lessons learned is the

> *OS Phase* **Avoidance STRATEGY 29**
>
> *Lessons learned represent the most important deliverable on any project. Lessons learned represent the legacy of the project manager.*
> *Collect lessons learned daily as you proceed with the project.*

only sure way to improve with time. It is much less expensive than constantly making the same mistake over and over."

## CHAPTER 30
## Managing Vendors

We must accept the *OS Phase* as a realistic possibility. Of particular concern is the reality that on medium to large-scale projects, the *OS Phase* could come at you from several different directions. Your own team could experience the *OS Phase*, but it might not stop there.

A lower tier group within your company could hit the *OS Phase*, or a critical sub-contractor could have the experience. The worst case scenario would be if all three of these groups hit it at about the same time.

The fact that your core team and others in your immediate sphere of influence manage their work properly does not necessarily guarantee that others supporting the project will have the same passion or *predictive processes* to avoid the *OS Phase*. Our vulnerability to impact from outside vendors grows quickly with the number of vendors or groups added. The significance of sub-team groups or contractor performance is not trivial.

A *simple* strategy for managing outside vendors or in-house groups is to characterize each as their own separate project. This focus will lead you towards emphasis of each of the tools we use for avoiding the *OS Phase*. You must be concerned with how they manage *scope*, as well as the fact that you must be certain to give them adequate *scope* so they can succeed. Attention towards quality as it relates to *scope* is vital for preventing disappointment when they complete their portion of the project.

With consideration for the relationship of *scope* with the *Stupid Triangle*, it will be important also to manage their expenditures and schedules, even if you have a fixed price contract. If any outside vendor fails or loses money, it might result in carry-over problems for your core team as well. Communication will be a key for success along with emphasis on their ability to meet the

> quality level described in their contract documents or work plan. Although you might not be privy to all of their risks and likewise yours with them, you need some assurance that they are actively managing *risks*. Surprises aren't good for anyone.
>
> If you pay attention to those groups or venders supporting your project, you are a step ahead of many others that take them too much for granted.

Continuing, without a break, Bruce introduced the subject of subcontracting. This subject was appropriate, considering the discussion of lessons learned.

"We've talked at length about how we should now manage projects, but we haven't discussed how I need to manage the various subcontractors still working on the project. I'm not sure that the statement of work for these contracts is even close to the detail necessary to adequately manage the scope of the remaining work."

Listening with great interest, Alice quickly noted an important point related to the statements of work. She turned to me and asked, "Earlier you referred to scope in terms of product scope and project scope. How do these different forms fit into the procurement activities for our contractors?"

Responding to the group, I worked to provide a relevant example for this project. "It would be great if more project managers thought of this difference before embarking on a contract, either as a buyer or seller. When you need support by an outside vendor, you prepare a Statement of Work describing the scope of what you want that vendor to supply. That scope is totally product scope. It is something that you need for the project."

Interrupting, Troy asked, "What about the time it took to prepare for the procurement? That time can be lengthy sometimes."

"Excellent, Troy, that's precisely where I was going with the example," I said, while noting special interest by everyone else around the table. The time spent preparing the procurement is project scope. Often we omit the effort for this type of activity from consideration when we develop our Stupid Triangle. The work has to be done but there is actually no budget allocation for it."

Continuing, I said, "Now for the vendor. They receive the statement of work and then have to perform the contract. The work description provided by the statement of work is product scope, but the effort for them to do the work is project scope."

"This seems to be very confusing, but I can see how important it is to understand," Alice added.

"Great," I replied, while noticing Alice's eagerness to understand more. "This distinction between product and project scope is important to understand because of its potential impact on the project itself. Depending on the type of contract, the subcontractors frequently suffer from their own eagerness and haste in agreeing to perform the work. If they bid the contract based on what they knew of the product scope and were likewise optimistic on what they have to do to accomplish the contract, the project scope, then the contract will eventually be..."

"...hosed!" Bruce blurted out, with everyone else acknowledging the reality of his comment.

Looking a little puzzled by the conversation, Barry asked, "So what? It's their loss, not ours. If they're dumb enough to bid too low just to get the work, then they chose their own poison. It was their decision, not ours."

"I disagree," Raj added, while taking an unusual position for a financial manager. "If we are in business for the long haul, we want our subcontractors or vendors to make money. If we understand the Stupid Triangle, I'm afraid the quality of the work might be compromised. It just makes no sense for them to fail."

"This entire conversation is totally illogical," Barry continued, while putting aside Raj's comment. "Surely that would happen only as a random occurrence and would not be planned by the contractor. We're technically contractors to our customers ourselves and I sure hope that we're not planning on losing money."

"We will never have to worry about losing money as long as you're around," Gene added, while bringing a sobering tone to the room. "Rich is the one we must watch for. We need to make sure he doesn't market these mountain adventures too cheaply."

Rich laughed at Gene's comment, but the thought wasn't lost entirely. Everyone in the room understood the significance of pricing on the viability of the whole concept and company. They knew that if their mountain adventure enterprise was first to market, they would capture market share, but they all realized that there would be competitors down the road and that meant more competitive pricing of the adventures.

"Getting back to the point of the conversation, we should be alert to this problem," Barbara commented. "My experience working with supply chain vendors has made me aware of many companies that provide contract services and equipment that are bidding projects with such a low profit margin, many are just surviving. In the haste to get new contracts, the sales person gets the job, throws it over the wall to the newly assigned project manager, and then it's discovered that the bid is too low, but it's too late."

"Sounds like a process we've seen with some of our vendors," Bruce added.

Joining in, Gene said, "Yes, we often referred to it as the *bid and run* process where I worked before my position here."

"Are there any special techniques for managing subcontractors to avoid this type of problem?" Rich asked me, while also looking to see if anyone else might answer.

"I suspect that it is difficult to keep contractors from being aggressive in the bidding, but we can use the techniques we've learned for managing projects to manage an individual contractor or group of contractors," I responded. "If we go back and review the slide that Alice presented at the beginning of our session this morning (Exhibit 30 - A), we see the project manager must be concerned with paying attention to the nine Project Management Focus Areas. We discussed those as pertaining to projects, but the reality is that they can pertain to anything we attempt."

"I can see how it would work for managing contractors," Barbara said, while pointing to the projection on the wall. "If we award a subcontract, we need to make sure they have a clear scope, so they don't shortcut quality. We need to communicate often and in a way that keeps their effort moving. We must ensure that they are paying at-

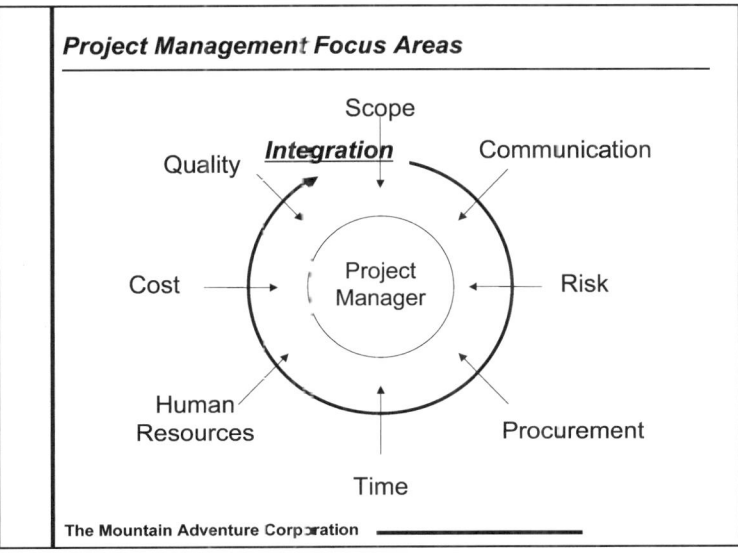

**Exhibit 30 - A**

tention to risks and have notified us of risks that affect their delivery. Most importantly, we must have a balanced triangle when it comes to schedule and cost and we need to make sure we know the roles and responsibilities of all of their team members."

"Wow!" Bruce exclaimed. "You said all of that without taking a breath."

"By now it just rolls off our tongues," Barbara acknowledged quickly. "It's funny, and I'm not sure if it's just me or not, but when a process makes sense, once you've looked at the details, it seems pretty easy to remember and easy to repeat to others."

With that, Bruce jotted down his ideas for the attributes of successful subcontract management onto the flip chart (Chart 30 - 1) and said, "I know what you mean,

**Chart 30 - 1**

Barbara. I don't think I'll ever be able to get these three attributes out of my mind. And now that I look at them, I guess they also apply to managing subcontractors."

Everyone laughed and acknowledged his comment, which was right on!

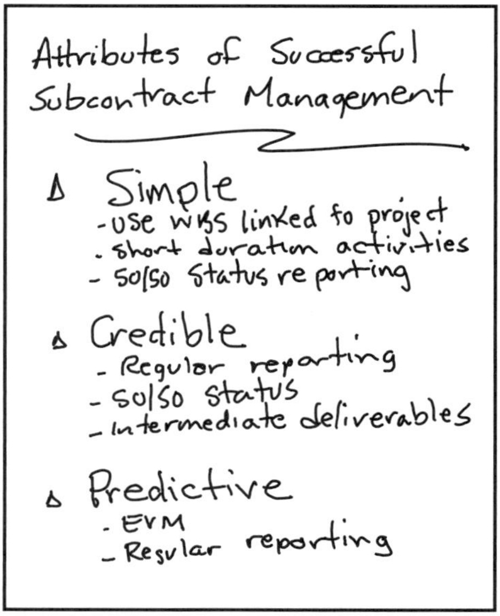

Rich was listening intently, relating the discussion of vendors to his own organizational responsibilities and then commented, "The concept of using these attributes is great. I would really benefit if we could list some examples of these attributes as they apply to subcontracting."

"I agree," Troy responded, as he made his way to the flip chart (Chart 30 - 2). "Let's spend a few minutes and see what we can come up with."

With everyone engaged, we went around the table and discussed some tools or processes that they could use. An unusual thing happened when everyone moved around the table to reunite the teams that developed the earlier attributes lists.

Bruce, Edward, and Barry listed the attributes for *simple*, while Troy, Gene, and Barbara thought through the *credible* attributes. Alice led Rich and Raj to create a powerful list of tools to drive the *predictive* behavior that we would want when involved with procuring outside services.

It was great to see Alice so positive about Earned Value Management after her earlier concerns. It wasn't completely obvious by her previous comments, when we discussed Earned Value Management, whether she really bought into it. Since it was at the top of their list, and I overheard her suggesting it, my earlier apprehension was unwarranted.

**Attributes of Successful Subcontract Management**

△ Simple
- use WBS linked to project
- short duration activities
- 50/50 status reporting

△ Credible
- Regular reporting
- 50/50 status
- Intermediate deliverables

△ Predictive
- EVM
- Regular reporting

**Chart 30 - 2**

After discussing the list for a few minutes, Barbara walked to the flip chart and began a very positive endorsement of the process. "It is so apparent that within the project management focused organization, these three attributes will appear in almost every process we discuss. That is probably my greatest revelation today. The Stupid Triangle moved Bruce, but these attributes really connect in the way I want to look at things now."

"It is amazing," Barry added, "how three words that have always been in our vocabulary, and used often in our discussions around this table the past year, meld together so well. They are almost a mission statement for the executive committee to embody and implement."

It was refreshing to see everyone in the room closely in tune with one another. Each has a special area of expertise, but from this day forward, they will judge each other on how they live up to these attributes while managing their respective organizational roles and responsibilities.

So that everyone would have a clear mind as we finalized the contracting discussion, I suggested a ten-minute break so that everyone could catch their breath. With quick agreement, the group dispersed, but it was obvious by their enthusiasm that they would be returning on time.

\* \* \*

Barry was the first one back in the room. He walked up to the flip chart (Chart 30 - 2), pointed to one of the predictive items, and asked, "The concept of intermediate deliverables is great for keeping the contractor on track, but won't that end up costing more in the long run?"

Alice walked in just in time to hear Barry's question. She responded, "That's right; the vendor will have to stop what they're doing to get the deliverables out the door. If we're only doing it to manage the vendor, then you have created an extra step that wasn't necessary before."

Everyone else returned to the room as Alice was presenting her response. Bruce could hardly wait for Alice to finish talking before he was ready with a comment. "Intermediate deliverables may increase the overall cost if you set up a bunch of them, but they will ensure that you get something to show for the effort in case you want to release the contractor early or in the painful event the project is canceled later on."

Barbara added, "The latter case shouldn't be an example here, but it does happen on projects where events happen or technology changes and the project is put on hold. If at that time nothing was delivered, it is a shame for everyone."

Gene had a lot of experience, mostly bad experience, managing vendors at his previous employer. After listening to the new discussion, he was quick to address his concerns. "My biggest problem is figuring out how to manage risks related to the vendor and their contract. Are there any strategies we've talked about here this morning that will work?"

Before I could answer Gene's question, Rich jumped in and shouted, "Use some Avoidance Metrics to identify or zero in on your areas of concern or risk."

Alice was surprised with Rich's pointed response. From her perspective, Rich had gone through a change of viewpoint today that was significant. Turning to Rich she said, "Excellent suggestion. In fact, the concept of using Avoidance Metrics for any facet of the project that 'might' have concerns is important. The value of Avoidance Metrics is significant and worth considering. In the case of our vendors, the Avoidance Metrics should be used to monitor vendor performance in those areas we deem as risks."

"It would help us to understand that if you could provide an example of an Avoidance Metric for our subcontractors," Edward suggested.

Bruce was first to answer. "Overdue deliverables would be an excellent measure. Another might be number of invoice errors. I think we waste way too much time trying to reconcile invoices that turn out to be in error."

"Those are perfect," Alice interjected. "Both of those measures are easy to capture and if they are increasing away from our target of *zero*, then they provide predictive indications that we are losing ground on the schedule."

Bruce added some additional thoughts to the discussion. "I'm sure as we sit down and look at the areas of frustration with subcontractors, we will derive a more complete list. But those two are good possibilities. If nothing else, when these measures start looking bad, we need to jump on top of them and look at them in terms of a risk to the on-schedule completion of the project."

"Should we hide our risk management interest from the vendors or should we confront them?" Troy asked, reading the minds of many in the room. "Up until now, any consideration of risks was not something we talked about openly to the subcontractors."

Subcontractor management was beginning to turn into a very active discussion. It seems that everyone in the room has experienced hitting the OS Phase as it related to managing outside services. This was great, because vendor management processes tie so closely to all of the processes we normally call into play for a project. Risk management was a big deal.

Not to let Troy's question drop, I asked the group the same question. "How often, and when, should we review risks with vendors?"

After a little mumbling and general lack of any answer to the question, Alice spoke, but directed her comments as more of a question. "We should definitely approach our vendors with concerns or risks. The mechanism coming to mind is in our monthly or weekly review sessions. It would seem that we need to use that as a forum to present items we are uncomfortable with and risks definitely fall into that category."

Alice's comments seemed to re-energize the group. Without any hesitation, Gene turned to her and said, "That's right. It's important that we manage our contractors the same way we would manage our internal organizations. We need to focus on risk and let them know how important it is to the project. The bottom line is we have to manage the contractors just like we do the project!"

---

*OS Phase* **Avoidance**
**STRATEGY 30**

*Manage vendors in the same manner that you manage a project, keeping in mind all of the project management focus areas.*

My confidence in the group grew with every discussion. I only wished I could hang around during the final stages of their project to see them in action.

# CHAPTER 31
## Strategic Chief Projects Officer

As we've discussed before, most project managers think their project is special. This in itself isn't bad. In fact, it is great that a project manager is proud of their project. An impact does arise, though, when we use the special nature of our projects to re-invent the processes necessary to support them. When you consider the number of active projects that occur at any point in time, it's easy to understand how this could have a major impact.

Project managers are encouraged to raise the bar and make it happen, which to many gives them a free pass to ignore or bypass any rule that gets in their way. If there is a lack of direction from the highest levels of a company, then the tendency for project managers will be to take matters in their own hands.

Companies, realizing the costs of redundant or poorly integrated computer technology, created the Chief Information Officer *role* to provide continuity within the company. A new position, Chief Projects Officer, could serve the same purpose.

The goal would not be for the Chief Projects Officer to be responsible for all projects in a company. That would be too difficult, considering the number of projects within the numerous organizations. The Chief Projects Officer, instead, would be responsible for assuring that projects use similar processes and standards. As a precursor, they would be responsible for building a company consensus on the processes and standards to adopt.

The Chief Projects Officer would be an advocate for prioritization of projects and for the allocation of resources necessary to support the various projects. Prioritization issues and available resources are generally the top two challenges facing large companies. It is important that someone is sitting with the other company executives when discussions related to projects surface.

> Many team members and project managers of the famous E-commerce boom thought their projects were quite special. They often told me that they couldn't use traditional approaches, but they eventually did...they went bankrupt....

Troy and Alice both agreed that their experience was not unique. They both recalled finding the same problems in their vendor's organizations and in other companies with whom they've interfaced.

The prevalence of poor project management processes could easily cause a person to become complacent. After all, if everyone has the same problem maybe we just need to adapt.

"Don't get me wrong," Troy commented. "Even in our company where we are performing only a handful of projects, there are a lot of different ways we approach project management."

"Do you think the variation in approach confuses senior management?" I questioned.

Gene seemed intrigued by the discussion and commented to the group. "The approaches we've discussed are workable and as an organization, we should implement them along with any other beneficial initiatives down the road. We must remember, though, that our commitment alone is not enough to ensure all future company level projects or even the smaller internal group projects are performed using the same processes."

"Barry, what do you think?" Rich asked.

"I, for one, agree that we need to start limiting the variations for managing projects in the organization, but I'm also reluctant to impose standards on everyone," he replied. "How will we always know they're the right ones?"

Alice took this opportunity to make a great point as she turned to Barry and asked, "Other than project management processes, what other company processes have so many variations? Do we have multiple accounting systems? Do we have various processes and forms for hiring new employees?"

Barry smiled and provided the obvious response. "The answer is NO. It just wouldn't make sense to have multiple systems for accounting and new employee hiring processes. When it's presented that way, you're right; someone has to decide what we're doing. Before today, it was much easier to ignore the problem and beat up the project managers when they failed. Isn't that right, Bruce?"

Bruce smiled, acknowledging Barry's comment, but remained silent.

This discussion was intriguing Raj who stood up quickly and started pacing along the wall. After a few moments of thought, he stated, "How in the world would any company survive if they had a bunch of different processes for all of their management activities? To accept variations in project management techniques teeters on gross incompetence. To think that we are losing money every day by wasteful processes is causing my chest to tighten."

"I agree," Gene responded. "I guess I've never thought about what it costs to do things differently. We're so accustomed to just doing it that way, that it didn't stand out as a concern. From our discussions today, I recognize some needs in our project management processes that weren't there before. The question would seem to focus on timing. Does anyone have a recommendation on when we should start driving the organization towards uniformity?"

"That's easy; the time is now!" Barbara answered, with a level of firmness that caused everyone in the room to sit up straight. "We have an opportunity to get the organization on board before a lot of bad habits are begun. We shouldn't waste any time."

Alice listened intently to the discussion. As the director responsible for project management, she had a vested interest, but decided to let everyone voice their opinions before jumping to any recommendation. She felt the condition of the project left her a little vulnerable as a reliable subject matter expert.

Rich, noticing Alice's silence and appreciating somewhat her dilemma, made a recommendation. "I propose that in addition to her role as an executive director, we add the title of chief projects officer to Alice's position description."

Everyone sat for a moment and let Rich's comment sink in.

Raj spoke first. "What would this new job entail and why would we want to make any change at all?"

"I'm interested in that answer, as well," Alice said.

Rich went to the flip chart and began writing. He listed all of the standard titles for executives. When he got to his proposed position, he underlined it for emphasis (Chart 31 - 1).

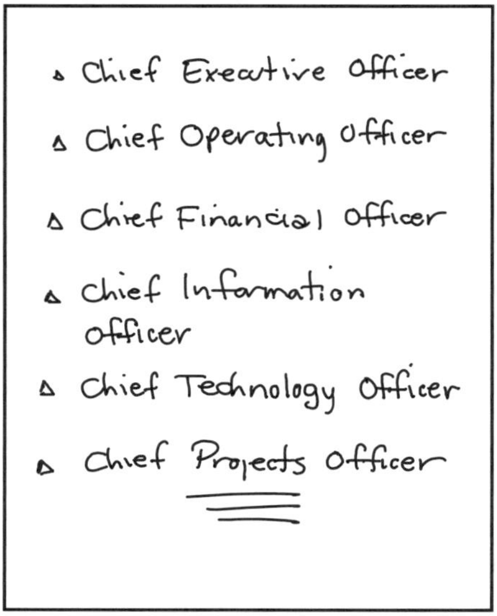

With everyone's attention, he said, "Actually, when you examine the chart, it becomes clear that companies have long since recognized the importance of labeling certain senior positions in the company to denote their primary responsibility. With few exceptions, this designation gives the individual in that position more respect from the members of the organization as a whole."

- Chief Executive Officer
- Chief Operating Officer
- Chief Financial Officer
- Chief Information Officer
- Chief Technology Officer
- Chief Projects Officer

**Chart 31 - 1**

Quiet until now, Gene added his thoughts, coming from his operations perspective. "If the organization handled the new position properly, this minor title change might turn out to be the most important strategic decision made in some time. It would show the entire company how important project management is to the success of everyone and not just the projects themselves. In fact, I think it will even provide the subtle message that consistency of process is important."

Although usually quite reserved in nature, Edward applauded loudly. "This is fantastic. This is the way it should be for all companies. I think we have stumbled on something big! And I mean big!"

"Before we get too carried away with this new job position, just exactly what would the role of Alice be in this position?" Barbara asked, as she turned to Rich and Gene. "Would all of the project managers report to her? Would she be responsible for writing and establishing all of the project management procedures throughout the organization? Just what will be different?"

Although my new friends originated the idea of having a chief projects officer position in their company, they turned to me, looking for what I might suggest as the next step if they were to adopt this new title.

Moving to the front of the room, I asked Alice to stand up and then reached to shake her hand. "Imagine coming to the executive committee meeting today to describe your horrible experiences with the OS Phase and now walking out with a new and extremely impressive job. There is no doubt that you have demonstrated to everyone just how competent you really are or you would not be standing here now."

Alice was noticeably embarrassed. She began to get a little anxious as she stood at the end of the table and seemed to ignore the discussion surrounding her.

I started the discussion by throwing out a few thoughts. "A chief projects officer role mustn't be a dictatorial role, but instead should play a facilitation role to the various projects in the organization. The position needs to be an enabler, not a restrictor."

"Hopefully Alice will put in place only enough procedures and directives to get the job done. It is important to be a support system, like information technology," Rich added with a big grin.

Seeing the analogy, in a joking manner Alice scoffed at the comparison. "The chief projects officer would drive organizational tools, establish best practices for the teams, as well as observe individual performance related to project management process implementation."

Barry was sitting at the edge of his seat and, without warning, came to the front of the room and began speaking, if not to the group, to himself, as he tried to convert years of his ingrained bias and opinions into a relatively new concept. "The thought of having a senior person responsible for project management techniques and processes within the enterprise is consistent with the CIO and CFO and CTO positions that are common in most companies. If a corporation is serious about developing a consistent unified approach, nothing short of establishing a CPO position will work. The organization's CEO becomes crippled waiting for project results and even then may never have the real assurance that everything is going as presented.

"Frankly, I'm disappointed that we didn't think of this sooner," Barry said in closing, as he took his seat next to Gene. "All I ever ask you to do, Alice, in your role as chief projects officer, is never allow administrative processes to delay a project. We've discussed that many times today. As a company, we are not in the business of creating schedules and planning. Granted, we have to create the business with one big project; in the end, projects will be attempts at new business or process improvements. Our business is selling and delivering exciting mountain adventures."

Gene was clearly having some serious ideas bouncing around in his head. Not able to contain himself anymore, he turned to the group and presented a very interesting recommendation. "I'm not sure if it would be appropriate for the team at this time to create any additional leadership positions, but in the future we might want to consider some new organizational titles for key project management focus areas. For example, if scope is as important as we say it is, then we should have a manager of scope for the organization."

Adding to Gene's words, Raj made additional proposals. "With that thought, maybe we should also have a manager of roles and responsibilities and a manager of project risks. Just as Gene said, we have financial managers (cost), quality managers, corporate risk managers, procurement managers, communication managers, human resources managers, scheduling managers, but no scope managers."

The recognition by everyone of the importance of project management was refreshing. In just a short amount of time, I witnessed the conversion of a conservative group of executives into a cohesive team that now understands the relationship of process performance to success in projects.

---

*OS Phase* **Avoidance**
**STRATEGY 31**

*Project management processes will not mature in any enterprise unless someone sits at a high leadership level and mentors the various organizations.*

*The chief projects officer position is new, and it could have a very powerful and profitable effect.*

## CHAPTER 32
## Multiple Projects

Just when we've accepted the appropriateness of using standard processes for managing all of the projects in our portfolio, someone will raise the issue of managing multiple projects. The inference is usually that managing multiple projects is special and requires a completely different set of processes and tools.

Wrong!

Despite the hype in the various project management circles, there is nothing special or magical about the techniques used for managing multiple projects. This simplicity is hard to articulate though. Most are convinced that managing multiple projects is a special situation and requires special or unique tools.

Even though managing multiple projects does present some challenges, it's important to dispel the "we're special" argument. The chances of succeeding with a program to manage multiple projects will depend on two important processes: resource management and project prioritization.

Unfortunately, reality sets in when we remember that good resource management *processes* are an exception rather than a rule and getting a prioritization *process* to work is something that most organizations fail at time after time. This is where the problem lies when attempting the management of multiple projects.

It is important to make sure there is some type of plan or strategy to accomplish these two functions. To proceed otherwise leads us on another step towards the *OS Phase*.

"When you consider what we've had to accomplish on this one single project, it makes me wonder how someone could ever manage several projects at the same time," Troy commented to the group.

"That's a very common question nowadays." Alice responded. "Everyone wants to be able to manage a dozen items at the same time.

To hear all of the hype, it's easy to believe that assigning several projects to an individual project manager builds character. Seems like a mistake."

"It sounds like you have a lot of thoughts in this area," Edward suggested.

"Is there just one technique or process that we should consider before managing several projects?" Troy asked.

The response to Troy's question is easy to present, but so often ignored. It was important to have everyone's attention before we discussed this critical concern. A few moments of silence on my part after the question seemed to quiet everyone else in the room, so I proceeded. "The processes associated with managing multiple projects are receiving the greatest interest by practitioners and authors. Organizations throughout the world continue to increase their focus on projects, but every step encounters staffing levels that are too low. Without even considering multiple projects, the organization will already have a challenge just to survive.

After these sobering comments, I went on to say, "The secret for managing multiple projects is to remember the tools and techniques that you used for managing a single project, and leverage the same processes on each of the multiple projects. The goal will be to combine some of the processes and save effort by eliminating any duplication."

"That sounds almost too simple," Troy commented.

"That very reasoning alone is what causes many organizations to seek out different solutions. We're back to the 'it's a special project syndrome' and that will confuse everyone in the organization," I said, with a serious tone in my voice. "And as far as being simple…it's not! In fact, the idea that we can easily manage multiple projects is a total misconception. Of all project management processes, multiple project management is the most difficult."

"I'm confused," Gene spoke, while getting a non-verbal acknowledgment of the same confusion from others at the table. "What makes it difficult if we are using the same tools and processes as we used with a single project? We've talked about how important it is to drive toward simple approaches today. Now we've moved away from that concept entirely."

Gene's comment sparked interest as to what my response would be.

After confirming that everyone was listening, I addressed Gene's question. "The opposite of simple is complex, not difficult. Something can be difficult to do just by its sheer magnitude, but the process itself is still simple. The term 'difficult' just implies that we will have to expend lots of energy to accomplish our result."

Laughing, Raj brought the point home. "What we don't want is a complex process that becomes difficult when we apply it to multiple projects. I'm laughing when I say this because we do it all the time."

"And then we eventually abandon the standard tool or process because we perceive that they are impossible to implement using the complex process," Barry added, becoming totally convinced at his own words.

"Exactly," I said emphatically. "The tools and processes are the same. The problem is that we have to use them."

"What's the problem, process or people?" Alice asked, referring to our earlier discussion on lessons learned.

Smiling, I turned to Alice and gave her an overdue compliment. "I'm impressed, Alice. Your question was perfect—it is important to find the area of deficiency. Understanding the difference between process and people is vital. There's no point in fixing the process if the people continue to mess up."

"Thanks for the compliment," Alice responded. "But you haven't answered my question. Is it a process or people problem?"

"Yes!" I answered abruptly to drive the point home. "If the processes are poorly defined, then that makes it a process concern. If they are appropriate for the circumstances, but not used, then it's a people problem. It's impossible to really know where to put the emphasis until we sit down and analyze both areas."

It was clear that Alice grasped the significance of the answer. "It sounds like we need to better understand the process first and make sure it's working, and then look at the people side of things."

"Absolutely!" I said, while joining Alice in a traditional high-five hand slap. "It sounds like you've just defined the job responsibilities for your new role as chief projects officer."

"We've spent a lot of time discussing processes and process problems. With that in mind, what is the biggest people concern we might face?" Troy asked.

"Priorities!" I shouted, not letting Troy's question hang in the air for even a second.

"That's right," Gene shouted back. "Every time we turn around we see the significance of setting priorities. Do you agree with this, Alice?"

"Yes," Alice quickly responded. "In order to avoid the OS Phase, we have to manage projects in a manner that supports the strategic plan of the executive committee. We can't afford having the organization going in too many different directions at the same time. If we're going to get the project successfully completed, it just won't work the way we're doing it now!"

After letting Alice's comments sink in, Troy added an additional perspective. "Priority setting on the project itself is clearly the accountability of Bruce as the project manager. But on the broader organizational perspective, the executive committee has to own the organizational prioritization process since their role is high level or strategic compared to Bruce's grass roots or tactical focus."

"That's a good way to look at it," I said, making sure everyone was listening. "As complex as the process of priority setting seems, it is common for the project manager and executive management to dismiss its significance. Everyone recognizes the existence of prioritization problems, but many laugh when the subject arises and then discount the problems."

Barbara expressed a thought that came to mind. "I was just thinking of an example that really describes this prioritization thing. I had one of my MBA professors describe prioritization from a different perspective. He concluded that an odd behavioral aspect of prioritization problems is the lack of recognition of problems by the person accountable for setting the priorities. They often have the impression that everything is just fine. When you sit back and examine them, priority changes seem to have little impact on anyone not brought into the process. As a perfect example, imagine someone sitting on the couch at home channel surfing. The person is constantly changing viewing priorities. This process of constant change is harmless until done in front of a spouse or others in the room. In these cases, the ones watching the channel surfing get frustrated quickly, whereas the person channel surfing is quite at ease with the process. Relating this television channel surfing to real time 'project surfing' process is an easy transition."

There's no doubt that project surfing is often experienced in large organizations," Barry added. "It's easy to imagine how frustrating this world would be to those at the working level, whereas those accountable for constantly changing the priorities often seem oblivious to any problem."

Alice liked the new term "project surfing." This entire conversation was very important to her. After internalizing the conversations, she added her thoughts. "Resources are not a concern if the prioritization process is working. If it isn't, then resource concerns exacerbate the problem to the point of being extreme. Many organizations have just enough resources to survive. If we take on more work than we have resources, the ultimate result might be catastrophic failure for the entire organization or company. The domino effect occurs often when one project is repeatedly delayed and continues to dominate the resources planned for succeeding projects."

"Anything we do in this area must be simple or it just won't work," Barry stated.

"That's right," Edward added. "Thinking of a simple example, imagine that we have two projects to accomplish. They both have scope. They both have humans involved and they both have risks. What we're looking for is where we can benefit from lessons learned and other scope management tasks. Where do we share resources and where might we find similar risks so that we have only a single action instead of repetitive actions…right?"

"Perfect observation," I said, while scanning the room to make sure everyone was still following the discussion. "If the projects are totally unrelated and do not share resources, then we can only benefit by the replications of the processes themselves, such as the scope management process. If you ask most project managers what their biggest concerns are related to multiple projects, the response would be managing resources. When we put our focus in this area, it's easy to forget the importance of sharing processes and risks."

"I agree," Alice responded. "But isn't it hard to identify resources months ahead and expect that we will need them on those exact dates?"

"It's next to impossible!" I said without hesitation. "But time after time, project managers and project management directors try to manage at that level and fail, or wished they had because their lives became very complex, not simple."

As a manager of many simultaneous, small information technology related projects, Edward was curious about the answer. "What's the solution? How do we manage the resources without getting everything too complicated? How do we focus forward and avoid the OS Phase?"

Before I could respond, Barry, uncharacteristically quiet up to the point, jumped to his feet, made a swirling motion with his hands, and laughingly said, "Rolling wave concepts, my friend, rolling waves! By looking at resource needs for the long term, but by making specific resource assignments for only six-eight weeks ahead, it's easier to pay attention to resources and avoid the complexities of the unpredictable future. The rolling wave, along with a strong prioritization process that we mentioned earlier, will help."

It was funny to see Barry so animated, but it had an impact on the group and his message was understood by everyone.

Rich and Gene were having a side bar conversation that led to both of them breaking out into laughter. Thinking that they had a comment related to the rolling wave concept or Barry's hula dance as he was demonstrating the wave, Barbara turned to both of them. In a curious voice, she asked them to share their conversation with the rest of the group.

Caught by surprise, but recovering quickly, Gene commented that he wasn't making fun of Barry, but was relating an experience he and his wife had last evening when they went out to a restaurant for dinner.

Now that everyone was looking in his direction, Gene then began to explain. "When Gloria and I arrived at the restaurant we noticed that the parking lot was only two-thirds full. The maitre d' caught us totally off guard when he predicted a forty-five-minute wait. The estimated wait was even more confusing because the restaurant was not full.

"After the maitre d's comment, Gloria peered into the dining room, especially in the front, where it paralleled the parking lot and there were many empty seats. Because of my nature and with a little prodding from Gloria, I strolled through the other areas of the dining room just to peek and found another dozen tables empty. When I challenged the maitre d', he said the problem was not a shortage of tables but a shortage of waiters.

"This didn't go over well with either Gloria or me. The maitre d' apologized and led us to a table."

Listening intently, but confused at the analogy, Alice asked, "How does your restaurant experience tie into our discussion on managing multiple projects or multitasking?"

"You need to learn patience, Alice," Gene said, while causing everyone else to break into laughter. "I was just about to answer that question."

Gene went on to explain that the waiter assigned to their table also was working on three others. There was little support staff that evening, so the waiter had to bring drink refills, salads, and condiments himself. As it turned out, a group of four entered just before Gene and Gloria took their seats so they had to wait a long time during each phase of the meal. What they both realized was that the maitre d' was attempting to stagger the diners so that any individual waiter didn't have more than one table at any phase of the meal. The desired approach would be to serve drinks to one table, salads to another, and meals to the third. Now that the tables weren't staggered, he had to hurry up and then wait, while each of the diners became frustrated at the poor service.

Interrupting the story, Troy commented, "I'm surprised at you, Gene. You picked the superficial answer. You blamed the problems on the waiter not being able to multitask. You missed the real resource problem.

"In college I worked in the kitchen at a large restaurant in Salt Lake City. It didn't matter how many servers were working, the most critical resource is the kitchen staff. Without any prioritization process and with short staffing, it's almost impossible to keep up with timely meal preparation. When pressured, the kitchen may deliver, but the Stupid Triangle enters the picture. When the time shortens and resources are too low, scope has to decrease. There is no other choice. Unfortunately, the decrease in scope manifests in terms of decreased quality."

"You've made a good point," Gene commented. "We only witnessed the waiter and never thought about his support team. The bottom line is the fact that the empty tables were an incorrect signal that resources were available. When everyone wanted to be the number one priority, the entire restaurant team had an impossible task of multitasking that became inefficient. This bad experience may have even resulted in some customers not returning to the restaurant in the future, adding to the irony of the whole situation. By accommodating Gene and Gloria, the restaurant may lose reputation and customers."

This was an excellent example for everyone present.

Barbara apologized for putting Gene on the spot, but thanked him for sharing the experience. Each of those present could draw the obvious conclusion to the office environment, where we ask project managers to add more and more projects, not staggered, but one on top of another, until they eventually fail.

Alice turned to me and asked my opinion of the discussion. Without hesitation, I reflected on some important related subjects. "My own personal view of everything improved when I became more process focused and less caught up in the daily emergencies. It would seem on projects that when everything became chaotic some process within or supporting the project was broken or malfunctioning. After studying the processes of project management over the years, it has become evident that the processes of project management are applicable to anything we do any day of the week, both at work and at home."

Barbara's experience with several other companies put her in a good position to comment as well. "From what I've encountered at different organizations it is safe to say that the way an organization manages their projects could be indicative of how they manage their company as well. When exposed to a troubled project that is so convoluted that those involved up and down the chain of command don't have a clue about its real status or how the project failed, it's not a major leap to imagine that this project is not alone. Remember, if the processes failed on this project, it would be a surprise to have them work elsewhere."

Alice summarized the discussion by adding, "This experience and your similar reaction to it makes it clear in my mind that we as an executive committee must ensure that we deploy projects to the organization in a manner that avoids this same type of failure. Managing multiple projects is very similar to managing one project. We will need the logical schedules first. This will help us to see if we can actually do all the projects and then see the impact of the resources."

Alice then went to the front of the conference room and started with a clean sheet on the flip chart. "We need to list some considerations for managing multiple projects. This way, I will have the benefit of your thoughts before we adjourn this afternoon."

With that challenge, we started around the room and with everyone's contribution captured, Alice ended up with a rather comprehensive listing (Chart 32 - 1).

The concerns vary between organizations but are typically similar to those on the flip chart. It was amazing to witness the energy level and thoroughness of this effort directed by Alice. She demonstrated the leadership role necessary for the chief projects officer position.

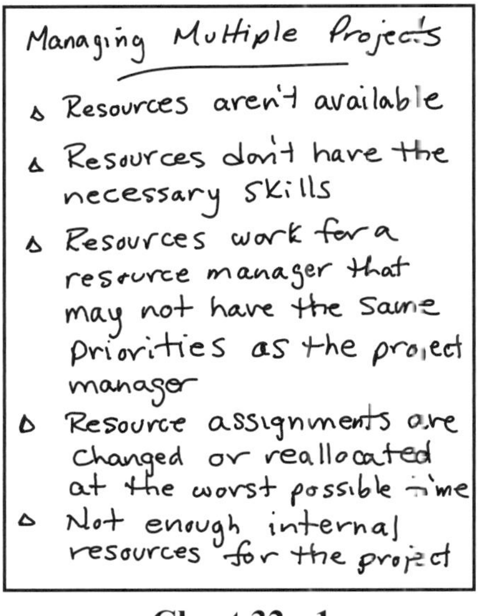

Managing Multiple Projects
- Resources aren't available
- Resources don't have the necessary skills
- Resources work for a resource manager that may not have the same priorities as the project manager
- Resource assignments are changed or reallocated at the worst possible time
- Not enough internal resources for the project

**Chart 32 - 1**

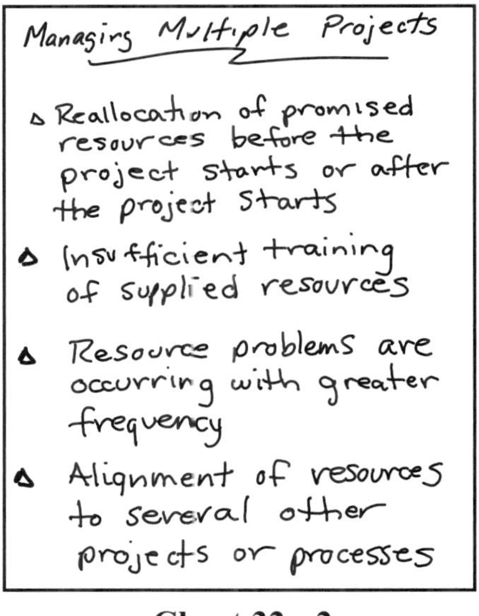

Managing Multiple Projects
- Reallocation of promised resources before the project starts or after the project starts
- Insufficient training of supplied resources
- Resource problems are occurring with greater frequency
- Alignment of resources to several other projects or processes

**Chart 32 - 2**

As Alice was hanging the second flip chart sheet on the wall (Chart 32 - 2), Gene approached the charts to describe an observation he had made. "We have a rather complete list of items related to managing multiple projects. I don't think we could have missed anything. This was a great effort. Also, as I studied the charts, it was impossible not to see the correlation of the bulleted items we captured and the Avoidance Attributes we've discussed today."

He reinforced his comments by writing the three bulleted attributes on the flip chart (Chart 32 - 3) and reminding everyone of their importance as he wrote still another new title for these multi-faceted attributes.

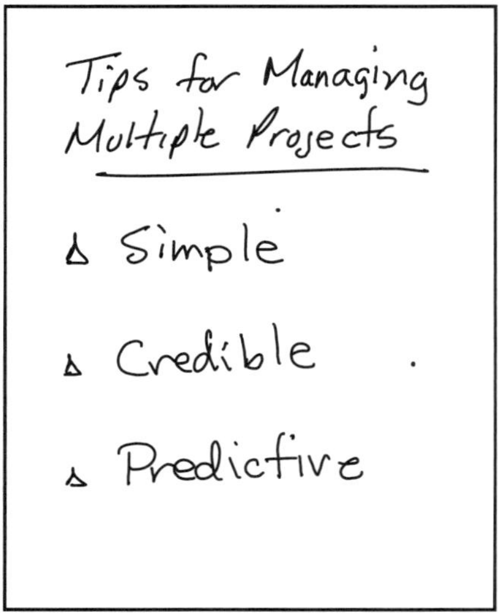

The discussion on resources stirred interest around the room. Bruce was following along, but was surprised we hadn't presented the scenario related to preparing a logic-based schedule before we prepared the resource schedule.

Sensing that the time was right to introduce this concept to the members of the executive committee, he asked Alice if she wanted to make the presentation. She declined with a smile and handed the ball back to Bruce. He took the handoff from Alice and did a great job describing all the details of our discussion from Saturday in Chicago.

Tips for Managing Multiple Projects

△ Simple

△ Credible

△ Predictive

**Chart 32 - 3**

Raj was the first to respond with his thoughts. He turned to Bruce, but made sure everyone else was listening. "The idea of preparing schedules based only on logic, before we analyze the effect of resources, is indeed fascinating. I can see that it is very important to understand the steps to complete any project before constraining the schedule with resources.

"I'm not sure of the others here, but this entire discussion of resources has my mind reeling. Something we have taken for granted so much of the time is indeed a major problem within the organization. In my previous job and even a little here, we seemed to follow Wall Street's advice and always trimmed bodies, but now I'm second guessing those decisions."

Barry joined in with another observation. "I agree with all of the discussion and would like to propose that we add resource management overview as one of our areas of responsibility. The executive committee should be keenly interested in the reasons for any difference between a logic-based schedule with unlimited resources and the delayed schedule using existing resources assigned. Depending on the nature of the project, the sheer fact that we're ignoring our potential of getting more projects completed, maybe with just an incremental increase in resources, is mind boggling. We've become so obsessed with cutting resources we may have lost out on some important opportunities. Unless we look at both schedules, we won't know what the impact really amounts to for the organization."

"That's right," Raj said, as he eagerly joined back in the conversation. "I wonder how many companies world-wide got so obsessed with downsizing to appease their boards that they actually impacted their ability to complete projects effectively and generate or save money for the corporation."

Gene was nodding in agreement. "At my previous employer, we reduced our staff down to little more than a lights-on operation. We could continue operations and maintenance safely, but if any of my staff ever had to support an improvement project or anything like that affecting the plant, all bets were off. There just wasn't enough staff to go around."

Alice responded quickly with an extraordinary recommendation. "It seems that somewhere down the road, as the company grows larger, we will need a resource manager that focuses on our effectiveness of resource management from the corporate perspective. This role would be different from Barry's responsibilities in human resources. He is responsible for hiring, training, development, and personnel concerns. The resource manager would be responsible for assessing the staffing levels and skill sets required in the future. When you sit back and think about it, there are managers in place for most aspects of the organization, but nothing for the overall management of resources."

"We have to be smart with our resource management and not reactionary to appease others that don't have the facts," Barbara added, while summarizing everyone else's thoughts. "Resource management is our accountability and we must be certain each step of the way that we're paying attention to the needs of the organization. If the company continues to grow, I hope that we consider adding another chair to the executive committee for someone totally responsible for assessing our overall resource utilization as Alice described."

"If you get your act together, that time may come sooner than you think," I concluded, while suggesting we take a few minutes to stretch and get some beverages.

Everyone expended a lot of energy during the discussion of resources and several key subjects remained on the table.

---

***OS Phase* Avoidance STRATEGY 32**

*Before you even think about managing multiple projects, you need to understand first the processes for managing a single project.*

*If you do get involved in managing multiple projects, ensure that you have a good resource and prioritization process in place.*

*Short duration activities support the resource management processes necessary when dealing with multiple projects.*

# CHAPTER 33
# Rewriting History—the Unpleasant Saga of Rebaselining

Delivering a project with the designed features on time and within budget seems so logical when we start out, but what happens?

There are few published statistics measuring the number of projects or percentage of projects completed within the original budget and schedule. The reason? Few projects finish with their original *scope*, time, or cost *objectives* still intact. Either we sacrifice *scope* in terms of a loss of features, functionality, or quality to meet the end date, or the schedule slips. Even worse, we throw resources at the project, often too late to do any good and most often in an unplanned and ineffective way.

If the project has a lengthy schedule, it is possible that the original champion and project manager(s) will be long gone. If they're still around, they will wear you down with many plausible excuses for missing the original *objectives*.

In each of these scenarios, a common suggestion is to rebaseline the project. Give it the proverbial second chance. Although feeling burdened at first in having to do it, project managers are excited to get a chance to start over.

Unfortunately, the project manager's ability to implement the new plan is put on hold until senior personnel in the organization decide on how best to "spin the news" about the current situation. The project manager is encouraged to "step up to the challenge!" "work smarter...not harder!" to "make it happen!" Management has raised the bar [again!] and the project manager should step up to the challenge!

What does all of this mean in terms of the new baseline? Unfortunately, it suggests that the new baseline be set at a politically acceptable level! Maybe not consistent with the forecast to complete the project, but instead consistent with what is politically correct.

> With all the hype and encouragement, the project manager again heads down a path of putting an unrealistic or unbalanced *Stupid Triangle* in place and will then proceed onward until the *OS Phase* surfaces again or management requests a new baseline.
>
> The *OS Phase* is easily triggered from constant rebaselining. If your project has undergone a rebaseline since its inception, the potential for getting to the *OS Phase* will be greater than if you haven't. If you have rebaselined multiple times since starting your project, reaching the *OS Phase* is a near certainty!

When everybody returned, we looked at the dwindling list of remaining items for discussion by the executive committee. Up until now, there wasn't any mention of how much the project would grow in cost, or the extent of the delay that was going to be proposed. Although everyone knew that those proposals weren't complete yet, it was only a matter of time before someone brought up the subject.

In an interesting turn of events, the biggest convert at the meeting today was Bruce. The executive committee members have listened and supported the discussions, but Bruce has gone through a complete metamorphosis. As we returned from the break, he was standing at the wall near the flip chart sheet with the Stupid Triangle drawn on it.

After the group gathered back in the room, he turned to Alice, but within earshot of everyone else, and gave some more insight into how he felt. "After spending all this time discussing the Stupid Triangle, it will be hard for me to ever imagine thinking about a project again without getting that triangular vision. I keep remembering the discussions. Find the scope and then determine the best mix of time and cost to get it done! Simple when you think of it, just plain simple!"

Everyone laughed at Bruce's bluntness and encouraged him to always remember the Stupid Triangle concept.

Gene shared his thoughts. "The Stupid Triangle provides substance for any evaluation of impact to either of the three baselines: scope, time, or cost. When someone in the position to ask requests a shortening of the baseline schedule, then scope is cut or costs increase by adding more people or increasing overtime. This is where I start to get heartburn about reactions I've had in the past.

"Given the situation I mentioned, the easiest response to a shortened schedule was to add overtime to get the job done. I knew there were other impacts by doing that, but they weren't in my face the way the Stupid Triangle displays them. Now when I consider the same scenario while looking at the Stupid Triangle, I realize additional staff or overtime reduces the schedule, but the extra effort will also increase the cost and might increase negative risks to the project. The extra risk means we might need more time and cost contingencies. The bottom line is simple. We can change any element of the Stupid Triangle, but when we do, we need to make sure that we adjust our forecast for the other two variables. We can't forget the cause and effect relationship, but at the same time, we don't want to over react and start a whole lot of rebaselining. The forecast tells everyone the project's expected outcome. If someone wants to compare the new forecast to the original baseline, then so be it, otherwise let the project team get about the project's business."

Ignoring Gene's comment, Barry displayed his infamous office manager personality by turning to Alice and asking, "Speaking of baselines, when will you be able to complete the rebaseline for the project? We need to modify what we have and get the new baseline in place as soon as we can."

With nods of agreement from the other executive committee members, except for Gene who was shaking his head in puzzlement at the question, Alice was on the spot to make a commitment for a new project baseline.

Alice looked straight at Edward without so much as a blink of the eye and said, "Define what you mean, Edward, by rebaselining. Some of us in the room apparently understand, but it's not clear at all to me."

Acting a little surprised, Edward responded, "It's clear to all of us that the current cost and time baselines for the project are not going to be met. What we need you to do is go back and correct any overruns to date and then re-estimate the remaining work on the project."

"We will need both time and cost elements re-estimated," Raj added.

"Why?" Alice quickly asked the team of Edward and Raj.

"Because we need to know what to expect from you guys for the rest of the project," Raj blasted back. "We might have a serious cash problem in a couple of months, so I need some good numbers if you want me to keep everything on track."

"If I can add my two cents, then we might be able to get to a consensus," Bruce added. "I don't want to hit the OS Phase anymore than anyone else in this room, but at the same time, I don't believe we have the necessary time to establish a completely new baseline. Why can't we just use the current structure of the project and then add a new forecast value that would have the same effect as a new baseline? Remember, any time we spend rebaselining is less time we have to work on the actual project."

"Bruce is right," Gene commented. "Why is it such a knee-jerk reaction to rebaseline every time we turn around? I don't think anybody was listening to my earlier comments. If you think about it, all we really want is the new cost forecast, along with the time period in which we will perform the work. Maybe it's just semantics, but we need to fix the way we do this process, and we need to deal with it now while we're changing the way we do business. We know where we are today and what we've spent. To rehash history seems like a waste of time."

Barbara began to smile as she added a personal experience. "In some government sectors where I've worked, requests for newly revised baselines occur with rapid frequency. It is often a joke among employees that their best core competency is that of rebaselining. When you think about that for just a few minutes, that's a frightening comment. In fact, if we go through a major rebaseline, it is possible that the new baseline will be totally out of range by the time the team obtains all of the approvals. It is important to remember that any project has the ability to change every day of the week. Our project is no exception."

"That's right," Alice added. "If we rebaseline every time something on the project changes, then we are in for many headaches. Change happens, and the project manager must focus on the changes themselves. Each change should be documented, then the project should move forward."

Joining the conversation, Edward spoke also from personal experience. "The worst practice related to rebaselining is when there are cost and schedule overruns to date, and the rebaseline initiative goes backwards in time, making estimates equal actual costs. It takes a lot of work to do this and when reflecting on why, it's easy to see that this process has no value-added for the project. The value is all about spin!"

I tried to close the discussion with a compelling reason for avoiding the rebaseline process. "There are many problems with rebaselining, not the least of which is that the time we spend doing the evil deed would be better spent working on the project. Rebaselining itself doesn't add any value. It takes the team away from facing the real problems. In most cases, rebaselining is performed because there isn't a good forecast. The best strategy is to make sure a realistic forecast is in place at all times. If the forecast is kept current at all times, the act of rebaselining itself seems almost pointless."

Unfortunately, Raj was not yet convinced with this new thought process. "I'll tell you why it's important," he said emphatically. "We have to provide an accurate baseline to our financial supporters. If we prepare a new baseline, the current performance on the project won't look so bad. Any overruns to date will disappear and the performance that led to the OS Phase will not be so visible. If we are going to have a credible proposal, we need to rebaseline and, in fact, we need to rebaseline quickly."

Bruce smiled and took the lead to explain to the group his new understanding of what an estimate is, and what a baseline is, and that sometimes they're the same and other times they are completely different.

After a few minutes of sketching out the details on the flip chart, Bruce turned to the group and explained his chart (Chart 33 - 1). "When we started the project we prepared an estimate for the entire project and it was approved and set as our baseline. In the grand scheme of things, it was a good representation of the expected project costs. As we moved forward in time, the baseline stayed the same, and our forecast on the project also remained the same. In fact, when we added some new sites at the request of the financiers, we never changed the baseline, now did we Raj?"

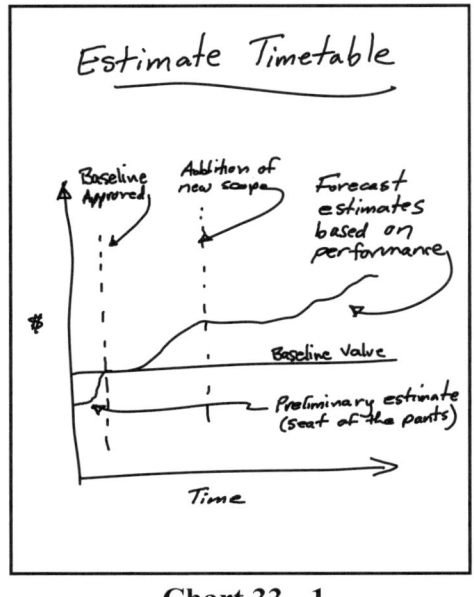

**Chart 33 - 1**

"That's different," Raj responded in an aggressive tone. "They asked for the change, and we documented it on change control documents and there wasn't any reason to go back and rebaseline from the beginning. We knew where we were going and we had permission to move forward."

"What's the difference between what you did for that change and what we're suggesting today?" Gene asked, with some aggressive sarcasm of his own. "It seems like you changed the story to fit the situation."

"You're right, I am guilty as charged!" Raj responded. "But that's my prerogative as chief financial officer. I'm in the position to ask for it and I did. My job is to get financing and to do that I need a new baseline, period!"

Alice was listening to the discussion as it bounced back and forth. It was time that she as the new chief projects officer stepped in and calmed the discussion down a bit. Stepping to the front of the room, she again gravitated to the chart with the three important Attributes that we've discussed frequently (Chart 33 - 2). "It's hard for me to stand here and say that these Avoidance Attributes are meaningful and will be a part of how we manage our organization and then hear that we

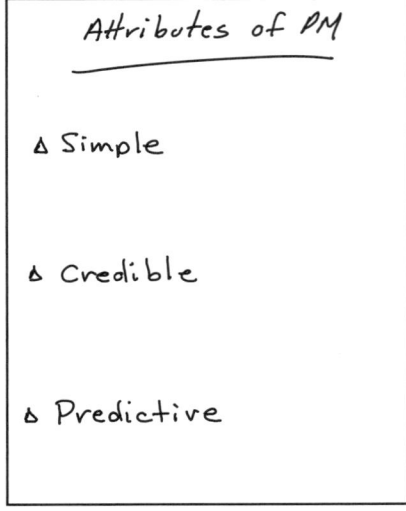

**Chart 33 - 2**

want to rebaseline so we hide our overrun to date. Somewhere that flies in the face of the purpose of the term credible. Looking at rebaselining in general, there is nothing simple about it. In fact, the difficulties involved with doing it will detract from what we have to do this week to solidify the forecast. As the newly appointed chief projects officer, I want to make sure that Bruce and all other project managers are being predictive in the way they do business each day. With that in mind, sending Bruce and his team off to rebaseline will detract them from what is important right now."

"We've created a monster," Edward said with a smile, as he turned and acknowledged Alice. "But, you know, I'm inclined to agree with you. We spend entirely too much time rehashing history. We need to look forward and get the project completed."

"That's right," Barbara added. "If Bruce can give us the details of his forecast, I will personally work with you, Raj, to put together a package of what you need to keep the financial folks happy. What we need when we finish here today is to turn Alice, Bruce, and Troy loose on getting the scope for the balance of the project work identified and then have them put the time and cost forecasts in place."

Alice turned to Barbara and thanked her for the support. Raj seemed pacified, at least for the moment. Rich was working in his mind with some new marketing angles and Barry was thinking again about Avoidance Metrics.

Before the team lost momentum, Alice suggested they begin a discussion about the form and format of the project's future performance meetings.

---

**OS Phase Avoidance**
**STRATEGY 33**

*If I could change one thing in the world, I would make it illegal to rebaseline projects. Constant recreation of project baselines might be the single most wasteful process in the entire suite of project management processes.*

## CHAPTER 34
## Are You Doing What You Said?

When it comes to reporting performance for a project or group of projects, the potential to spend a lot of time and effort is sometimes overwhelming. Few project managers would challenge the need by executive management to understand how projects are performing. As we know, only the project manager has the true sense of what the project has accomplished, and, more importantly, the project's forecast. Unfortunately, the basic need for information has resulted into a full-scale assault on the project manager's available time to support this process.

It's not uncommon to witness organizations that come close to being completely shut down for several days to accumulate, analyze, and report on project performance information. The point of diminishing return is past and it's not looking any better in the future. What should be a routine process of gathering details and passing them upstairs has turned out to be a formal process, likened to preparing initial project baseline documentation. It's impossible sometimes to indicate projected variances without having to spend countless hours of preparation, so that all bases are covered, only to sit in a monthly project review meeting that lasts a mere fifteen to twenty minutes.

The time and cost to prepare performance reports must be included in the original baseline, thus the **Stupid Triangle**. This is where the challenge begins. Most people at the senior levels of the company do not realize what it takes to prepare the information they ask for and will pooh-pooh any suggestion that it is a big deal at all.

If the *role* of the chief projects officer accomplished anything across a large enterprise, it would be to streamline the performance reporting processes. The cost savings, although difficult to capture precisely, could easily pay the salary of the chief projects officer, with plenty left over for the necessary golf outings.

Once we begin working on the project, we are the stewards of the effort until the project is complete. It is important to give it our best and finish what we started. It is important that we provide the correct performance every time it's required. Stop telling management what they want to hear, but instead tell them what they need to hear.

"Before we leave the meeting this afternoon, we need to gain closure on the format of Bruce's performance report," Barry said, while getting a nod from the other executive committee members.

"Why leave it just on Bruce's shoulders?" Rich added. "I think as an executive committee, we need to set a standard for all projects. I don't know about everyone else here at the table, but I'm personally getting frustrated at the wide variation in reporting presented to us on a regular basis. I would think we could come to a consensus on a format and frequency and then leave it alone."

Alice took the opportunity to make a major impact in this area. She jumped to her feet before anyone else stood up and said, "I'm ready to get this taken care of ….NOW!! We just can't afford to continue on the way we've been going. We have the frequency decided, that is, once a week for large executive committee monitored projects. The format of the presentations, however, is such a mixed bag that I personally spend a lot of my time trying to figure out what the report is saying. In the past I think we've all tolerated it, but after this session I'm having a complete change of heart."

Alice's passion caught the attention of the group. Years of frustration were setting her tone and her close relationship to the recent failure made it personal. With everyone's undivided attention she continued. "The term OS Phase may have begun as a cynical depiction, but since last Friday it's been a reality for me personally and it affects everyone else in the room, as well. We must fix our project management processes. I can find some solace in the reality that others before us have experienced the OS Phase. I think we need to stop for the day and let Bruce, Troy, and me put together a plan, or maybe I should say an Avoidance Plan, and get everything back on track. A critical part of that plan will be our recommendation for weekly performance reporting."

"Simple should be the rule of the day when it comes to completing this requirement," Troy added. "I have always found it amazing when a project manager gathers information to report to management and they don't have it already at their fingertips. If a project manager is at all savvy, they would be reviewing any information that higher ups need on a regular basis before they had to submit it at the end of the reporting period."

Troy continued to drive the point home. "Why would I want any higher-level manager to get information at the same time that I looked at it for the first time? Speaking of risk! To do this would be foolhardy."

Barbara was soaking in all of Troy's comments and then added a few of her own. "The worse part of performance reporting is the reality that the report completed this month is for this month only. It will provide trending information and someone may go back and review performance later for some type of performance analysis, but in reality, no one, that is NO ONE, will ask you next year about the performance of the project this month. Performance reporting is a moment in time, paralleling our forecasting processes. If we could somehow use the same information to manage a project as we use for reporting, we could save a lot of time."

Edward couldn't let the moment pass without tying the discussion to his world of information technology. "Performance reports are similar to buying most technology hardware. It looks good today, but won't be worth as much a couple of weeks later. We can't afford for Bruce or any other project manager to waste a lot of time on performance reporting if it's not consistent with what is being done by the project manager to keep track of the project."

Alice had some additional thoughts relative to the problem at hand—that of getting the project back on track. "Since the chances of changing performance reporting requirements are remote at best, we must help Bruce define the data collection process for the performance reporting process. If we don't do it now, this effort will take a lower priority and become lost in the shuffle. It is vital that we support Bruce and make it clear up front what process steps will be required each reporting cycle and prepare the appropriate time and cost estimate for each report."

"That's right," Gene added. "We have to remember that projects do not exist so that someone can spend time reporting on performance. It must be thorough, but it must be simple."

Looking around the room it was clear that everyone was in agreement with the proposal. Bruce was ready to take the lead and move forward based on the recommendations of the executive committee.

Alice turned to Bruce to make sure he was comfortable with the plan. Bruce confirmed his commitment to the project and to his support of the executive committee, but wanted to go over the performance reporting concepts before leaving the meeting. "It would be reasonable for me to develop a proposed performance reporting format, but since I have everyone cornered in the conference room, I thought it would be great to get a few ideas from everyone."

"Good idea," Raj said. "As we discussed a little while ago, we are the recipients of the performance reporting process. It makes sense for us to outline our thoughts before we leave this morning."

With that suggestion, Raj went to the flip chart and drew out his recommendation (Chart 34 - 1).

Barry and Rich were looking at the chart with great interest and before they could comment, Barbara said with her usual firmness, "I like it!

"It's simple; it provides information relevant to the project, and, most importantly, it focuses on reporting whether or not the project is proceeding according to the new commitment."

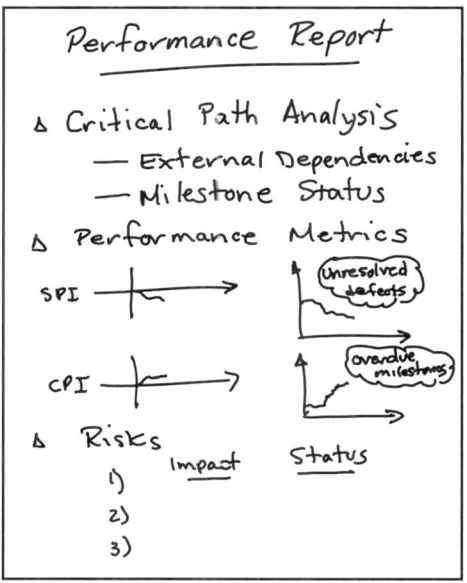

**Chart 34 - 1**

Gene agreed with Barbara's assessment and said, "Without any further discussion, I think we should let Bruce consider these thoughts and recommendations and turn the project into the successful initiative we all knew it was from the beginning.

"We will look at Earned Value Management as a way to evaluate performance and we will continue to use the schedule to assess our ability to meet the end date of the project."

Rich added, "And we need to look hard at the processes being put in place and make sure we are giving Alice the comments and support she needs as we proceed with Troy's project and the other smaller initiatives in the company."

"Sounds like we finally need to get on the same page and start to become efficient," Gene added. "Now that's a process we can all get used to!"

With everyone's agreement on Rich's recommendation and Gene's energetic challenge, the meeting adjourned.

Watching Alice talk with committee members as they left the room, it was clear to me that her plan was going to be simple. She was going to do everything in her power to avoid the OS Phase forever.

---

*OS Phase* **Avoidance**
**STRATEGY 34**

*A monthly status report in a corporate environment should take hours, not days, to prepare. The best approach is to keep the most current performance information on an electronic bulletin board or web site. Any member of the organization with proper clearance should be able to get whatever reports they want whenever they want them.*

*Status reporting itself adds little value to the project. Automate the process whenever possible. Always remember—it's all about data!*

# The Organization in Crisis—
# The OS Phase Expanded

CHAPTER 35

# Organization-Wide Implications

In my profession, I have a chance to meet professionals from hundreds of different companies. If I were to consolidate my gut feel with regard to how companies are managing the *processes* of project management after listening to their comments, I could summarize it into one word...chaos!

Without actually looking up the word chaos in the dictionary, I suspect part of the definition might say or imply "without *process*" or "with too many *processes*." Either way, there is a glaring *process* problem in most business sectors. This is occurring in spite of the hundreds of books written related to *process* improvement. Despite what appears to be improvement in some companies in the areas of traditional Total Quality Management *processes* or the newly revamped Six Sigma quality improvement *processes*, relapses are common. Chaos prevails! Why?

One of the biggest problems is the confusion between complexity and maturity. For many who are trying to raise the level of process maturity in their organizations, the addiction to complicated *process* flow charts and both lengthy and numerous procedural documents seems to be all too common.

Every project has to be *special*.
Every company has to be *special*.
But don't forget, *special* costs a lot of money and time and won't put a company into any better competitive position than if *processes* are kept *simple*. If a *process* isn't a core business, it's not a competitive advantage to be different.

Corporations don't have to report about projects. They report balance sheet items that don't relate to projects. Given a choice, no one wants to report bad news. It has become a culture to mask bad news. Project performance is easy to mask. We'll just leave it at that!

# ORGANIZATION-WIDE IMPLICATIONS

> With all of the current scrutiny on corporate accounting, maybe we should insist that annual reports provide information on project performance. Sounds *simple*, but it's not. The addition of project performance would be difficult to implement because it would mean that we would have to develop standards and get everyone affected to agree to them.
> Never mind…it was just a thought!!
> To many project managers, the concept of chaos is a blessing because it helps to mask accountability and dilute real problems.

It's odd, but even after the long meeting with the executive committee, everybody didn't just run back to their offices. Bruce, Troy, and Raj headed off to talk about some near-term financial requirements, and everyone else was still engaged in other related discussions.

Those remaining in the conference room were listening to something Gene was saying. Of everyone present from the executive committee, Gene had been the quietest of the group. But, he seemed to be the most intrigued at the discussion surrounding the new attitude towards management of the project. As manager of operations, he has a stake in when the project will be complete, but his involvement today demonstrated someone in his position with much more interest than would be expected.

After I put away some notes, I walked up to the group to hear the conversation, which was heating up. I had missed some of the earlier conversation, but as I was joining the group, Gene's enthusiasm definitely caught the attention of Rich, who is famous for getting to the point quickly. "Gene, if you don't mind me saying it, your mind seems to be traveling at top speed and I'm curious why you've become so excited."

Smiling at Rich, Gene responded just as quickly and just as bluntly as Rich. "What I've realized is that nearly everything my team performs on a regular basis could benefit from using the same processes as we've discussed here today. That's amazing when you think about it. If we could get everyone, and I mean everyone, to start thinking in a simple, credible, and predictive manner and get them all to focus on process and data management, life might become simple again."

Rich smiled and responded back to Gene, "I think we all had that thought today. After all, a process is just a process. The simpler the processes we have, the easier it will be for everyone to follow them."

"Therein lies a potential problem," Barbara added with a smile. "If all of the processes are simplified and projects begin to perform better, the need for our high-paying positions in the company may go away."

We all laughed at Barbara's comment.

"We could actually work ourselves out of a job!" Barry added with an unusual amount of levity in his voice. "I'm seeing the same vision as Gene. If we can apply these concepts to non-project related work, then the transition of working on projects to working in operations or information technology could improve our performance significantly."

It was as if everyone in the room had won a large lottery. The sidebar discussions increased to a level of frenzied excitement you'd expect to see on a stock market trading floor. This recognition of the benefit and importance of the processes and concepts was gratifying and would prove to be immeasurable to everyone throughout the organization down the road.

---

*OS Phase* **Avoidance**
**STRATEGY 35**

*The concept of simple, credible, and predictive is not just for project manager*s*. Everyone in the company can benefit from these concepts.*

---

Although there are many organizational challenges for companies, I believe those that understand the significance of the concepts discussed will drive their own companies in a direction that will raise them far above the competitors.

# CHAPTER 36
# Reaching Maturity in Project Management

The term maturity is a part of many methodologies today. The concept of maturity can be used to assess the capability of one organization compared to another. In the family environment, we use maturity to evaluate our children as they grow into adults. We compare an expected maturity level to what we observe. The correlation to the corporate world is similar. We set certain levels of maturity or expectations related to an organization's performance and then we evaluate the organization's achievements based on *simple* observation or more formal evaluation techniques.

The idea of maturity is *simple* if we let it be that way. We need to remember that perfection will be possible only after much trial and error. It is unlikely that we can be perfect the first time we do anything. Actually, if we were perfect the first time we did anything, life might become rather boring. If, instead, we learn from experiences and get better as a result, eventually we will be able to develop processes that will work perfectly if we just follow the proper steps. We will then be ready to move to the next level.

Many believe that there is an ultimate level to achieve. That is wrong. Even the most mature organizations can find ways to improve as long as they realize that fact.

There are many ways to reach maturity in project management. All paths, however, require development of similar processes. But that in itself is not the best measure. We reach maturity when we have not only similar processes, but when we have similar processes that are *simple*, *credible*, and *predictive*.

To help the organization achieve maturity, sponsorship by someone that has successfully made the passage will make the journey much easier.

We have learned to recognize that having a project sponsor or mentor is important for the success of any project. What we miss sometimes is the hidden relationship between the process of sponsorship and maturity. When we reflect on our own behaviors, we might think that by working independently we mature quicker. That's wrong.

Sponsorship must not be another name for micromanagement. Nobody wants someone looking over their shoulder every minute. What we do benefit from is someone that can give us direction and then stand back and watch from a distance. That is the desirable state for a sponsor. A great way to achieve maturity in anything is to have someone rooting for you along the way. As our youth grow up, we as parents will often have more success if we follow a *role* of sponsor instead of the strict disciplinarian parent. The hardest part of being a parent, though, is to stand back while your child struggles with the difficulties of adolescence.

Sponsorship is important within the environment of small entrepreneurial companies, especially those experimenting with new concepts and technologies. In order to come up with new ideas, executive management must allow creative and unrestricted thought development.

It is all too common for organizations, or even entire companies, to attempt improvement in their project management maturity level by just changing their project management tool. When they do this without fixing the *process*, their success is limited. Watching these massive, but futile upgrades, makes me think of a golfing event that occurred several years ago when I lived in Idaho.

On this sun-filled weekend day, I was using a set of $50 yard-sale clubs that had a unique design for the driver and 3-wood. It seems that the designer of the club bent the shaft at a 20-degree angle to compensate for a hook or slice, or some other golfing buzz word.

On this particular afternoon, my drives were pathetic. To say my golf game was not at all mature would be one of the largest understatements of a lifetime. I didn't take golf seriously enough to understand where I needed to improve.

My drives off the tee were short and in the rough! After a drive of about fifty yards on a 510 yard Par 5, I began cursing the stupid driver. My partner that day, a man I'd never met before that afternoon, took the driver from me, proceeded to the tee and slammed a drive of at least 250 yards smack down the middle of the fairway.

His comment to me when he walked back from the tee has stuck in my mind for years. He said, "I think it's the mechanic that has a problem, not the tool!"

My only reaction at the time was to let him play through!!!

His comment was blunt and quite humbling...but it was correct.

The tool was capable of supporting anybody that knew how to use it effectively. Maturity isn't reached by buying a club that a professional golfer endorses; it's reached by learning and improving the complete process.

Having a strong passion for your project doesn't imply any level of maturity. Passion is great, but we have to be sure to direct it properly. If it is...then life is good!!!

Maturity is all about dealing with small problems before they turn into chaotic events. Maturity is all about establishing processes to manage projects in a ***simple***, ***credible***, and ***predictive*** manner.

A genuine sign of reaching maturity is when you realize that it wasn't that difficult to get there!

Following Bruce's meeting with Raj, he joined Troy, Alice, and me for lunch. It was exciting to see the renewed enthusiasm in everyone's eyes and voices. Last Friday the world was crashing down on these three, and now they were ready to put together a solid plan for the future of the project.

"You're all very fortunate that you have a solid organization structure within the company. Constant organizational change has little benefit and the only thing certain is that the change will waste lots of money and resources," I commented.

Alice was pleased with the compliment. She took a few minutes to share her thoughts of the company. "As part of the original team, I knew that the formation of the company would depend upon how the executive committee operated. There was a lot of thought put into their roles and responsibilities. Keeping management levels to a minimum, the executive committee itself operates as the principal managing authority. The committee has an odd number of members, each director has an equal vote and a majority vote is required on any policy or fiscal decision. There are no restrictions on how each director should organize their own organizations. The important thing is to get their responsibilities completed. As we learned, the responsibility assignment matrix will be an excellent tool in the future for us to improve the process of integrating the committee's workload."

"Well spoken, as usual," Troy added. "I've not seen many companies functioning as well as we have in the past. Now that we understand the OS Phase and the techniques to prevent it from reoccurring, we can move forward and get better."

Alice was pleased with Troy's comment and responded, "We'll be able to improve the maturity of the organization if we get everyone's support and keep the proper focus on process and people."

Reflecting on the key points of the meeting, I reminded them of the importance of getting the revised Avoidance Plan completed and approved before getting into too many details. "Remember, the first step is to describe how you plan to achieve what you need to do...."

"But keep it simple!" Bruce added, with the sudden burst of energy I was getting used to seeing. "We need to complete it by Wednesday and I think we can accomplish that if we keep it simple."

Troy looked at Bruce, trying to be serious, and asked, "Did you just give us an arbitrarily set deadline? I mean, where did Wednesday come from?"

"I think you've been caught," Alice said, holding back a smile as she turned to Bruce.

"We've matured a lot in just a couple of days. It seems that we became slightly lethargic as an organization. We took too much for granted and no one, including myself, rocked the boat enough."

"That's going to change," Bruce interjected. "I'm excited to get started on making everything simpler. That was the most important thing I've learned today."

Joining the discussion, Troy added, "I learned that when you do everything in a simple manner, the ability to be credible and predictive is itself simple."

"That's perfect," Alice exclaimed. "Unfortunately, when it comes to defining the terminology and principles related to project management, there seem to be endless literary sources from which to choose. Project management is indeed a very big business."

Poking fun at myself, I added, "I've often joked that there are as many books and consultants for project management as there are for losing weight."

Smiling, Troy gave a perfect response. "I hope that managing projects is more exciting than losing weight! I've been there, and it's not much fun."

The lighthearted comment drew high-fives from everyone. The team spirit was great to see!

I reminded the three musketeers that I needed to return to my hotel and begin preparing for my next engagement. We did establish a follow-up meeting to review the Avoidance Plan for the Mountain Adventure project and Troy's upcoming project.

After exchanging goodbyes and handshakes, I left my three new friends at the table. As I exited the restaurant, I could hear their enthusiastic conversation even as I reached the maitre d's station. It wasn't going to be easy for them for quite awhile, but over the long haul they should be able to focus more on the project and less on the project management processes. When that happens they will have made it, and interestingly, over time, they will forget their OS Phase experience. That's the only saving grace about having bad experiences; we usually develop amnesia.

After a quiet ride to the city center of Dallas, the taxi dropped me off at the Meridian Hotel. As I approached the elevator just past the bell stand, it was impossible to ignore the vocal and somewhat heated conversation of several executives sitting on the couches in the center of the lobby.

Their discussion sounded almost like they had hit the OS Phase!

Maybe I'll stop and talk to them for just a minute to see what's wrong!

> *OS Phase* **Avoidance**
> **STRATEGY 36**
>
> *Whenever possible, ignore close-by conversations while waiting for a plane or walking through a hotel lobby.*
>
> *Never strike up a casual conversation about someone's project problems.*
>
> *Remember what your parents always told you: "Don't talk to strangers!"*

# Epilogue

It's been six months since I first met Alice, Troy, and Bruce at O'Hare Airport in Chicago. We have kept in touch since that time. I was pleased to learn that Bruce directed the project to a successful conclusion. From Rich I heard that sales are much greater than expected due to an intense marketing effort.

The July issue of the nationally published *Mountain Adventure* magazine had a great article highlighting the entrepreneurial spirit of the entire company and describing how they used their focus on processes to get the project completed. Bruce's team made the front cover. He was even smiling! I framed the cover sheet and sent it to Bruce with my congratulations.

With the project completed, my wife and I are guests of Gene and his wife Gloria at the Grand Canyon. We are preparing to embark on our very first adventure. Gene wanted to join us to make sure that we had a flawless experience.

Alice e-mailed me last week and was pleased to report that Troy's Island Adventure Project was moving smoothly and that her golf game was really improving. I still need golf lessons and have a set of bent clubs for sale!

Barry's book on avoidance metrics is a best seller. It turns out that he co-authored it with Barbara. Both of them are currently traveling around the country on a book tour.

Edward and Raj put together a proposal for a new business venture that markets the database concepts they built for the project. The software suite is simple, credible, and predictive and is capable of supporting any type of project ever conceived.

The term OS Phase hasn't made it into the formal project management text books…yet!

www.avoidingtheosphase.com

# Glossary

| | |
|---|---|
| ACWP | Actual Cost of Work Performed |
| BCWP | Budgeted Cost of Work Performed |
| BCWS | Budgeted Cost of Work Scheduled |
| CV | Cost Variance |
| CPI | Cost Performance Index |
| CPO | Chief Projects Officer |
| ERP | Enterprise Resource Planning |
| EVM | Earned Value Management |
| MCS | Management Control System |
| PMI | Project Management Institute |
| PMIS | Project Management Information System |
| PMBOK® | Project Management Body of Knowledge |
| RAM | Responsibility Assignment Matrix |
| RACI | Responsibility, Authority, Consult, Inform |
| SMART | Specific, Measurable, Attainable, Realistic, Time Bound |
| SPI | Schedule Performance Index |
| SV | Schedule Variance |
| UAT | User Acceptance Testing |
| WBS | Work Breakdown Structure |

# A

**Acceptor**
The Acceptor is the person you want to be responsible for reviewing and accepting a task as being in compliance with requirements.

**Actual Cost of Work Performed (ACWP)**
What we've spent on all work performed to date. This value represents the actual costs linked to the same time period as the values for the work scheduled and the work completed or earned. This term is also referred to as Actual Cost (AC).

**Analogous Estimate**
An estimate based on an analogy of similar work.

**Attribute**
A positive characteristic, trait or personal strength.

**Authority**
The ability to make project decisions as long as they fall within the boundaries defined in the approved project authorization document.

**Avoidance Attributes**
Suggested attributes of project managers (Simple, Credible, and Predictive).

**Avoidance Matrix**
A 2 x 2 matrix that designates whether an object "Adds Value" or "Doesn't Add Value" compared to whether the object is "Required" or "Not Required."

**Avoidance Metrics**
Measured performance areas vital to the project. Sometimes called Critical Success Factors.

**Avoidance Model**
A well-understood and documented model that stresses the importance of capturing and managing all project scope, roles and responsibilities and risks, and assuring that the status of each are current, correct, and complete.

# GLOSSARY

**Avoidance Plan**

A written document that includes a summary description of the project, a description of how the project team will execute the project in terms of the relevant Project Management Focus Areas and all relevant project details / documents or references to those items. See also Recovery Plan.

**Avoidance Triangle**

A pictorial representation of the relationship between the project scope, time, and cost baselines. Sometimes referred to as the Stupid Triangle.

## B

**Baseline**

A point of reference used as a comparison. Often referred to in conjunction with the project's scope, time, and cost approved values at the time of project approval. A common cliché used to describe a baseline is *a line in the sand*. Any project characteristic or feature could have a baseline established.

**Behavior**

Personality or actions exhibited by project stakeholders.

**Buzz word**

A cynical reference to a term or word (s) used (often excessively) by a project stakeholder to emphasize an idea or concept.

**Budgeted Cost of Work Performed (BCWP)**

The value of the work actually completed to-date. The Budgeted Cost of Work Performed will be weighted based on the percentage complete of each work activity. This term is also referred to as Earned Value (EV).

**Budgeted Cost of Work Scheduled (BCWS)**

The summation of the budgeted values of work that was scheduled to be completed to-date. This term is also referred to as Planned Value (PV).

## C

**Chief Projects Officer (CPO)**
The company official responsible for assuring that projects use similar processes and standards. As a precursor, they would be responsible for building a company consensus on the processes and standards to adopt. The CPO would also be an advocate for prioritization of projects and for the allocation of resources necessary to support the various projects.

**Compliant Behavior**
Something that someone will do because they "have to," not because they "want to," and definitely not because they feel that it adds value.

**Contingency Reserve**
A time or effort-based (cost) budget that is allocated to be used for project risks that occur on a project. The value of the contingency reserve can be calculated based on an evaluation of the identified risks.

**Cost Performance Index (CPI)**
An Earned Value Management term that evaluates cost performance in terms of an index. Perfect performance is 1.0 and cumulative trending results are a great predictive indicator.
**CPI = BCWP / ACWP**

**Cost Variance (CV)**
An Earned Value Management term that represents the mathematical difference between what was earned on the project and what was spent. Perfect performance would be 0.0.
**CV = BCWP - ACWP**

**Critical Path**
An output of a project schedule that represents the consecutive sequence of project activities and their associated schedule values (early start / early finish / late start / late finish / total float) that forecast specific project milestone dates as well as the forecast project completion date. Used also to describe a project schedule, i.e. Critical Path Schedule.

# GLOSSARY

**Critical Success Factor**
A metric that represents an important project performance value that is predictive in nature and indicative of whether a project objective will be met. See also Avoidance Metrics.

## D

**Deliverable**
Something that the project delivers and will on many occasions result in payment or reimbursement. Once all of the deliverables are completed, the project is done.

## E

**Earned Value Management**
Provides metrics that evaluate how well the schedule as a whole is performing to the target schedule and how close actual costs are coming in based on the budget for work performed. An incredible benefit of Earned Value Management is how well it links with critical path analysis for the schedule and appropriate cost performance analysis. It is one of the best predictive tools available.

**Estimate**
An approximation of any project baseline value. Estimates should have a corresponding accuracy level and basis.

## F

**Forecast**
A current estimate or a prediction of any project baseline value based on project performance.

## H

**Hosed**
A slang term representing a person or project's condition when something hasn't gone as planned. Often precedes entrance into the OS Phase.

## L

**Lessons Learned**
Lessons Learned are the captured details and experiences of projects. Lessons Learned are most often characterized as either positive (good experiences) or negative (bad experiences).

## M

**Magic Pill**
A cynical term to characterize a generic solution to project management concerns. The real magic pill is recognizing that in order to make sure everything proceeds smoothly we need to define the process for managing the scope (stuff).

**Management Control System (MCS)**
The group of processes, supporting computer systems or databases that make up a company's or organization's way of doing business. The effectiveness of the MCS, or, actually, the lack of effectiveness of the system, is one of the biggest contributors to the OS Phase.

## O

**Objectives**
Measurable criteria that must be met if a project is to be considered successful.

**OS Phase**
The time period when a project, which seems to be on track, begins to fail or has failed.

**OS Phase Characteristics**
Symptoms for conditions that typically precede failure.

**Overtime**
Work above and beyond a typical work week. This work is typically at a higher pay rate for non-salaried workers. Using a lot of overtime is usually a sign that a project is in trouble. If it isn't in trouble yet, given enough overtime and eventual team member burnout, it will be.

# P

**Performance Report**
A project report that summarizes a project's status, progress, and forecast. Features on a performance report are usually customized based on the type of project and specific stakeholder requests.

**Primary Preparer**
The person held singly accountable for getting the task completed; used in Responsibility Assignment Matrix.

**Process**
A series or flow chart of activities that have all of the characteristics of a project except that they are repeated and do not have a formal end date, like a project. Some processes are formalized into procedure documents. Projects consist almost entirely of processes.

**Product Scope**
Scope related to the product or the result of the project itself. Product Scope is what the customer wants.

**Project Phases**
Projects are often broken into time phased periods that are consecutive and cover the entire duration of a project. Some project phases can actually be managed as a project. Examples of phases are: conceptual or requirements phase, design phase, building or construction phase, testing phase, final turnover, systems integration phase. In cases where the project has failed, they typically also have the OS Phase.

**Project Management**
The job of managing all of the processes necessary to complete a project.

**Project Management Focus Areas**
Project processes are organized into manageable and similar groups. These groups are called Focus Areas and represent the most important areas of process where the project manager should "focus."

**Project Management Information System (PMIS)**
The computerized portion of the Management Control System. The PMIS is necessary for providing the project with information related to the project in a timely and accurate manner.

**Project Scope**
The portion of the total scope that represents what it takes to give the customer what they want. This would be better designated as Avoidance Scope since it includes all of the work necessary to avoid hitting the OS Phase.

## R

**Recovery Plan**
Similar to the Avoidance Plan but with specific emphasis on remaining project scope and the necessary project recovery efforts. This plan is used after a project hits the OS Phase or is stopped before it does. See also Avoidance Plan.

**Requirements**
A condition or a thing. Requirements represent an item that must be delivered or a condition that has to be met. Requirements do not include work and are included in product scope.

**Resources**
Any person or thing that is needed for a project.

**Responsibility Assignment Matrix (RAM)**
A RAM is a matrix that displays and tracks roles and responsibilities for a project. The RAM is beneficial not only as an informational document, but as an action document, a tool that keeps everyone on their toes.

**Risk**
An element of scope that we don't want to have happen. When risks are present on a project, some type of schedule or cost/effort contingency reserve must be allocated to accommodate the impact of the risk.

## Reviewer
Designation in the Responsibility Assignment Matrix that determines who will check the accuracy of the process or activity (review).

## Roles and Responsibilities
Designations for project stakeholders documenting their individual level of involvement on the project.

## Rolling Wave Schedule
A process of constant knowledge gathering. Managing the targeting of short durations to near term activities, where we do have the necessary detail. Future activites, at the project manager's discretion, do not have to be broken down until the team gets closer. Depending on the overall duration of the project, a weekly review of future activities should reveal those that are ready for commitment.

## S

## Schedule
An organized grouping of project activities, each containing estimated durations and sequencing attributes. The work associated with any schedule activity is the same scope as that defined for the Scope of the project. See also Critical Path.

## Schedule Performance Index
An Earned Value Management term that evaluates schedule performance in terms of an index. Perfect performance is 1.0 and cumulative trending results are a great predictive indicator.

**SPI = BCWP / BCWS**

## Schedule Variance (SV)
An Earned Value Management term that represents the mathematical difference between what was earned on the project and what should have been earned. Perfect performance would be 0.0.

**SV = BCWP - BCWS**

## Scope
Anything that takes time or costs money or effort.

**Scope Creep**
Scope that is added to a project and is not processed through any type of change control process that would include a corresponding Time or Cost component. Scope Creep usually results in project Time and Cost overruns.

**Stakeholder**
Any person that has any association or connection with a project. Stakeholders range from members of the project team to eventual customers. Executives or managers that have input or will offer feedback to the project team are also stakeholders.

**Stuff**
A cynical name for Scope.

**Stupid Triangle**
The Avoidance Triangle is often referred to as the Stupid Triangle not because it's stupid, but because any time we ignore the relationship between scope, time and cost, we're stupid.

**Subject Matter Expert**
A person that has a specific knowledge about an activity, work package, or process depicted on the project RAM.

## T

**Triple Constraints**
See Avoidance Triangle

## U

**User Acceptance Testing (UAT)**
An important part of the development of any software or web-based system that occurs near the end of the project as a final step, the scope of which typically includes a test plan, test scripts, test itself, defects, corrective actions and a final report.

## W

**Work Breakdown Structure (WBS)**
A structure that breaks down the work. The WBS is a hierarchical

representation of the project's scope. Each lower level of the WBS represents more specific project deliverables. Levels of the WBS are added until the elements of the WBS are at a level that is manageable. The lowest level deliverables on the WBS are called Work Packages.

**Work Package**
The lowest level deliverable in a work breakdown structure. Work Packages are further divided into schedule activities that are used to identify the critical path schedule for the project.

# INDEX

## A

Acceptor 131-132
Actual Cost of Work Performed (ACWP), *see also* Earned Value Management 287-295
analogous estimate, *see also* estimating 197, 200
authority 160-161, 166, 177, 356
Avoidance Attributes 246-258, 260-261, 334, 342
Avoidance Matrix 300-304
Avoidance Metrics, *see also* Earned Value Management 267-268, 270-273, 276-283, 290, 295, 316, 343
Avoidance Model 69-70, 75-76, 98, 115, 130, 135, 138, 172, 212, 222, 260, 305-306
Avoidance Plan 163, 166-167, 222, 237, 281, 283, 346, 356-357
Avoidance Triangle 41-43, 46-48, 50, 55, 61-64, 67-68, 70-72, 86, 97, 100-102, 109-110, 112-114, 119, 124, 127, 131, 145-147, 156, 172, 180, 196, 207-208, 218, 232, 248, 256, 259, 269, 309, 311, 315, 332, 338-339, 344

## B

baseline 16-17, 54, 78, 136, 147, 151, 192-194, 218, 283, 292, 337-344
behavior, *see also* compliant behavior 203-213
blame 16, 18, 26, 29, 111-112, 154-155, 189, 226, 234, 244, 253, 262
brainstorm 58, 136, 148, 246
Budgeted Cost of Work Performed (BCWP), *also see* Earned Value Management 287-295

Budgeted Cost of Work Scheduled (BCWS), *see also* Earned Value Management 287-295
budget estimate, *see also* estimating 193, 197
buzz words 13, 99, 231

## C

Chief Projects Officer (CPO) 319-324
compliant behavior 104-106, 252, 262
computerized data management systems, *see* data manaement
computerized project management tools, *see also* Project Management Information System 91, 128, 134, 173, 179, 226, 231, 239
contingency reserve 146-147, 196
control estimate, *see also* estimating 197
Cost Performance Index (CPI), *see also* Earned Value Management 293-296
Cost Variance (CV) 291-293
cover-up, *see also* spin control 9-10
Critical Path 157, 280-283, 347
Critical Success Factors, *see also* Avoidance Metrics 268

## D

database management software 134
data management 226, 231, 239-244, 290, 352
definitive estimate, *see also* estimating 195, 197
deliverables 45-55, 64-67, 72, 88, 96, 107-109, 113, 165, 198, 228, 269, 276, 315-316
Delphi technique 58

# INDEX

## E

Earned Value Management  280-296, 314, 348
   Actual Cost of Work Performed (ACWP)  287- 295
   Budgeted Cost of Work Performed (BCWP)  287-295
   Budgeted Cost of Work Scheduled (BCWS)  287-295
   Cost Performance Index (CPI)  293-296
   Cost Variance (CV)  291-293
   formulas  291, 293
   Schedule Performance Index (SPI)  293-296
   Schedule Variance (SV)  290-293
Enterprise Resource Planning  91
estimating, 190-202, 208, 288
   estimate accuracy  197-198, 200
      budget estimate  193, 197
      mid-level quality estimate  197
         rough order of magnitude estimate  192, 196
   estimating techniques  195-198
      analogous estimate  197, 200
      bottom-up estimate  197-198
      control estimate  197
      definitive estimate  195, 197
      parametric estimate  197, 200
      sideways estimate  198
      top-down estimate  197
   forecasts  91, 93, 101, 192, 198-202, 256, 343

## F

fraud  83

## H

human behavior, *see also* behavior  111, 206

## K

Knowledge Areas, *see also* Project Management Focus Areas  30

## L

lessons learned  122-123, 228, 297-310, 327, 329
lessons learned contributor  123

## M

Magic Pill, *see also* Avoidance Model  66, 69, 135
management by objective  51
Management Control System (MCS)  87-90, 226, 245
management processes  28-29, 32, 40, 44, 67, 69, 74, 88, 90, 98-99, 108, 111, 113, 135, 142-143, 147-148, 153, 157, 159, 168, 191, 219, 227-229, 233, 236-237, 245, 247, 262, 317, 320, 321, 324-326, 336, 343, 345, 357
motivation  12-13, 203-204, 209
Multiple Projects  325-336
multitasking  185-186, 331-332

## O

objective  51-63, 105, 165-166, 260, 267, 270, 273, 276
organizational behavior, *see also* behavior  115
overtime  86, 88, 339

## P

parametric estimate, *see also* estimating  197, 200
perfect project  14-15, 31, 74-75, 154, 215
perfect project manager  154, 214-223
performance metrics  80, 248, 256, 267, 278, 290, 347

performance reporting 16, 76, 78-79, 83, 85-93, 97, 112, 184, 206-207, 245, 251, 252, 344-348
   criminal implications 83
   embellishing performance 21, 79
precedence diagram 173
Primary Preparer, *see also* RAM 119-120
process 28-29
product scope, *see* scope
project baseline 16, 54, 151, 339, 344
Project Management, 30-1, 45, 86-8, 91, 162, 198, 214-23
Project Management Body of Knowledge (PMBOK®) 30
Project Management Focus Areas 30-31, 232, 312
Project Management Information System (PMIS) 87- 88, 91-93, 198, 226, 231, 243, 291
Project Management Institute (PMI) 30-31, 45, 162
project manager 214-223
   attributes 219-223, 245-258, 260-261
Project Phase 6, 18, 21, 207
project plan 161-163
project surfing 329

# R

rebaseline 337-43
recovery plan 20, 157-158, 235
requirements 6, 33, 34, 37-40, 42, 45, 53, 61, 96, 100-101, 106, 113, 132, 153, 180, 257, 259, 300-302, 346, 351
resources, *see also* skills matrix 43, 71, 90, 92, 116-118, 128, 149, 150, 174-178, 180, 188, 201-202, 229, 259, 319, 324, 329-330, 332-337, 356
responsibilities, *see* roles and responsibilities

Responsibility Assignment Matrix (RAM) 118-125, 127-141, 149, 155-156, 161, 172, 208, 212, 272, 281, 283
   acceptor 132
   accountability 137, 155
   approval codes 131-132
   authority 161
   behavioral tool 208, 212
   blame 155
   coding the Matrix 119-120, 122-123, 131-133, 139, 143
   input for preparer 122
   lessons learned contributor 123
   primary preparer 119-120
   RAM as a validation of scope 127
   risk associated with RAM 149
   review and concur 131-132
   support to preparer 120
   subject matter expert 123
RACI Chart (Responsibility, Authority, Consult, Inform), 118-119, 128-129
risk 75-6, 135, 142-52, 208, 310
   associated with project baseline 147
   behavioral tool 208
   categories 149
   demonstrated by RAM 124
   incorporated into Stupid Triangle 146-147, 259
   risk assessment 143
   risk management 76, 147-148, 259-266, 272-273
roles and responsibilities 67, 114-126, 128-130
   management of roles and responsibilities 116, 118-120
   risk related to roles and responsibilities, 149
Rolling Wave Schedule 187-188
rough order of magnitude estimate, *see also* estimating 192, 196

## S

schedule, 163, 167-178, 179-189, 208
  behavioral tool 208
  deficiencies, 181-182
  estimates, *see* estimating.
  length of tasks 182-186
  performance analysis 290-291
  Rolling Wave Schedule, 187-189
  Schedule Performance Index (SPI) 293-296
  scheduling software 168, 172, 179
  sequencing of activities 173-174, 181
  resources 174-178
  variance 290-293
  work processes 186
scope, *see also* stuff 29, 33-38, 40, 42-44, 45, 46, 61-64, 69-70, 96-113, 114-115, 135, 146, 168, 174, 196, 261, 295, 306, 309-311
  association with risk 146
  managing scope, *see also* Scope Management Process 39, 164-165, 226
  product scope 34, 310-311
  relating to RAM 121, 124
  role of scope in starting a project 158, 167-168
  scheduling scope, 174
  scope baseline 136
  scope creep 43, 111, 218, 265
  scope definition 96, 110, 136
  scope management process 29, 43-45, 70-72, 97-98, 108, 115, 166, 174, 329
  scope management technique, 165
  scope validation, 126
sideways estimate, *see also* estimating 198
skills matrix, *see also* resources 201
SMART objectives 57
spin control, *see also* cover-up 10, 13, 18

stakeholders 38, 54, 61-64, 72-73, 126, 138, 142, 255, 301, 369
stuff, *see also* scope 8, 32-41, 44, 46-48, 63-65, 69, 96-97, 101, 112, 125, 129, 136, 167, 187, 214
Stupid Triangle, *see* Avoidance Triangle
subcontractors 281, 310-317
subcontractor management 317
subject matter expert, *see also* Responsibility Assignment Matrix 73, 118, 122-123, 321
support for preparer 120-121, 128

## T

top-down estimate, *see also* estimating 197
triple constraints 35

## U

User Acceptance Testing 48-49

## V

vendors 309-318

## W

Work Breakdown Structure (WBS) 103-110, 140, 165-166, 174, 181, 198-199, 208, 240, 295
Work Package 108